D1488321

· *Shucked* ·

Shucked

Life on a New England Oyster Farm

E RIN B YERS M URRAY

ST. MARTIN'S PRESS ❧ NEW YORK

www.stmartins.com

Book design by Claire Vaccaro

Oyster illustration by Meighan Cavanaugh

Library of Congress Cataloging-in-Publication Data

Murray, Erin Byers.
    Shucked : life on a New England oyster farm / Erin Byers Murray. — 1st ed.
    p. cm.
    ISBN 978-0-312-68191-3
    1. Oyster culture—Massachusetts—Duxbury. 2. Island Creek Oysters
(Firm). 3. Farm life—Massachusetts—Duxbury. 4. Murray, Erin
Byers. 5. Duxbury (Mass.)—Social life and customs. 6. Duxbury
(Mass.)—Biography. I. Title.
    SH365.M4M87 2011
    639'.410974482—dc23   2011024839

First Edition: October 2011

10 9 8 7 6 5 4 3 2 1

For Dave,

who has made me the luckiest

CONTENTS

III. Filter Feeder

IV. Half Shell

Acknowledgments

This book would not have happened if it weren't for the efforts, encouragement, and support of so many people. I owe enormous and heartfelt thank-yous (and a couple beers) to them all:

First and foremost, to Skip Bennett for saying yes, for letting a novice boater work on his crew, for trusting me to tell the story, and for giving me so much to strive for.

To Shore Gregory for his friendship, constant encouragement, and teaching me how to say no.

To Andrew Yberg for being a patient teacher.

To everyone at Island Creek, including the growers, my crew, the wholesale team, and especially CJ, Chris, and Cory for wrapping me up in the big bear hug that is the ICO family.

To Garrett Harker for hosting that fateful crab festival and, along with Jeremy Sewall and Tom Schlesinger-Guidelli, letting me join in on those first cautious new restaurant steps.

To all of the chefs who are part of this story, shared their recipes, and fed me along the way, including Seth and Angela Raynor, Jasper White, the Boston scooter gang, Jody Adams, the team at Eastern Standard, the women at French Memories and Snug Harbor, Paul Kahan at the Publican, and especially Jonathan Benno as well as the entire team at Per Se.

To Sascha de Gersdorff for being a thoughtful reader and tireless cheerleader.

To the women in publishing who gave me a stepladder to get started and inspiration on the page, including Alexandra Hall, Annie Copps, Christie Matheson, and Rachel Baker.

To my agent, Danielle Chiotti, for believing my story had heart.

To my editor, Daniela Rapp, for having a firm hand and kind words.

To Nicole Kanner, Jenn Korn, and Karen Carp for being steadfast sisters and giving me wine when I needed it most.

To Jim Williams for teaching me how *not* to open my first oyster, and along with his wife, Carol, teaching me how to eat it.

To my sister, Shannon, for her lifelong guidance, constant companionship, endless encouragement, and, along with her husband, Brian, bringing Gracyn Byers White into our world.

To my mom, Dottie, and dad, Kelly, who have given me all of my tools and talent, for a lifetime of love and support, an adventurous upbringing, the wisdom to make a home wherever I land, and of course, for never leaving their seats on the roller coaster.

And finally, I have to thank Dave, who knows that there aren't enough words to adequately express my appreciation or my love. He is my best friend, my soul mate, my most honest critic, and my rock.

· *Shucked* ·

INTRODUCTION

On a steamy midsummer night in August 2008, I was invited to a dinner party at Eastern Standard, a high-ceilinged brasserie in the heart of Boston's Kenmore Square. The restaurant's proprietor, Garrett Harker, a tall, silver fox who oversaw one of the most gracious dining room staffs in the city, was also a Baltimore native, and where he came from August was crab season. He was throwing a classic, newspaper-on-the-table, Chesapeake Bay–style festival complete with blue crabs flown up from Maryland, buckets of Old Bay seasoning, and cans of icy cold Natty Boh. It was just my kind of party.

Within minutes of walking in, I met a young, tan, bearded kid wearing sunglasses and a Red Sox cap who looked like he could have walked off the campus at nearby Boston University. He shook my hand firmly and said that his name was Shore Gregory and he was the director of business development at a company called Island Creek Oysters. I immediately did a double take. Not only was a guy named Shore working for an oyster company but he looked like he should have been playing hacky sack on the quad, not directing anyone's business.

I was familiar with Island Creek, having eaten their oysters at restaurants around the city. Started in the early 1990s by waterman Skip Bennett, the fifty-acre operation sat forty-five minutes south of the city in a hamlet called Duxbury and quietly nurtured 5 million of the country's most coveted oysters. They were on every oyster bar menu in Boston and I'd seen the Island Creek boat, a traveling raw bar complete with its own cast of male shuckers, set up at high-end fund-raisers. The farmers of Island Creek had a reputation for being a charming bunch of fishermen who loved to have a good time.

Shore introduced me to his young cohorts, a languid blond named CJ, the company's delivery truck driver, and Matthew, another guy in a cap, who handled sales.

We sat down to piles of crabs and as we picked through our shells, I interrogated Shore about his job. He patiently walked me through the history of the company, filling me in on how Skip got started and later, how the dedicated farmer won the hearts of local chefs like Chris Schlesinger, owner and chef of Cambridge's legendary seafood spot the East Coast Grill. After September 11, Shore explained, Skip's wholesale accounts stopped buying oysters—restaurants everywhere were struggling to pay their bills. Instead of giving up, Skip drove his truck up to Boston, knocked on the back door at the East Coast Grill, and asked the chef if he wanted to buy some oysters directly. Schlesinger, a long-time supporter of local farmers, said yes and then passed Skip's name along to his chef friends. Skip gained a reputation for being a backdoor delivery guy and producing some damn good oysters—and it helped him grow the business into the incredibly successful outfit it was today. Shore also described the farm's yearlong cycle and a bit about how oysters grow. As with wine, he told me, the source of an oyster's flavor comes from the precise location where it's grown. They called it "merroir."

I said the word out loud, feeling it roll around on my tongue. There was something fascinating about it, something evocative. I loved the idea behind it: sense of place. I wanted to know more. I pulled Shore aside at the end of the night and set a date for a tour of the farm.

At the time of Eastern Standard's crab dinner, I was the Boston editor for DailyCandy.com, a wildly popular lifestyle and shopping Web site. My job was to scour the city for trendy ideas to drop into the in-boxes of well-off female readers. I was always out and about, my job providing me with a parade of reasons to dress up and socialize: store openings, restaurant fetes, fashion shows, lunches.

But between parties, e-mail blips, Facebook bites, and mad dashes to my daily three o'clock deadline, I had shoved much aside to make room for publicists, editors, and shopkeepers. I was more intimately connected to my BlackBerry than Dave, my husband of two and a half years (I only know this because he told me so in an e-mail).

The job, in so many ways, was a dream job. It afforded me a lavish lifestyle; I worked from home, ate well, and took time off to travel. Dave, a lifelong musician, was also a bartender, so mine was the stable career, offering insurance and steady income. We had a hard time coordinating our schedules or finding time for a date, but at least we lived comfortably. It should have been the perfect setup: a crammed social schedule, a good marriage, a condo, a career.

But instead of feeling satisfied or content in that life, I felt achingly empty, lost. It was as though I was missing some essential element—as though I'd never discovered who I really wanted to be. By the time I realized it, I was too busy to find out.

I'd had a lucrative career trajectory, but along the way I'd shelved one of my early passions: writing about food. My first editorial job was at *Boston* magazine, where as an editorial assistant, then a staff writer, part of my beat was covering the city's food scene. It thrilled me to write about a new restaurant or track the city's (and country's) food trends. Small plates were hot and craft cocktails were just starting to appear on bar menus. A new league of young chefs was parading into Boston's hottest kitchens and I was there to interview them all. I learned about ingredients, studied up on white truffles, discovered which wine grapes thrived in our New England climate, and searched for the perfect lobster roll. When interviewing a chef about where he sourced his favorite ingredients, I tracked down every purveyor, farm, or retailer he listed. The stories behind an ingredient—where it came from, who prepared it, why it tasted that way—spoke to me more personally than any other topic I tried.

And then I took the job at DailyCandy, which was more

of a general lifestyle publication, and food became less of a priority. Instead of exploring a spice shop, I needed to study up on handbag designers, the latest spa treatments, or getting the scoop on shoe sales. Aside from a few free-lance pieces, I rarely got the opportunity to cover food. And without an excuse to hunt down stories about the next popular heritage breed pig, my passion for food and I were starving.

I decided to enroll in a part-time program at the Cambridge School of Culinary Arts, where for twenty hours each week (on top of my DailyCandy gig) I perfected my knife skills and studied the language of food and cooking. It fed some of my cravings but the program was over in six months and something still nagged me: I had no idea *where* my food came from. I got that vegetables, meat, grains, and fruit were harvested, shipped, packaged, and put on my table, but I had no understanding of the business of food, of what it felt like to watch something grow, or how my breakfast, lunch, and dinner got from the ground into my gaping mouth.

A few weeks after that night at Eastern Standard, I escaped my cramped home office, as well as an avalanche of deadlines, with story scouting as an excuse to spend the afternoon cruising around Duxbury Bay on a flat-bottomed boat: my introduction to the world of Island Creek.

As we disembarked into knee-deep waters, I steadied myself in a pair of unwieldy waders while Shore, clad in sunglasses and a faded T-shirt, pointed out large clusters of recently planted oysters. Around us, Island Creek farmers, mostly burly guys wearing worn-out baseball caps, were busy checking their crops. Shore picked up a horseshoe crab. One of the guys started a seaweed fight. It felt like science camp.

"You'll have to come back this winter," Shore said, leading me through the warm, translucent waves. "The ice gets so thick we have to come out with chain saws to cut through it."

He introduced me to the rest of the staff and I was impressed to find two twenty-something women working alongside the guys. With their bulky blue gloves, arms smeared with mud, messy ponytails, and weathered faces, they looked tough, imposing. But they smiled as we approached, meeting my awed gaze with friendly hellos. They showed me how they picked oysters by hand, plucking the mottled shells straight from the mud. I watched carefully, fascinated by their intensity. I thought about the dozen odd jobs I'd held in my life (working the counter of a putt-putt course; DJing at a local radio station; slogging along as a production assistant on television commercial shoots) but they looked about as boring as bank telling compared to what these girls were doing. The food journalist in me wanted to know more—what it was like to work on the water all day, to watch an oyster grow. But they had work to do and my questions were holding them up.

With every conversation, I felt more and more removed from the circus that was my job. While I was buried under fashion catalogs and beauty samples, these funny, kind, and genuinely disarming farmers got to work on the water all day long growing food. I wanted in on the action.

"This is incredible," I said, back at the boat.

"It's a good life," Shore said, tossing an oyster up and down with one hand. I looked out toward the farmers who now stood clustered together in conversation. Their laughter skittered out over the water, reaching us in waves. Suddenly, I couldn't stomach the idea of going back to my desk.

"Looking for more help?" I asked, running my hands through the water.

"Why?" he countered. "You want a job?"

I tried to read his eyes behind the dark glasses.

"Kind of," I said, half joking.

"Great," he deadpanned, turning toward the boat. "You're hired."

For days after my Duxbury visit, I fantasized about the farm. Shore might have been kidding but somehow our interaction had planted a seed. Out there on the water, my food curiosities were satiated. But now, I wanted the whole story—the history, those women, winter on the oyster farm. And that word "merroir." I wanted to know that sense of place.

It was time for me to make my escape, I realized. The parties, the deadlines, the emptiness; it was time to drop it all and do something real.

I began scheming up a scenario where I quit my job and worked on the farm for a year. This wasn't just idle daydreaming: I put numbers on paper, tracked our savings, and figured out just how Dave and I could survive if I overturned our entire lives. A few days later, I approached my husband.

"I want to work on an oyster farm for a year," I told him point-blank.

He was quiet at first, incredulous. He knew I'd been unhappy and looking for a change, but tossing my perfectly good life away to work for an hourly wage . . . in the mud?

"*You're* going to give up your cushy life to be a farm girl," he jabbed, trying to make light of my plan. Yes, I said defiantly. Why not? I was fully capable of the work (I mean, other girls were out there doing it, why couldn't I?) and I was willing to sacrifice the job. More than anything, I wanted a life-changing experience, I said.

"I need this," I conceded imploringly. He pulled at his beard. He asked me a million questions about what this would mean for us, how we would make it work, and what I would do on the other end of it. I had very few answers, only enthusiasm.

"I'll tell you what. If you can figure out how to make it work financially, I'm all for it," he said at last.

That was all I needed.

A few weeks later, I invited Shore out for a drink and told him I wanted to work on the farm for a year. He studied me, like Dave had, waiting for the punch line.

Instead, I gave him my reasoning. I needed a break from my career, I explained. I wanted to see where food came from firsthand. I wanted to watch the process from beginning to end. He, too, pulled at his beard.

"You need a sturdy back to work on Skip's crew. And the stamina for some long hours and really hard work," he said. He paused, then added, "If you think you can handle that, then this might actually work."

I waited anxiously for him to report back with Skip's response. Suddenly, I couldn't bear the thought of *not* taking this plunge. When Shore finally called, he told me it would take some convincing. I set up a time to have dinner with Shore and the farmer himself.

"Have you ever driven a boat?" Skip asked when we finally got together. His hair was still mussed and his cheeks were bright red from a day out on the water.

"Once, when I was a kid," I told him reluctantly. I realized that I wasn't his typical farmhand hire. But he heard me out and we ended up talking for hours. He wanted to know what I hoped to gain from the experience and how I might be able to contribute off the water. He listened carefully and weighed my reasonings before telling me that he would think about it.

A few days later, Shore called me with good news.

"Skip's on board," he said, sounding pleased. He asked if I could start in March, the very start of the growing season.

I

Spat

*He is small
but he is free-swimming . . .
wherever the tides
and his peculiar whims may lead him.*

—M. F. K. Fisher, *Consider the Oyster*

CHAPTER ONE

FNG

March 9, 2009

Most people don't wake up and just *decide* to be oyster farmers. Not most sane people anyway. Especially on icy, raw, rainy March mornings when it's blowing stink off the coast of Massachusetts.

But essentially, that's what I'd done. And when my alarm went off and I heard a bullet storm of rain pellets chipping away at my windowpane, I immediately wondered what the hell I'd been thinking.

But my fate was sealed (job quit, mud boots purchased), so I tried to momentarily ignore the elements and get dressed. What on earth was I supposed to wear now that I'd tossed aside a perfectly decent, well-paying job as an online life-style editor for an hourly wage to dig shellfish out of the mud? I pulled out an assortment of clothes: long underwear, sturdy jeans, two long-sleeve shirts, two pairs of socks. Wrestling into the layers, I thought back to one of my first conversations with Skip Bennett, Island Creek's forty-three-year-old founder and head oyster farmer.

He'd been vague.

"You'll be out on the water," he said. "A lot," he stressed with a raised eyebrow. "Think you'll be comfortable working outside all day?"

We were having drinks at B & G Oysters, a jewel-box oyster bar in Boston's South End that carried his product religiously, and I couldn't quite read my dark-haired companion's smile. Was that trepidation? Amusement? Incredulity? He was, after all, talking to someone who had a manicure but absolutely no maritime experience, and he'd just hired her to work side by side with his surly, weather-beaten farm crew for a year.

"Yes," I half lied. Well, I mean, I *could* be comfortable working outside all day. I'd once taught swimming lessons to little kids for an entire summer. Surely some of that experience would come surfacing back. Right?

"You'll be culling," he said. I nodded. I had no idea what culling was.

The oyster farmer looked down into his drink and smiled. "It's okay. We'll figure it out once you get there."

Pulling on a pair of old jeans that morning, I thought of everyone else I knew—my husband, Dave, former colleagues, my dad—who would spend the day yawning away hours at a desk and here I was dressing for summer camp (albeit one that started at an ungodly hour). I kissed my sleeping husband and slipped out into the dark.

The rain came down harder as I made my way onto Route 3 southbound, and it occurred to me that my mud boots weighed heavier on the gas pedal than my everyday stilettos had. In no time flat, I was pulling into Island Creek Oysters World Headquarters. I was early.

Set about four miles away from the actual waterfront of Duxbury Bay, Island Creek's main office is a pretty humble affair. Tucked away at one end of a semicircular oyster-shell driveway is a squat, shingled, one-story house that serves as the wholesale company's office. A barn next door is used as a garage and toolshed, and at the other end, abutting the road, sits a shanty of a seafood shack trimmed with hedges, BENNETT LOBSTER AND SEAFOOD painted on the window. The entire property, I later found out, belonged to Billy Bennett, father of Skip, who had long ago retired from owning a nearby tire-and-gas business to become a lobsterman, which he did commercially for several years before retiring again to become an oyster farmer. A waterman in every sense of the word, Bill Bennett had worked hard, long days his entire life. And at sixty-nine years old, he was enjoying every minute of it.

The one-story house had been converted into an office a few years before I arrived; some of the Island Creek farmers had even lived there, including, a long time ago, a twenty-something Skip and his former wife, Shannon, who gave birth to their oldest daughter, Samantha, in what had become the conference room. With a broad, high-ceilinged great room up front, it was now a workspace, complete with desks and a fax machine.

The morning I arrived, it was relatively quiet. With a rainy gloom settling over the world, the blaze of lights and blasting heat of the office were a welcoming hug.

Lisa Scharoun, a trim, effortlessly fit forty-something with a pixie face and blond hair to match, was the farm's office manager. She greeted me with an up-and-down glance.

"Well, don't you look fashionable?" she said curtly. I looked down. Despite my best efforts to "dress down," I realized that with my jeans tucked into green Hunter Wellies and my hair pulled back neatly, I could have been wandering down Newbury Street for some rainy-day shopping.

It was a punch in the gut.

"Here's your time sheet," she said, handing me a piece of paper.

Looking for a familiar face, I encountered the opposite: a round kid wearing glasses, with a big frown under his goatee.

"You're gonna have to move your car," he said, stonefaced. This was Cory, the shop manager.

We ran out into the rain where he shouted at me: "That's Billy's spot. No one parks there but Billy." He pointed to another open space.

Cory waited for me to move the car, then walked me behind the fish market, where we came to a small, concrete processing room filled with two walk-in refrigerators and a few stainless steel tables: the shop. The lights were bright and cold and the air smelled of Windex. My host, much less surly now that we were back indoors, walked me around the space before introducing me to two twenty-something guys standing in the corner.

The taller, Nordic-looking one was Andy Yberg, who went by Berg and had a surfer's build, lean and occasionally awkward, along with shoulder-length blond hair. When he smiled, his chapped lips revealed a faint underbite.

"Nice boots," he said, pointing to my feet; he had on the exact same pair, making me feel slightly less bruised by Lisa's jab. He nudged the bearish, bearded guy standing next to him, Andy Seraikas.

"Call me Andy, or A2. I go by whatever," said Andy number two. His sky-blue eyes were framed by long lashes and he spoke softly, giving his defensive linebacker frame something of a teddy bear finish. These were my crewmates.

"Cory already has a nickname for you," A2 said with a grin.

Behind me, an extremely animated Cory was doing a jig. "It's FNG, Fucking New Girl!" he boomed, hopping from one foot to the other. The guys laughed. I shot Cory a look, freezing him mid-hop.

Berg eyed me with brotherly concern.

"You ready for this?" he asked.

Yup, I nodded. It was now or never.

Back out in the rain, Cory waved us off as the Andys and I piled into our rig, a white-cabbed truck with a gated flatbed. A few miles down Duxbury's main road, Route 3A, we made a right onto Harrison Street and passed the manicured greens of the Duxbury Yacht Club golf course. As we crested a small hill, I got a glimpse of Duxbury Bay, shrouded in a soupy fog. We pulled into the town's harbor parking lot, which sat behind a tiny town center, where a row of pickup trucks faced the quiet waterway. As I climbed down from our truck, the saltwater air hit me hard and fast. It was refreshing—and shockingly cold.

At one end of the parking lot, a little hut spewed a plume

of fragrant smoke out of its chimney: the harbormaster's central command and the only sign of life.

Inhaling the smoky mist, I followed the guys past the hut through the silence. The Duxbury Bay Maritime School, the largest maritime school on the East Coast, was in the process of constructing a massive new building directly on the waterfront. The half-erected structure dwarfed the school's former digs, an aging shack that looked like it would crumble any minute. Directly in front of the shack sat a giant dirt heap. And directly in front of that sat a forty-by-twelve-foot float perched up on some makeshift pilings: my new office. The guys had a million names for it: the Oyster Plex, the Clubhouse, Our Girl. Because the farm was still in winter mode, we weren't "on the water" quite yet. Our setup, a flat deck with a graying, shingled house on top, would eventually sit in the middle of the bay attached to a mooring. But she'd been out of the water since December, and for now, looked like Dorothy's windblown house plunked in the middle of a parking lot.

The guys climbed up the side of the dirt pile with ease. It took a few tries but I finally got up and followed them into the house.

"Smells like oysters," A2 said, throwing a glance at the FNG. He grinned at me like he could tell what I was thinking: Ew. My nose filled with the pungent dankness of decaying seaweed. Nothing could have prepared me for that first whiff. It was a slap across the face, sharp and sweet all at once. My eyes welled up for a split second, and I breathed in again, this time more deeply, taking in the sweetness. It was layered and complex, like inhaling shaved truffles or a barnyardy Pinot Noir. Each breath added new depth. Marshy wetland. The beach. Raw meat. It was stinky and aromatic, like a cheese cave—intoxicating.

Berg nudged me out of my trance to get around me so he could turn on a spitting, propane-fired space heater, which changed the smell again. Pit-smoked lobsters covered in rock weed. A New England clambake.

I looked around my new home. There were orange plastic crates filled with oysters stacked along the walls. A rack of sturdy shelving was stuffed with rusting metal rakes, fishing line, first-aid kits, and sunscreen. Down the middle of the makeshift garage, two dirt-caked picnic tables were set end to end on top of upside-down crates.

I stood on one side of the table while Berg stood on the other, facing me like a bartender. He was patient while I got my bearings. But it was time to work.

"Throw these on over your clothes," he directed, tossing me a pair of orange waterproof overalls. I wrestled them over my jeans, careful not to knock anything over. He handed me a pair of royal blue astronaut gloves, which my hands found to be clean and snugly lined.

My now-waterproofed, Oompa-Loompa self turned back to the table. Berg had emptied a full crate of muddied, seaweed-strewn oysters onto the surface between us. Another whiff, this time filled with the sour stench of mud. I picked up an oyster to examine it.

My experience with the little buggers, up until this point, had been limited to your typical, on-the-half-shell restaurant presentation: glistening on a bed of ice. Naked and brimming with meat, they weren't nearly as intimidating as the pile before me. But here, caked in fouling and dirt, the closed shells looked more like gnarly rocks and had few if any appetizing qualities.

"Better get used to these," Berg said, reading my gaze. "Now, you wanna learn how to cull?"

Culling means sorting the pile by size. Island Creek grows a standard Eastern oyster, the only oyster species native to the East Coast (it sometimes goes by its Latin name, *Crassostrea virginica*). Because oysters grow at different speeds, a single harvest might bring in several different size oysters (the ones we were looking at were almost two years old but I saw that some were the size of a silver dollar while others were as massive as my fist). In order to sell a consistent size and shape to its customers, Island Creek sorts the oysters into three standard sizes: "threes," "selects," and "Per Se's." Threes, also called "regulars," are just over three inches in length and have a deep, rounded bottom shell, called the cup. These, Berg explained, could be a little elongated, even spindly looking, just as long as they had a deep cup and were longer than three inches. The other two sizes are a little smaller (three inches exactly) and the difference between them appeared to be next to nothing, except for a specifically rounded shape. The latter two would be a little harder for me to identify, he said.

Berg sorted while he talked, holding up specimens as examples. He came to one that looked perfectly good to me (a three, perhaps?) but tossed it into a crate by his feet.

"What's wrong with that one?" I asked.

He picked it up and pointed out a tiny crack in the shell, where inside I could see a sliver of cream-colored meat.

"By the time this gets to a restaurant, it'll be dead," he said. "Instead, we'll put it back in the water and within a few months, it'll repair itself and we can drag it back up and sell it later."

Hold the phone. These things repair themselves? I'd slurped back hundreds of oysters in my day but knew next to nothing about the animals themselves. They could physically regrow their shells and fix their own imperfections, thereby turning themselves into sellable oysters? I had a lot to learn.

After watching Berg sort a few more, I picked up an oyster to consider it carefully. I examined the shell. No cracks. I smelled it, inhaling its musky dankness. Sweet dirt. Seaweed. Ocean air. Oyster.

Berg handed me a measuring tool, a wide, flat, three-inch metal ring. I tried to slide the oyster through the ring lengthwise, but it wouldn't fit. Bigger than three inches. I followed Berg's lead and tossed it into the "threes" crate. Berg watched my hands closely.

"See how this one's a little smaller, with a deep cup?" he said, taking another oyster from me and holding it at eye level, showing a full inch of cup between his forefinger and thumb. I nodded.

"See how it's rounded like this? You can see how it would sit well on a plate."

I nodded.

"That's a perfect select," he said, dropping it into the crate.

I was utterly confused, hoping desperately that something would soak in. The cull, I would learn, was not a

cut-and-dried process. Technically, it was the very deliberate act of sorting oysters by size and shape. But in actuality,
it was about acting and reacting, about decisiveness, and
about feel.

A fellow crewmate would tell me later that culling taught
her how to exist in the moment. "You have to act fast, you
have to stay focused," she said. "It's not about what's in the
crates to come or what you've already finished. It's about
what's right in front of you."

The tools required are a well-trained eye and, in the
state of Massachusetts, a three-inch ring used to measure
the length of the shell. The state does not allow the sale of
native sub-three-inch oysters, and similar to lobster or fishing regulations, it's a rule that is meant to encourage shellfish harvesters to throw back the little ones, which should
then grow larger and potentially procreate, adding more of
the species to the environment. It is, in the opinion of the
farmers, an outdated law that may have made sense when
the Massachusetts coastline brimmed with wild oysters (well
before Island Creek's time) when anything sub-three-inch
was likely too young to harvest. But for the modern oyster
farmer who repopulates the waterway with a new oyster
crop every year, ensuring an unending supply, the law can
be a headache.

Still, it was the law that day, so Island Creek worked
around it by selling their plum-sized, deep-cupped precisely
three-inch oysters, their "selects," out of state. In fact, they'd
made quite a business selling those near-perfect specimens,
which chefs loved, to the top restaurants in the country

like Le Bernardin, Masa, Alinea, Craft, and a popular little spot called Per Se.

Chef Thomas Keller had been buying Island Creeks since opening his legendary New York restaurant Per Se in 2004. Actually, the introduction came just before the acclaimed restaurant's opening, thanks to a serendipitous kitchen fire that destroyed hundreds of thousands of dollars in equipment and stalled the operation for several months. Keller's kitchen staff, left out of work temporarily, traveled to various locations doing research. Rory Hermann, a sous chef at the time, ended up in Duxbury in the dead of winter and stumbled upon the growers at Island Creek. After spending a few frigid days on the farm, he hand-selected several of Skip's deep-bellied oysters and brought them down to the now-ready-to-open Per Se to try them out with Keller's signature dish, Oysters and Pearls, a silky combination of tapioca pudding infused, and topped, with oysters and finished with a dollop of caviar. It turned out that Island Creeks were a perfect fit. Today, Skip culls out that specific size and shape, calls it a "Per Se," and ships thousands a week to Per Se and Keller's other hot-spot restaurant in Napa Valley, the French Laundry.

But Keller and his legendary dish were the last things on my mind as I stood holding the three-inch ring in one hand and sifting through a pile of unwashed oysters with the other. All I could think about were my feet, which were frozen solid. And the fact that I'd only been at it for an hour. I watched A2 out of the corner of my eye. He'd been culling quietly alongside us, giving advice here and there, but had gone through several crates by himself already. I looked down at the pile between Berg and me, which was dwindling slowly. My frozen feet and I would have to pick up the pace and push through.

"What about this one?" I asked, holding up a particularly mangled oddity.

Berg took it from me, flipped it around in his glove to feel its heft, and held it up to the ring.

"I'd sell that," he said, tossing it into one of the sorting crates. Training my mind to see the oyster for more than just a bumpy mottled shell would take weeks, maybe even months.

"You learn it as you go," Berg reassured me with a telling look; his patience with my newbie status hinted that he, too, had once looked at oysters with untrained eyes. It wasn't just about the length or the shape, he added. It was about meat content, how it would rest on a plate, and even the sturdiness of the shell. Were there cracks near the edge? Had the metal dredge rake punctured a hole in it? Would it look good on a bed of ice? I wasn't just tossing oysters around. I was looking for ones with potential.

It took some time for me to figure out what all the fuss was about. But while culling felt like mind-numbing work, if I wasn't on my game, wasn't paying attention to every oyster in my hand, I might destroy an entire order, or worse, multiple orders. Consistency to the point that every oyster in every bag looks the same is what Skip hangs his hat on, Berg explained. Some oyster farms have machines that do this job, but not Island Creek. Thankfully, the cull wasn't the last quality-control check, or even the next to last. Oysters at Island Creek are generally handled around fifteen to twenty times during their brief year-and-a-half-long lives. After the cull, they are washed; tapped together a few times to make sure they are full of healthy, living meat; counted out by hand; put into bags; and usually spot-checked again before going out on a delivery truck to restaurants around the country. Of course, all of that hands-on care and attention comes at a nice premium. Island Creek can sell oysters at around seventy-five cents apiece, more if they're shipped across the country. Gulf oysters, Blue Points, and other generic East Coast varieties would be lucky to get fifty cents. Chefs willing to pay for Island Creek's artisanal quality get consistency, flavor, and almost 100 percent yield every time.

Berg casually threw out numbers, but my brain was having a hard time processing so much new information. There seemed to be a never-ending supply of crates to cull through. And I was overwhelmed.

"Coffee?" he finally asked.

My gloves were already off.

We walked past the crumbling Maritime School toward the main road, where we found ourselves facing a small town center. The short row of buildings looked like it could have been there for a century, very quaint and almost untouched, like a little piece of the past. Nestled among the businesses, between a real estate office and a wine shop, sat French Memories, a classic French bakery and café. The guys and I made our way indoors, where the smell of fresh coffee and baking bread brought the blood back into my toes.

Frenchie's is the farm's unofficial watercooler. Island

Creek Oysters is actually made up of a number of grow-ers, about twenty total, who all grow oysters within Dux-bury Bay; many have their own farm crews, like Skip does. But while Skip's barge was set close to the harbor, during the winter the other farm crews worked off the water—in rented garages, mostly—and came down to the harbor daily, sometimes stopping by Frenchie's for a quick lunch or cof-fee break. It was where we'd run into other crews, chat about the weather, catch up on each other's work, and share a cup of coffee. The Andys knew the staff there well: Behind the counter, a handful of chirping, kindly women stood at the ready, asking us if we wanted some croissants or a few cookies to take with us. They greeted the Andys and introduced themselves to me warmly.

A group of grandfatherly gentlemen sat together at a table, all bundled in wool sweaters, chattering over coffee. It was only about nine A.M. but it looked as though they and the rest of town had been awake for hours. As I filled my self-serve coffee cup, I got a few nods of acknowledg-ment, except for one fellow who stared at me oddly. I smiled and shuffled away, glancing down at myself; I'd removed the rubber suit before leaving the float but I was still filthy. My boots were covered in slick grime and there were bits of seaweed clinging to my sleeves. Berg and A2 were equally mussed up. I grinned at the three of us. Just a couple of oyster farmers grabbing coffee.

Back on the float, A2 turned on some music. He was a music junkie, he admitted, with tastes that veered from Kanye West to Jason Mraz. I was just grateful for some tunes to fuel our work. I hummed along to Billy Joel and tried to soak up the moment, the feel of the oysters, the space. As we worked, the guys nattered away, slowly revealing bits of their lives. Fresh out of the University of Rhode Island, they lived together, along with the goateed Cory, in a little rented house in Manomet, just south of Duxbury. With a degree in marine sciences and an interest in aquaculture, the surferlike Berg had gotten a job at Island Creek right out of college; A2, a landscape architect major and Berg's bearish college buddy, tagged along, taking up an interim job on the farm crew while he waited for something to stir him into a more permanent career. A2 seemed shy at first but had a sarcastic streak and a whip-smart sense of humor. He tossed out movie quotes or pounced on Berg's commentary, adding his own comical barbs whenever the opportunity allowed. I could tell that while he was perfectly content working on an oyster farm for his first year out of college, this wouldn't be his life's calling, like it was for Berg. He was interested but it wasn't his passion. Berg, meanwhile, had an answer for everything when it came to oysters. He was serious, with a tough exterior, and cracked only when A2 got under his skin with a silly joke. Together, they were an odd couple, bickering over who left dishes in the sink or trading sarcastic jabs.

"We spend a lot of time in here together. *A lot*," Berg explained at one point.

Their curiosity about my life came out in spurts. Did I eat oysters? Where did I live? What was I doing before? But it was my former writing life that piqued A2's interest.

"Wait, you would go out to eat, write about it, and someone paid you for that? Unreal," he stated, mildly impressed.

While I'd gotten the formal spiel about the farm and its setup from Shore, I wanted to know more about the other growers, and especially the other farm crews. All twenty of Island Creek's growers worked independently, Berg explained. Skip had been the first to start growing oysters in Duxbury but he was quickly joined by a friend from Maine named Christian Horne, and later a guy he grew up with named Don Merry, as well as his own father, Billy. In fact, all of the growers were close friends of Skip's and had grown up on the water. As the company grew, Skip and the other guys started hiring seasonal workers, mostly buddies or local high school students, to help with the daily tasks: harvesting oysters, culling, bagging. Eventually, Skip hired a couple of year-round employees, a skeleton crew, which is what Berg, A2, and I had become.

To handle the business of selling the oysters, Skip had also created the wholesale arm, called Island Creek Oysters, Inc., which is now the farm's sales vehicle—an independent entity that buys oysters directly from the growers for a fair, flat rate, and then in turn, sells the oysters to restaurants around the country. Because the growers are independent, they each run their own business: hiring their own crews, buying their own equipment, and managing their own oyster stocks. Skip, an independent grower as well as the owner of the wholesale company, is in charge of both entities; he'd delegated day-to-day management of the crew to Berg and of the wholesale arm to Shore, allowing himself time to float between the two.

Once they harvest and bag their oysters, the growers (and crews) take their bags up to the shop, where Cory works. Cory is the wholesale arm's quality-control manager, so he usually gives the oysters one final check before routing them onto the delivery trucks for the day. CJ, the languid blond I'd met with Shore the previous summer, was, at the time, in charge of getting the oysters from the shop to the sixty or so restaurants where they were served around Boston. CJ was a beloved Boston personality who, like Skip, got a kick out of walking through the back door of a restaurant and straight into the kitchen. He usually walked away with a to-go box of food or an invitation to come back for dinner.

I heard the sound of footsteps outside the house and a minute later Skip appeared, his tall frame and thrown-back shoulders filling the doorway. He was bundled up in a knit ski cap and a thick, woolly sweater.

"What's up, guys!" he said, smiling.

Our boss moved around the space easily, picking up oysters as he chatted with Berg. He had the body of a quarterback, muscular and confident, toughened by a lifetime of working outdoors. The skin around his eyes crinkled slightly when he laughed. He was loose and relaxed, completely comfortable in his own skin.

He picked up an oyster, clasping it around its rim. "These look good, Berg. How's our new employee doing?" he asked, smiling at me from across the table.

"She's getting the hang of it," Berg replied for me.

"Have you tried one yet?" Skip asked me, pulling a knife off the shelf. Before I could answer, he'd popped an oyster open and held it out to me. I took off my gloves to hold the jagged shell and inhale the salty specimen. I'd been handling the rough-edged exterior of the animals all morning; seeing and smelling the cream-colored meat was almost shocking. I slurped it back and chewed, relishing the hit of briny water and burst of sweet meat. Skip plucked another few out of a crate and shucked one for himself and each of the Andys.

"They taste amazing right now," he said after a few chews. "This is the best way to eat them, right out of the water," he said. "Quality control, right, Berg?"

Berg nodded, happy to see his boss pleased.

Skip pulled on a pair of gloves and started to cull across the table from me. After sorting a few, he held an oyster out for me to inspect.

"What would you do with that one?" he asked.

I took it from him and measured it with the ring, wondering if this was a trick question.

"Uh, I guess I'd put it in the threes crate," I said reluctantly. He took the oyster back and held it up so that it was eye level.

"I think you're right," he said. "Just a little game I like to play with new folks," he added with a smile. I could tell that he was a kid at heart, as young in spirit as his crew was in age.

He stayed and culled for a few more minutes, then took off his gloves and announced he had to head back up to the office. "Hey, are we hitting the tide tomorrow?" he asked before walking out the door.

Berg pulled a tide chart out of his back pocket, flipping through the pages. "Sure, looks like a good one in the afternoon."

Skip hesitated a moment and looked over at me. "Think you'll be up for a trip on the water?"

"Sure," I replied, trying to sound nonchalant.

"We'll make sure she's ready," Berg called out, but Skip was already out the door.

We spent the rest of the afternoon culling, until Berg called it quitting time. The sun never emerged and despite working in a heated space, I was frozen stiff. Berg drove me back up to the shop to pick up my car, and as I got out, told me I'd done well for my first day.

"Hopefully you'll be back tomorrow?" he asked with that brotherly smile. Yes, I told him. After a good night's sleep.

That night, I tried to download my day to my husband, Dave, who admitted he understood only about a quarter of what I was telling him. Helping him get his head around the space, the process, and our actions would take some time. I still had a million questions myself: When would the float go in the water? What was it like to harvest? And how in the world would I hold up in this cold?

As I peeled myself out of my clothes, I did a mental checklist of how I felt. My feet were still tingling and there was a dull ache in my lower back. Was I cut out for this? The guys moved so effortlessly, lifting and hauling crates. Would I slow them down?

On the other hand, I already felt like one of the guys. By the end of the day I'd gotten them to drop the FNG business. Nicknames were big at Island Creek. Besides Berg and A2, I'd eventually come to know Bug, Benny, Squeege, Hans, X-Man, The Don, Jeeves, The Rook, D.G., Hewie,

F.O.B., Zeech, The Vick, Killer, Gard, Pogie, and Sam. It was like living in a Mob film. I needed one of my own, so A2 and Berg tried some out to see what stuck: E. E-Rock. E-Bear? Time would tell.

The next afternoon, the clouds over the bay hung low and thick as we walked down the dock toward Skip's twenty-three-foot-long blue skiff. We were headed out for my first trip on the tide.

"You sure you don't want to put on something warmer?" Skip asked over his shoulder. I looked down at the thick Army green waders I was wearing. They were a size too big and cinched around my waist with a bit of rope. I also had on a fleece ski cap, thickly lined gloves, a layer of long underwear, and two pairs of socks. But suddenly, I felt completely vulnerable.

"The hardest part is the ride out," he assured me as he climbed aboard. "It's just like riding the ski lift. Once you get out there, you're fine."

He paused a little too dramatically. "But the ride definitely sucks."

I stepped onto the boat awkwardly, grabbing a metal bar that framed the console to keep from falling on my face while Skip, Berg, and A2 muffled their laughter. Turns out, I wasn't much of a boater. As Skip pulled us away from the dock, I clutched the bar to steady myself. We bumped across the chop toward the middle of the bay.

We were surrounded by land on all sides. The Powder Point Bridge took up a long stretch of the view to the north while Duxbury Beach, a barrier that protected us from the Atlantic Ocean, sat to our east. It stretched down like a spindly finger, ending at Saquish Point. Directly in front of that sat Clark's Island; Skip pointed it out, explaining that the Pilgrims actually landed there before reaching Plymouth.

We slowed to a crawl as we neared the acreage of the bay floor that Skip leased from the state (public waters are all state and federally controlled so growers "lease" certain acres for shellfish farming). The tide was quickly draining out of the bay, a ten-foot drop that happened during every new and full moon, revealing the naturally occurring raised flats. We were a few days into a new moon cycle so the tide wouldn't stay out very long, but it would give us enough time to harvest by hand, a process that was only possible a few days out of the month. Normally, when the tide was up, Skip or Berg harvested by dragging; they pulled a handmade metal dredge with a net attached to the back along the bottom of the bay floor behind the boat, then used a small mechanical winch to haul the net, usually full of oysters, into the boat. But today, during one of the coldest, darkest days of March, we were out on the lease to pick oysters by hand.

It was a slow process compared to dragging. But in Skip's opinion, it was easy money. You could hit all the spots that you couldn't reach with the dredge and pull up only the ones that were perfectly sized, he told me as he nudged the boat out of the waterway and onto the muddy bank of the flat. At the southerly edge of the lease, the tide had pulled back to reveal dull coffee-colored mud dotted with black bits of shell. Here and there, tiny divots were filled with water, reflecting the ever-darkening sky. The entire expanse was settled thickly with a blanket of jagged-edged oysters—too many to count. Tufts of slippery kelp and seaweed stood out from the brown-on-brown surface. But once my eyes adjusted, I picked out vivid oranges, dashes of grassy green, and spots of neon red—from various underwater sea life and the oyster shells themselves.

The Andys lowered themselves into the shin-deep water, each grabbing a stack of empty crates. The idea was to fill as many crates as we could before the tide came back up, drowning the lease, the oysters, but hopefully not us.

I held on to the side of the boat and lowered myself into the water backward. The cold rush of water suctioned the rubber to my shins. My boots immediately sank in the mud. I yanked to pull one out and stumbled forward, grabbing the boat to level myself.

"You okay over there?" Skip asked. He was a few steps ahead of me, practically gliding in his boots.

I trudged after him, wondering how long it would take to master the wader walk. A few steps in and I was panting. I'd managed to grab an empty five-gallon bucket from the boat but was ready to ditch it in order to steady myself. I eventually reached the guys and higher ground where the water had drained completely.

The guys dropped the crates in the middle of a huge patch of oysters. A2 grabbed a few crates and led me to a spot that seemed particularly packed with shells. I shuffled behind him, feeling the crack of shells under my feet, but A2 assured me they were strong enough to bear my weight. The sheer number of oysters made me nervous. Just how many were we expected to pick today?

"Only fill the crate with the good ones," A2 said, leaning over to pull an example out of the mud. I followed his lead, pinching at an oyster with my crab-claw glove. The mud slurped as I pulled, releasing a bubble of sour air.

I examined the mud-caked shell. It was a perfect teardrop with a sharp hinge at the bottom and bumpy ridges across the back. I tossed it gently into a crate. I picked up another so misshapen it looked like a boomerang. Eager to do my job well, I showed it to A2; he shook his head, meaning I could leave it in the mud. My mind drifted back to the cull, with Berg's voice running through my head. Deep cup, round shape. I knew I should be looking for good threes, but with all the shells buried in the mud, it was hard to tell good from bad.

I kept at it, tossing oysters into the crate, shoving aside an errant flap of kelp or picking slimy strings of seaweed off the oysters. I reeled back when a long, purple centipede-like creature crawled out of the mud, oozing milky white goo. Skip walked up.

"I was hoping we'd see some of these," he said, picking up the seaworm and laying it across his glove. "They come out every year about this time to lay their eggs."

Everywhere I looked, there was life, from a tiny, flapping fish to air bubbles in the mud. Random spritzes of water occasionally shot out of the ground.

"Razor clams," A2 informed me.

Soon, my fleece and waders were covered in mud and my lower back was killing me. I stood up to straighten it and studied the guys as they bent over in concentrated work. They each had a different stance.

Skip had a football center–thing going, like he was ready to hike the ball: legs wide, knees bent, elbows supported on his thighs. He was picking what was between his legs or directly in front of him and kept the crate to his side. He'd pick and toss in one quick motion, then take a step forward and do it again. He'd been digging clams his whole life and it showed.

Berg was hinged at the waist, placing one foot in front of the other. He moved quickly, his hands flying. He never once lifted his upper body.

A2 had a more casual stance. He was down on one knee, leaning on the edge of a crate while he picked and later, down on both knees, picking what was directly beside him. It looked comfortable but not terribly efficient.

I decided to try Skip's method and opened my legs wide. As soon as I bent my knees, the pressure in my back disappeared. I squatted, feeling the burn in my glutes.

Not too long ago, I had spent a lot of money at a well-known yoga studio, where in hundred-degree heat a yogi put me and my designer yoga pants into this exact same pose. Nothing about this moment felt like a yoga class—except that I was sweating my ass off. Well, that and I was trying hard to control my breathing. Lean over, inhale. Toss the oyster, exhale. Apparently, that had been money well spent.

I stood up to look around again, realizing that in the time it had taken me to fill a single crate, the guys had filled five apiece. Skip was on his way over to check on me.

"Getting the hang of it?"

"I think so," I said. I was dying to ask how long we'd be out there but kept my mouth shut, worried I would sound whiny. The cold was creeping painfully through me. As he walked away, I shook my hands to get the blood flowing. A light mist had started to fall, causing the water to crystallize on the mud. The temperature was dropping.

I leaned over to keep digging and tossing. The oysters we were picking were close to two years old, but I also found massive specimens, what the guys called jumbos: They were sometimes four, six, or eight inches long, and their shells felt gnarly from years of growth. They'd been missed in earlier harvests. But a surprising number of restaurants ordered jumbos specifically because they're great for frying or cooking in soups and stews. I decided to put a few in the crate in case Berg wanted to bag them up.

Skip and Berg took a break from picking to walk around the lease, bodies huddled beside each other in conversation. From the way Berg stuck close to Skip's side, it looked like a teacher-student lesson. Like Obi-Wan giving guidance to Luke. The two were feeding off each other's energy.

I was daunted by the idea of filling another crate. Shouldn't the tide be coming back up? Suddenly, a man appeared out of nowhere. He was without boat or explanation but was bundled up in wader boots and a winter jacket, carrying a camera.

He introduced himself as David but didn't move forward to shake hands. Looking down, I saw why: My gloves were covered up to the wrists in mud with an oyster in each hand. He was the farm's official photographer and wanted a few shots of us picking.

Later that night, after a very long shower, I checked my e-mail and found that he'd sent me a few images. There was one of me arm-deep in the mud with a smile plastered across my face. I remembered feeling cold, confused, and completely out of my element. But apparently, despite the millions of goose bumps, the fear, the nerves, and the self-consciousness, I was also having fun.

How to Shuck an Oyster

Before I picked up an oyster knife, I watched others shuck. I would ask them to do it slowly so I could study their steps carefully. Skip eventually taught me the method below, and after a few practice runs, it quickly became my fail-proof shucking method. The trick: Don't use force, use finesse.

1. First, find a really good shucking knife. Island Creek uses a French brand called Déglon, which is what I learned to shuck with and will never go back. With its supersharp blade and plastic handle, it's sturdy and works efficiently.

2. Put on a glove or wrap a thick towel around your hand before you grab your oyster.

3. Place the oyster cup, or rounded side, down on a flat surface, using your gloved hand to hold it in place.

4. Holding the knife horizontally, place the tip into the hinge (the pointed tip of the oyster) at a forty-five-degree angle. Carefully jimmy the knife into the hinge using just a little bit of pressure, twisting the knife a few times to release the hinge. You'll feel the top shell pop slightly once you've released it.

5. Once the top shell pops, turn the blade of the knife toward you so that it's now vertical—this twist will separate the two shells. Then, holding the oyster in your gloved hand, slide the knife horizontally against the inside of the top shell to sever the adductor meat from the shell. Remove the top shell completely.

6. Slide the knife underneath the meat inside the cupped shell to release the second adductor muscle.

7. Slurp it straight from the shell. (As CJ, our lovable delivery guy, says, "Oysters come with their own bio-degradable plates.")

CHAPTER TWO

PAIN

There were more cons than pros to being an oyster farmer year-round. The winter brought shorter workdays, sure. But all I saw were cons: cold, ice, wind, and solitude. Not to mention my two biggest challenges: frostbitten feet and the cumbersome task of hauling crates.

The crates Island Creek uses are French, made of an indestructible orange plastic, and designed specifically for shellfish farming. Each one holds some three hundred oysters and when full weighs around fifty pounds. When stacked one way, they nest together to save space; stacked the other way, the top crate rests in the nooks of the bottom crate in a way that won't crush its contents.

Sounds simple enough, but it took me weeks of doing it four or five times a day to get a handle on the stacking system. Each crate was like a puzzle piece and I had to concentrate *really hard* to fit them together. I only had a split second to drop one in place, release the fifty pounds of weight, keep my fingers from getting crunched between the crate and whatever surface was around it, and then pivot away so that whoever was carrying the crate behind me could stack theirs, too. I lost count of all of my pinched fingers and, after a few days, stopped apologizing to A2 for constantly being in the way while he tried to stack. I started to hate the crates. But they were useful tools that I would eventually feel more of a kinship with than the oysters themselves. Berg joked that if he ever got a tattoo, it wouldn't be an oyster. It would be two orange crates, one on each bicep.

Because our float was sitting in the middle of a parking lot, we didn't have access to a water supply or a hose. This meant we culled oysters on the float and then hauled our crates back to the shop, where we would bag them up inside Cory's space. Each day we loaded around twenty crates, or about one thousand pounds of culled oysters, onto the farm truck, then unloaded them at the shop to wash, count, and bag everything. It didn't feel like farming. It felt like we were in the moving business.

On my first day, I stacked three crates onto the truck before I was gasping, arms aching as I lifted with my shoulders to get the crate waist high. On my fourth attempt, I heaved a crate too sharply and a dozen oysters crashed to the ground.

"Easy on the 'sters," Berg scolded, no longer amused at my beginner status.

My second day, I stacked five pretty quickly but then stumbled to lift the sixth. A2 stood behind me, craning his neck to watch me wrestle it into place. My hands cramped. I eventually moved out of the way and took a breather while he stacked the rest.

By day three, I couldn't lift my arms above my shoulders. The simple act of grasping the crate handle was excruciating.

The end of my first week couldn't come fast enough. When I finally slumped into my car on Friday afternoon, I felt like I'd endured boot camp. As I pulled onto the highway, that whimper that had stuck so long in my throat finally pushed itself free. My muscles screamed. I was a wreck from all of the standing, lifting, and constant motion. And I still hadn't wrapped my head around the process. Every night, I'd gone home with the intention of doing some research online to figure out just how an oyster grows but would crash into bed instead. I had the basics. Harvesting oysters. Culling. Crew camaraderie. Where that fit into the big picture of an oyster's life or even how the farm operated, I had no clue.

One night, scrubbed clean and feeling somewhat refreshed, I had dinner with an old DailyCandy colleague. We met at a new Beacon Hill hot spot where under expensive chandeliers we munched on lamb pizzas as I regaled her with stories about my new job: the pain, the discomfort, the mental fatigue. She giggled at the thought of me in my mud boots lifting heavy crates all day long.

"You're a farmer, girl," she said, a little wide-eyed. "You get to play in the mud. Who wouldn't kill to do what you're doing right now?"

She's glamorizing it, I thought. *She thinks it's fun! And frivolous!* It took me most of the night to realize that not so long ago, that had been me: utterly clueless about the amount of work that goes into farming.

I woke up early the next morning only to find that the blood had drained from my hands overnight. I wrung them out, trying to get rid of that funky rag doll sensation. My wrists were stiff and pain shot through every muscle in my fingers. Holding my toothbrush was a chore.

Dave tried to be sympathetic. What had started out as an exciting, life-changing experience for us both (him, in that he would be living intimately with someone who had the atypical job of farming oysters for a living) was quickly revealing some harsh realities, my pain being the worst.

"Better get used to those aches and pains, farm girl," he teased, and then very kindly gave me a ten-minute neck rub.

Figuring out how to combat sore muscles was all-consuming. Each morning, I'd down a few Advil with my breakfast—sometimes two, sometimes four—but the effects always wore off before our coffee break. I'd take baths instead of showers and soak for full hours. A massage would have been nice, had I an ounce of extra time—or money. My body was being torn apart and rebuilt at an impossible rate.

A few weeks later, I woke up to my alarm, turned my body, and felt the jolt of broken tissue ripple across my back and neck. The pain stiffened me upright. Had I torn something? I'd been lifting more and more crates and feeling stronger. When did I pull something? I twisted again, trying to untangle the knot. I stretched, holding my breath in anticipation of the pain. Slowly, I loosened. It wasn't serious. I couldn't turn my neck easily, but I could get up.

I was dismal and cranky all morning. It was pouring rain and my jeans were soaked through before our first trip to Frenchie's (I'd been culling without the orange jumpsuit for weeks, finding it too bulky to wear on the float). A2, who usually had me giggling with some story about his roommates while we culled, read my generally morose attitude and finally suggested a break. I tossed my gloves on the table and practically shot out the door. Without thinking, I sat on the edge of the float to jump down, realizing seconds too late that I'd drenched my butt and my underwear on the soaking wood.

"*Goddammit!*" I screamed. "It's freezing out here. I can't lift my arms. This weather sucks. Now my ass is all wet."

A2 reeled back like I'd punched him. "Whoa. You okay?" he asked cautiously. It was the first time I'd shown any sign of frustration.

"I'm fine," I spat back. "I just need coffee."

A few hours later, we were stacking crates on the truck, getting ready to head up to the shop for the afternoon. I grabbed a crate from inside the house and walked toward the truck, which sat level with the float. As I stepped onto the truck, my toe caught the cleat fastened to the edge of the float. I stumbled face-first, dropping the fifty-pound crate. One leg slid forward, lodging itself between the float and the truck. My other knee folded beneath me and took the brunt of my weight as it was crushed against the truck. My neck landed on the edge of my fallen crate, bruising my windpipe and instantly knocking the breath out of me.

A2 appeared beside me, pulling me up to my feet. "Holy

shit! Did you break anything? Are you okay?" he shouted, panicked.

I leaned on him, rubbing my throat. My neck was sore and I'd battered my legs, but I could tell by his face that it looked much worse.

"I'm fine," I breathed. My eyes welled up, mostly out of embarrassment. A2 put his arm around me, hugging my shoulders.

"You scared the crap out of me. Take it easy, okay?"

I hobbled to the bathroom to check my injuries. In front of the mirror, I put my head in my hands. My body wasn't cut out for this work. I should have been at home, at my computer, sipping hot tea. Instead I was soaked to the bone, freezing and falling face-first into a pile of oysters. What was I trying to prove?

I looked at my red-eyed reflection in the mirror. "Pathetic," I mumbled to myself. Somewhere inside my head, a voice mocked: *You asked for this.* I wiped my eyes and went back to the float.

That night, I came home to an empty house. Dave was at a concert with his buddies. There were leftovers, which I heated up and scarfed down without tasting any of it. I poured a glass of expensive Pinot Noir (wine was one luxury I refused to give up), changed into a bathrobe, and drew a scalding-hot bath. Savoring every inch of heat, I sank into the tub, laid my head back, and closed my eyes. Tears streamed down my face as I thought back to the days when I didn't carry crates around for a living. My dream of escaping to something thrilling and radical felt like it might turn into a hellish nightmare. What was I doing there? I wiped away the tears and tried to think of nothing except breathing for as long as my mind would let me.

Over an hour later, I emerged limp and pruny. I decided to answer some e-mails I'd been avoiding only to find my in-box cluttered with disturbing news. A close friend and former colleague had been laid off by her magazine employer. There were rumors that more publications were about to do the same, a move that would leave a lot of my friends desperate or clinging to their jobs. I read through more notes before shutting off the computer—I didn't know how to respond.

The next morning, I woke up refreshed. I stretched lazily to find that my injuries weren't nearly as bad as they could have been. Coffee tasted good. I made myself an extra egg for breakfast. I sang along to every song on my drive to the farm.

As I crested the hill on Harrison Street, a thrill raced through me. The bay was glinting in the sunlight and I'd lost that hint of doubt—I knew exactly what I was doing there. I thought about the day ahead, about A2 and Berg and their banter. They'd settled on a new nickname for me: Pain, short for E-Pain, in honor of the rap artist T-Pain. The float was our haven, one without desks, soul-crushing e-mails, or fear of layoffs. It was just us, our laughter, and the oysters.

We'd gotten into a routine: cull on the float in the morning, move up to the shop after lunch for washing and bagging.

Meals came from Bennett's General Store across the street. I came to crave their salty chicken corn chowder, a creamy, red-pepper-flaked affair that both satiated and warmed me. (My appetite had grown immensely. Meals were now fuel.) After gorging ourselves, usually standing up, we would take over the shop, crank up the heat, close the garage door, and turn on the music. No matter how many bags we put in, afternoons at the shop seemed to fly by (whereas on the float, mornings could drag on forever).

Cory was often around, full of shouts and smiles. He liked to cheer us on—"Yeah, crew!"—or give us a round of applause just for showing up. I got to know the farm's other familiar faces, like CJ, whose long blond hair was usually pinned down by a ski cap and whose sleepy eyes always made him look either stoned or hungover (usually it was neither, just sleepiness). He would load up the truck slowly, offering us a "Hey, dudes," while we stacked crates around him. (I'd been so fascinated by CJ and the delivery job that afforded him the opportunity to snack his way through Boston's most notable restaurant kitchens that before arriving on the farm, I'd actually written a feature article about him for one of the city's nightlife magazines.) There was also Jeeves—a name A2 had given to the two guys who worked for Billy Bennett, Skip's dad. Individually known as Joe and Steve, they worked inside Billy's seafood shack, which was attached to Cory's shop. Joe was Billy's grandson, Skip's nephew, and Steve was one of his college buddies, but they were usually mistaken for twin brothers.

Between this new cast of characters, the trucks rolling

in and out, farmers dropping off their bags, and the wholesale team dashing around, the place was a beehive. But I liked the energy. It made me feel like I was a part of something bigger.

Island Creek sells its oysters in stiff, plastic mesh bags, similar to ones you'd see filled with onions or potatoes in the grocery store. These were bright yellow with the company's logo printed in white and green across the middle, a black cinch tie at the top. To bag the oysters, we first needed to hose them down to get the mud and grime off. A2 and I would take turns, hosing down crate after crate over a drain in the middle of the shop (we washed them with freshwater—which can be hazardous to oysters if they sit in it for too long, but because we were just rinsing them off, this freshwater didn't harm them). Once they were clean, we would count them into one-hundred-piece bags, then stack the bags up directly in the cooler. I wore my orange overalls and blue gloves while I washed. The pants felt baggy and they brushed together when I walked, but when I stood they were like an oversized wetsuit. Berg had also found me a waterproof blue Grundéns jacket that was fleece-lined and had a pointy hood. When I wore it all together, I was indomitable. I would stand with a hose in one hand, my other hand on the crate in front of me, and spray the oysters down, jerking the side of the crate now and then to get the oysters to flip over so I could cover all sides. Spray, spray, jerk. Spray, spray, jerk. Move the clean crate aside, grab a dirty one from the stack. It was mindless, easy work but once the music went on, I lost myself in the act of washing.

After we washed, we counted. I wasn't fast, but I liked counting right from the start. We'd dump the culled oysters onto a metal table where they would scatter across the stainless steel like jacks. Each one was clean of mud and seaweed, its vibrant greens, oranges, and browns shining in the watery light.

I loved running my bare hands over the shells, feeling the weight of the oyster in my palm. Their sharp edges and knobby ridges felt like tiny joints and bones. They were heavy and solid. They felt alive.

Berg made me watch him count a few bags before trying it myself. He took two oysters, tapped the cupped sides of the shells together, gave them a hard shake, and put them in the bag. Two more oysters, tap, shake.

"What's with the tapping?" I asked.

"You can hear when they're hollow—see?" He picked up a dead one and tapped it against another shell. It sounded like tapping the side of an empty tin can or a porcelain statue, a hollow *tink tink*.

"We call those clackers," he said.

Then he took two good oysters and tapped them together. I heard a *thunk thunk*, like hitting two blocks of wood together—sturdy, dull, thick with meat. "These are good," he said, and tossed the dead one aside.

"These are returns," he said, pointing to a crate. I picked a few up and could see, with the mud washed away, that some had tiny cracks in the shell. When he shook the shell, water shot out. Those were leakers. They'd be returned to the water, where they would repair themselves by regrowing their shells around that spot.

Confident in my counting abilities, I picked up an empty bag and a wide-mouthed plastic funnel and got to work. Two oysters, tap, shake. Two. Two more oysters, shake, tap. Four. Two more oysters, *thunk, thunk.*

So focused on listening for the hollow sound, I lost count. I started over. Oysters, tap, thud, toss. I got all the way to twenty without screwing up but then started examining the shells more closely. Twenty-four. Or was that twenty-six? No, definitely twenty-four. I got to sixty-eight when my mind flipped. Sixty-six. Sixty-eight. Eighty. Eighty-two. Eighty-four. Damn. I'd missed the seventies. I looked at Berg, who was watching me.

"Lose count?" he said, his lip curling into a grin. "It's okay. Just start over. And go really slow. I like to count by twos to fifty. Some people count to fifty twice. Whatever works for you. Just make sure it's right."

I dumped bag number two and started over, counting to fifty twice. I finally filled the bag with one hundred pieces but then worried that I hadn't been concentrating on the oysters. With every subsequent bag, I focused harder.

About a week after "Pain's Fall," the sun came out and the air warmed up to fifty degrees. We opened the garage door and set our washstands outside on the driveway. My feet were warm, my hands had loosened up. A2 threw on some hip-hop and I happily belted out the lyrics. The sunshine was invigorating.

I looked down at my outfit—orange pants, green boots, blue gloves, black hat—and started giggling uncontrollably.

I put down the hose and bent over in a full belly laugh. A2 rolled his eyes.

I imagined walking into a boutique in this getup. As other women balanced precariously on pointy heels, I would bang my way through the store, knocking over handbag displays. I would remove my gloves to shake hands with the owner. Shoppers would stare at me, covering their noses from the smell. "What?" I'd ask innocently, staring them down.

My fantasy drove it home for me. I was more comfortable in these clothes than I'd ever been in a pair of heels.

I've officially done it, I thought. My city-girl life was far behind me. I was an oyster farmer.

The Island Creek Oysters Mignonette

Oyster farmers, I quickly came to learn, are offended by cocktail sauce. Originally created to mask the taste of bad shellfish, the sauce now represents an affront to all the hard work and energy farmers put into growing a perfectly delicious—and nowadays straight-from-the-water-fresh—product. Oysters are really best eaten naked or with a mist of lemon. But, to dress up the presentation, the guys taught me how to whip up this spicy mignonette, a recipe they culled from their friend—and the first chef ever to visit the farm—Chef Jeremy Sewall.

1 tablespoon jalapeño pepper, minced
¼ cup shallots, minced
1 tablespoon fresh-ground black pepper
½ cup dry white wine
½ cup white wine vinegar
2 tablespoons fresh cilantro, chopped
1 lemon cut into 8 wedges

Combine jalapeño, shallots, pepper, wine, vinegar, and cilantro in a small bowl and stir with a fork. Keep cold (on ice or in refrigerator) while shucking and plating your oysters. Top shucked oysters with a spoonful of cold sauce. Serve with lemon wedges.

MAKES ENOUGH FOR ABOUT 2 DOZEN OYSTERS

CHAPTER THREE

OUR GIRL

I became obsessed with the weather. I checked it first thing in the morning, studying the five-day forecast for signs of sixty degrees and sunshine. We suffered through buckets of rain—hard, gross, pounding showers—then were rewarded with mid-fifties and sunshine. I asked Skip's father, Billy, about the forecast regularly, too. A smaller, more weathered version of his son, Billy was always passing through the shop on his way to or from the water. He wore a baseball hat set high on his forehead, revealing watery blue eyes and the wide-mouthed smile of a happy clam. He'd spent a lifetime on the water and the deep lines in his skin proved it. He kept a weather journal, as he had been doing for years, and some days he'd stop to chat with us, perching his foot on an upside-down bucket while he told us when the wind would turn or what to keep an eye on.

"Saw terns flying on the water today," he'd say, revealing

the flattened Rs of his thick Massachusetts accent. "Bet the herring are soon to follow."

I tried to sharpen my own sense for these things, perking up when I smelled rain in the air or felt the wind change directions. It was my first time working outdoors, completely exposed to the elements, and without even training it, my body was becoming a barometer.

What I didn't feel coming was the storm brewing at home.

Dave was growing frustrated with me. We were months into my routine and our time together had become limited to a few hours between when he got home from his day job (he was now an operations manager at a music booking agency) and the time I crashed headfirst into bed at 8:30 P.M. Plus, he was still bartending, holding on to a few shifts a week to make up for the fact that I was only earning about half of what I'd made at my old job. Those extra hours were draining for him.

But I hardly noticed. I was too busy keeping a farmer's schedule—up at dawn, in bed by eight or nine. All of my waking hours were spent in Duxbury. I wanted to learn as much as I could about this new world—and that meant getting to know all of the players. I'd grab beers with Shore after work, mostly to gain a better understanding of how the farm operated but also because our conversations were long and intense; he understood what I was going through mentally and physically and was becoming a friendly shoulder to lean on. I was also bonding with A2, Berg, and Cory, occasionally spending evenings at their Manomet condo just to hang out and watch some TV. Frankly, I was sacrificing time with Dave in order to kindle a passion for something else. And while we'd struggled with mismatched schedules before, instead of my BlackBerry coming between us, this time it was my newfound relationship with the farm.

"It's fine," Dave joked one night, rubbing my back as I fell asleep on the couch. "I'll just sneak out to the bar after you're in bed. You'll never know I'm gone."

The following week, it was sharper: "Guess I'll just watch the game by myself."

Eventually, it was downright bitter. "Just once, it would be nice to go to sleep *and wake up* next to my wife."

The few hours we did spend together, I'd yawn my way through a conversation about his day or try unsuccessfully to teach him about some oyster fact I'd learned (while fascinating to me, dorky oyster knowledge held almost no interest for him). Our chats grew shorter and more soured by his rising anger over having to take public transportation everywhere. We only had one car and his commute had swelled to more than an hour, as he had to rely on a bus, then subway, to get him all of five miles from our Brighton condo to his Somerville office—and some days, from his office job over to the bar for a second eight-hour shift. Most weeknights usually ended with him cursing as he walked through the front door only to find his wife splayed on the couch, half asleep, no food in sight, and our two-year-old pup, Rex (a loving but sheepish mutt whom we'd rescued shortly after we were married), needing to go out. I, meanwhile, relished my commute against traffic every morning and selfishly tried to ignore my husband's unhappy demeanor.

Dave and I met at *Boston* magazine. He was a tall,

bearded, vaguely hipster musician moonlighting as an ad-sales guy; I was a young upstart, wrestling my way from the advertising department, where I was a lowly sales assistant, to the editorial department, where I hoped to become a lowly editor's assistant. Our friendship blossomed as we discovered a mutual love for indie, atmospheric pop music and commiserated on being transplanted Southerners: Dave was from Knoxville, Tennessee; I claimed Southern rights by being born in Georgia and having my entire immediate family spread between Texas and the Carolinas. We became happy-hour companions. We went to tiny, smoke-filled clubs, drank Budweisers, and watched local songwriters croon onstage. He dated my roommate. I was one of his band's most dedicated groupies, buying the guys beers after a set (sometimes to an empty room). He tagged along on my first few nerve-racking restaurant reviews.

Eventually, we both found ourselves single and spending all of our free time together. Our friendship had swelled to a point where we might as well have been dating. So, I invited him over to watch football and eat black-eyed peas with me on New Year's Day—our first official date. It ended, perfectly, with a kiss good night at my door. Within a month, I confessed to my mom that he was someone I could see myself buying china with. Our best friendship had easily transitioned from a buddy-buddy one to a passionate one. He was a romantic and I was smitten. A year later, he surprised me by showing up at the tail end of a press trip through Vermont. I was supposed to take a bus back to Boston the next day—he was there, he said, to give me a ride home. But really, he came to give me an engagement ring.

We got married, barefoot on a South Carolina beach, a year after that.

Musician Dave did his best not to give up on the dream of playing music full-time. But as he and the band grew older, Practical Dave emerged, pushing him to transition to something stable, something on the business side of the industry. He eventually landed a job at a small but well-known music booking agency working with some legendary blues and zydeco artists. He continued to gig with the band until his bandmates, all best friends, moved on and away. By the time I started on the farm, he hadn't been onstage in months. Instead, he was bartending a few nights a week at a Belgian beer bar called the Publick House, our favorite worn-out old haunt. Whatever camaraderie he lost when he left the band was quickly rediscovered with the bar crew. I would visit him during shifts, regaining my groupie status, to watch as he cracked everyone up singing beer-themed songs or reciting movie lines. I called his bar buddies the Band of Merry Misfits.

We'd had our moments of distance during my Daily-Candy days. But those suddenly felt like paper cuts compared to the rift my new life was causing. He was frustrated that all of my time and energy were now devoted to the farm—and that I didn't seem to care about what he was suffering through on a daily basis in order to allow me to have it. We got into it one Saturday morning, yelling across the living room at each other about schedules and money. It turned spiteful as he accused me, rightfully, of sidelining our marriage for this new job. I evaded it by violently (and wrongfully) accusing him of not supporting my quest for personal happiness. Barbs like "What are we doing in this relationship, anyway?" rang through the air. And then, suddenly, Dave brought up having kids. It came out of the blue, like a sucker punch. He spat out the one question I was terrified to answer: "So what—do you not want to have kids now? Or is it that you don't want to have kids with *me*?"

We'd talked about starting a family during our first year of marriage but decided to put it off so we could build our careers and do some traveling. But as time passed, having babies became less appealing. At least to me. Being a food writer was directly at odds with what having children entailed. I had wine to drink! Dining to do! Nine months without alcohol followed by nineteen years of responsibility? Pass.

There was more to it than that, of course. My sister, Shannon, fifteen months older than me, could not get pregnant. She and her husband, Brian, put in a grueling, three-year effort that involved needles, supplements, charts, thermometers—hardly the kinkiest of sex toys—but had finally conceded that their bodies just weren't made for having babies. They were going to adopt, she announced at Christmas that year. They wanted a baby and there were plenty out there to give a home to.

While I was thrilled for my sister's newfound conviction, her struggle was less than inspiring. Her reproductive troubles didn't necessarily have anything to do with me. But something about her situation made me feel weak. What if we had that much trouble getting pregnant? Would we ever consider adopting? We hadn't even started "trying" technically, but the thought of it just exhausted me. I was terrified of what we might find out.

"It's not you," I countered, trying to bring the argument down a few decibels. I had simply shelved the idea of having kids for the time being. Did he really want kids badly, all of a sudden? That made no sense to me, I explained. He had two jobs, one of which was being a bartender, and now I was a farmer. Where in our world would an infant fit?

I put it in simple terms: lifestyle, money, and timing. I loved him, I urged. Of course I wanted little Murrays running around.

"Just give me time," I pleaded. "Give *yourself* more time."

We dropped the fight, but I could sense that this wasn't a closed topic.

My time on the farm started to feel more like an escape than ever—from everything. There, I could put the gloves on and work. There, I could focus on nothing else but what was directly in front of me.

I was transitioning into a worker, a machine. My hands moved over the oysters with incredible speed as my eyes became trained to find the flaws. A tiny crack or chipped shell would stand out from the rocky pile and I reached for it, knowing exactly where to toss it, while my eyes flicked back to the pile in search of more imperfections. I only stopped to admire the beauties: a deep cup and perfect roundness. The signature Island Creek.

An intense, twelve-hour day in the middle of the week

before Easter made the transformation complete. We started on the float, culling as usual, while the sky poured an incessant rain around us. I felt bad for Berg: He was out on the boat, exposed to the elements, harvesting oysters with nothing but his pointy-hooded Grundéns jacket and overalls to protect him. Around ten A.M., I checked the thermometer hanging outside the float. Forty-five degrees and falling.

"The gas station guy told me it would snow today," A2 said smartly. I didn't want to believe him or his gas station guy, but worried they might be right. I fired up the space heater just in case. For once, A2 didn't make a crack about me being "Pro-Pain."

Lunchtime came and we made our way to the shop for a wash-and-bag session. Our routine had been to bag up only the oysters we needed for the daily count, usually around forty or fifty bags—that day we'd culled way more crates than necessary but figured we could wait and turn them in tomorrow. A2 and I could bang out fifty bags that afternoon, no problem. We got organized and I got busy washing. A few crates in and my mind wandered to what I'd have for dinner. I had some good energy, I thought. I might even be able to pull together a respectable meal for Dave. Tomato sauce flecked with sausage? I could serve it over farfalle with a fistful of grated parmesan and a few basil leaves. Some crusty bread on the side. Something about the threat of snow made me crave a carbo load. Peeking out the window, I caught a few snowflakes flying past. A2 just looked at me with a proud, closed-mouth grin (we'd already started bickering like siblings—I hated when he was right).

We were, for the most part, protected and warm in the shop, but my hands were starting to feel the burn of freezing water. I wanted nothing more than to get through my stack of crates and home to that hearty plate of pasta.

A2's phone rang. I heard Berg's voice through the earpiece and watched as A2's face fell. I shut off the hose as he hung up.

"Berg-man wants us to keep going," he said, sighing in frustration.

"Keep going? What does that mean?" I put out dumbly.

"It means we keep going, keep washing and bagging. All of it," he said, pointing to the full tower of crates. I did a quick calculation in my head. Fifteen more crates meant four more hours. At least. It was already three P.M.

The princess in me shrieked. "Does he expect us to get this done today? I mean, it's just the two of us! Seriously, Berg?"

I was preaching to the choir. A2 was pacing.

"I was going to the gym after this," A2 said, fire in his voice. "What the fuck, Berg."

I turned the hose back on and tried to ignore the stack behind me. The calculations kept running through my head. We called it oyster math: determining how many bags of one hundred would come out of a haul of crates. It would take me hours to wash all of those oysters, less if I half-assed a few. I kept washing but tossed each crate harder than the last as the anger welled up inside me. For once, I thought, I was going to get through the night without collapsing in exhaustion. For once, I was going to get home in time to make a decent dinner and share a conversation with my husband. But not now. Now I'd get home close to eight P.M. There would be no stopping at the grocery store, no satisfying meal. No Dave time.

I fumed. Unfair! I didn't even have a choice, which made me angrier. Why would we suddenly need so many bags in one day? There were greater forces than us making these calls—but who was making them was still a mystery to me. Was it Skip? The wholesale team? A few more crates and I was belligerent. I wasn't getting paid enough to stand here and wash oysters for twelve hours! Writing suddenly seemed so much more civilized. People in the real world didn't drive their employees to the point of mental exhaustion and physical strain like this. I was outraged.

I stopped just short of stomping my foot, crossing my arms, and screaming.

A2 was equally miffed. But instead of unleashing his inner toddler, he walked to the stereo, fiddled around with his MP3 player, and turned on Kanye West.

As Kanye's silky vocals and anthemic beats slid out of the speakers, I felt myself loosen. I mumbled to the music until it triggered something. I worked in sync with the beat, moving crates around like a dance. I turned to see A2, his back to me, head down in rhythmic concentration. He raised one arm, oyster in hand, pumping his fist to the lyric. I nodded with the beat.

I'd never known Kanye's music before meeting A2. I found it lovely and surprising to get an introduction to hardcore hip-hop from a scruffy white kid from New Hampshire. Growing up, he'd told me, his friends were into NASCAR and country music. He picked up rap. I once asked Berg for an explanation.

"I have no idea," he said, shaking his head. "No one does. The kid loves hip-hop."

We got through a few more songs, then turned on another album, and before I knew it, Kanye had been on for hours. With each thumping song, I moved farther down the stack, finally arriving at my final three crates. I looked at the clock: six P.M. A2 had slowly kept up, counting out oysters as fast as I could get them washed. Behind him, the bags were stacked up to my thighs. I did a rough count: one hundred.

"Do you realize we just did one hundred bags?" I said, tapping A2 on the shoulder. He spun around to admire the work.

"Shit," he said.

I got busy writing up tags and organizing the pile.

An hour later, with our bags packed tightly into the cooler, A2 and I leaned against the stainless steel counter, dazed from our marathon afternoon. Berg's rusting black Dodge pickup truck pulled up to the garage door and our soaking wet boss stumbled out of the front seat. I guiltily took back all my terrible thoughts.

Berg had taken a beating out there. Pulling his coat off, he asked A2 for the number.

"One hundred and three for the day," he reported proudly.

Berg stopped mid–jacket removal and his jaw dropped a little.

"Whoa," was all he could manage. "Really?"

Easter week had crept up on the wholesale company. Orders were coming in fast and furious and they needed oysters in the cooler for the next day's delivery. Our 103 bags would fill all of the additional orders and then some. Berg high-fived us for doing our little part to save the day.

I made it home in time to find Dave tossing peas and some butter into a huge pot of bowtie pasta. He took one look at me and smiled sympathetically.

"That bad, huh?" he asked, handing me a plate.

I apologized for not being home earlier, downed two helpings, then kissed Dave for putting aside his frustrations and doting on me. After which, I promptly fell into bed.

That week, we finished with a final count of 426 bags—about 200 more than an average week. Our chests puffed out as we caught up with Skip on Friday afternoon. Our boss was impressed. He handed each of us a hundred-dollar bill.

"The bonus system," he said, grinning happily at his productive crew. "You guys killed it this week."

That morning, Skip had dug up a few baskets of steamer clams. It was his favorite pastime and, he confided in me that day, his own version of therapy since it allowed him to spend a few hours alone with his thoughts. The oyster farmer had more than a few projects on his plate; between the wholesale company's business dealings, his own oyster lease and farm crew, boats to fix, oyster seed to order, and two daughters he adored more than life itself, his mind raced as he tried to balance it all. But during those moments out on the water, when it was just him, a basket, and a few hours to dig up clams, he could sort through it all to find focus—and peace.

He loaded each of us up with a bag of his steamers, as well as a sack of freshly shucked sea scallops. I topped the pile with a couple dozen oysters and called Dave to tell him we were having an Easter feast. Back at home, I stashed the scallops, steamers, and oysters in the back of the fridge, putting each bag on a plate and setting all of them over a bed of ice. Berg had instructed me not to set any of it directly on the ice: freshwater would kill the oysters and steamers; the scallops would freeze.

Sunday afternoon, I pulled everything out, inhaling the fragrance of salt and seaweed. I'd come to crave the scent of the ocean. Peeling each silky scallop apart from its chewy foot, I listened to Berg's voice in my head: Wrap them in bacon, seal it with a toothpick, and bake in a super-hot oven until just opaque.

I dumped the steamers into my fat orange Le Creuset braising pot over sizzling garlic and red pepper flakes, then poured one of Dave's hoppy, brown ales over the top, closing the lid just as it all came to a boil. Within fifteen minutes, we were heads down at the table, dipping steamer after steamer into a vat of butter, slurping oysters straight out of the shells, and nibbling the smoky scallops from their tooth-pick stakes. In the background, the lull of the Masters commentators signaled the arrival of spring. On the table, our feast signaled the arrival of a new era of eating for Dave and me, as well as a new period in our relationship. This food, which we shared and now communed over, came directly from the waters that were now, I suspected, about to pull me even farther away from my former life.

By late spring, I'd become one with our landlocked float. I got to know its nooks and crannies and spent a lot of time wondering how it was constructed. It kept me warm, protected me from the rain, and greeted me each morning with that *whap!* of nose-tingling sea smell. I liked to get to work a few minutes before the guys and warm up the space heater or organize crates. Now that I was comfortable with what went where and what was to be culled, I could set things up as soon as I arrived, getting a head start on the day. I'd turn on my iPod to something melodic and quiet, then start culling in peace. Those moments were usually shattered when A2 showed up, grumbling about having to be awake. However brief, I enjoyed them and the feeling of being completely at ease in a once-foreign space.

And then, just like that, it all changed. Our Girl was going into the water to be attached to a mooring in the middle of the bay. It had to happen eventually. And it terrified me. My big fear was getting seasick. I'd never been seasick before. But spending eight to ten hours on a rocking surface might be just the sort of thing that sets off the need to hurl into the ocean. Plus, I didn't know how to drive a boat. Would I be stranded out there? Would I be comfortable asking the guys for a ride every time I had to pee? For the first time since starting on the farm, I felt like a girl.

A2 and I were up at the shop when the move took place. I was told later that the forty-foot platform did some rocking and swaying as it was lifted up by the Maritime School's ancient, creaking boat lift. Everything inside had either been removed or secured so that things wouldn't topple. Once she was safely in the water, they tied her up to one of our little skiffs and Skip pushed her out to the mooring, way out toward the channel of the bay.

The next morning, I arrived at the harbor and found our old dirt pile abandoned. The guys were nowhere to be found. I waited in the parking lot for a bit, staring out at the tiny dot on the horizon that was to be my new home.

Mark Bouthillier, one of the other growers and a young, freckled father of two, pulled up in his pickup. I'd been getting to know the growers and their trucks one by one, usually with meetings like this at the harbor.

"Where's your crew?" he inquired.

"No idea," I replied.

"Hop in," he beckoned, offering me some warmth from the forty-degree chill. I heaved myself into the truck and we sat, watching the water, drinking our coffee. Finally, after fifteen minutes of small talk, he suggested I call my boss.

"Hey, Pain, where you at?" Berg answered.

"I'm sitting here waiting for you guys. Are you on your way?"

"Oh, sorry about that. We're already out here," he said, then paused. "Looks like you missed the boat, Pain."

Mark laughed when I told him. "Better get here early tomorrow," he offered. I hopped out and ran down to the dock, watching as Berg steered our skiff, the blue Bateau, toward the dock.

When he finally reached me, he was laughing. "Sorry, I figured you would call," he explained.

"Did I miss something? What time did you guys get here?"

"A2 wanted to start earlier today. I wasn't sure if it would be too early to call you. But you're here now, no big deal," he said. Miffed to have my first experience on the water be so awkward, I arrived at the float in a sour mood. A2 looked at me, apologetic.

The space felt different. The view was remarkably better—water on all sides, a Miles Standish monument, the town's tribute to its founder, rising up to our south—but I was all out of sorts. Things felt more compact, our stuff had been moved around. We spent the day figuring out our new systems.

We no longer had to commute up to the shop to do our washing and bagging; Berg brought out a small, gas-powered pump that pulled bay water up through a hose, which we used to wash off the oysters. I let A2 figure out the pump while I readjusted the workspace for counting. Using the table to cull, then clearing it to count, felt counterproductive at first. But those added steps actually created a more sustainable system for us—and for the farm itself.

It occurred to me, probably for the first time since starting on the farm, how environmentally friendly our floating barge was for the farm. I'd learned early on, from Shore, Skip, and Berg, that growing oysters in a sustainable way was Island Creek's mission. Oysters themselves are incredible for the environment: They filter up to forty gallons of water per day, a process that cleans the water of impurities like carbon and nitrogen, which find their way into the water from runoff and lawn fertilizers. During my first visit to the farm the previous summer, Shore had impressed me with the fact that because there are now so many Island Creek oysters on the bottom of Duxbury Bay, the bay itself is completely filtered every nine days.

The farm is ecologically minded, too. These floats, when anchored in the middle of the bay, allow work to be done in one contained environment. Oysters are either picked by hand or with the use of boats that run on low-horsepower motors, then brought to the floats, where, with nothing but man-made energy, they're culled and put into bags. The only step in the process requiring additional energy is washing the oysters, which Skip figured out how to do in a low-impact way with that gas-fueled motorized pump. Transporting the oysters to the shop and then out to the restaurants required only gasoline—and not very much since the freight was small and could be sent in bulk. Between the environmental gains made by the oysters themselves (filtering an entire bay full of water almost weekly) and the minimal use of fossil fuels (gasoline and a small amount of electricity), Island Creek Oysters was practically carbon negative.

Once I got used to our new surroundings and realized how much less labor-intensive the work would be out there (no more hauling crates!), I came to love being on the water even more than being on land. We had more visitors out there: Mark pulled up on his skiff at one point to make sure I'd made it, then gave my crew a hard time for ditching me. Christian Horne and Gregg Morris, growers who shared a boat at the time, revved past us, leaving the whole house rocking in their wake.

But the bathroom thing was definitely an issue. Berg asked me three different times if I wanted to go in. Finally, I caved. Being helpless sucked.

"Probably time for you to start driving the boat," he offered once we boarded the Bateau, and he stepped away from the wheel. We were midway through the harbor. I stiffened in fear. Drive? Skip's boat? All the way back to the dock? It was probably less than a mile but felt impossibly far. Berg wouldn't budge.

I stood behind the wheel of the twenty-three-foot skiff, timid and uncertain.

"The wheel's pretty sensitive," Berg cautioned. "Watch how you turn it." We were probably going all of five miles per hour but I could feel the power of the engine shifting to the left and right.

"Watch the channel markers," he said, pulling the wheel for me gently. We were still a dozen yards away but it took the boat longer to react than I thought. I shifted us down a gear, slowing to a crawl.

"Pain, there aren't any boats out here. Pick it up a little," Berg laughed. As we neared the docks, I panicked. How was I supposed to park this thing? I slowed down again, waiting for Berg to take over. He just stood there, watching.

"You've got to use neutral and reverse, they're your

friends," he offered. I dropped down to neutral as we coasted closer to the dock. "Turn the wheel to the left and pull into reverse," he said as we inched closer. It felt counterintuitive. Cars didn't respond this way. But I turned left and dropped into reverse. Hard. The boat's rear jerked to the side.

Berg sprung into gear and pulled the shifter back to neutral. I'd almost careened into the dock backward. He straightened out the wheel and landed her safely on the edge.

"Easy, Pain. We'll try again later," he said, patting me on the shoulder.

Despite my poor attempt at boating, the day went off smoothly. We got our bags done and just as we were loading them onto the boat, a flotilla of skiffs pulled up around us. The growers wanted to celebrate the start of summer; Shore came out, too, along with Skip and Cory, bringing with them a cooler full of beers.

It was the first time I'd seen Shore out on the water since my first tour of the farm. He greeted me with a high five and a cold beer.

"Feels good to be out on the open water, huh?" he asked. We hardly saw each other during the day but he'd been keeping a close eye on my progress, usually checking in during one of our after-work beers. I still had no idea what went on in the office or how he spent his days. In fact, the Andys referred to Shore and the rest of the wholesale team as "suits" (we, on the other hand, were "boots") and usually gave the suits a hard time about being relegated to the confines of the office. It was a rare meet-up between the two worlds and I could tell Shore was happy to be out on the float.

"Beats sitting behind a desk," I answered with a wink.

Berg's Bacon-Wrapped Scallops

One of the perks of working on an oyster farm is all the free oysters you can eat. But working on the water among fishermen also gave me access to an abundance of other sea goodies, too, including scallops caught right off the coast of Massachusetts. The day Skip sent us home with several pounds of freshly caught scallops, Berg, off the top of his head, rattled off this recipe for wrapping the little gems in bacon. Here, in his own words:

> *1–2 pounds of large sea scallops*
> *Bacon slices (one per scallop)*
> *Toothpicks*

Get your oven hot, about 450°. Make sure it's completely preheated, so be patient. Pat each scallop dry, then wrap each one in a slice of bacon and pin it all together with a toothpick. Bake 'em on a cookie sheet and make sure you watch 'em carefully. Once the bacon's browned and crispy, pull them out. Careful: They're super-hot.

SERVES 4 AS AN APPETIZER

II

Growth

An oyster leads a dreadful but exciting life.

—M. F. K. Fisher

CHAPTER FOUR

MAMA SEEDA

May came in quietly, bringing with it a new crewmate named Will Heward. An X-ray scientist for General Electric, Will was "taking a break" from the corporate world to work at Island Creek. He had a wiry frame, nervous laughter, and intense, wild eyes. He'd also grown up in Duxbury.

Something seemed off with Will. When he first arrived at the float, his hands darted about as he explained that stress at work had been bad. *Really* bad. So bad that his health was suffering. He was anxious. He wasn't sleeping. He was on medication. And he needed a time-out. He was there, he told us, to figure out what he wanted to do with the rest of his life.

Will's timing was perfect. After months of working as a threesome, A2, Berg, and I had grown tired of our own stupid jokes. We needed fresh material, which Will could no doubt provide. He was a frenetic talker, launching into monologues about his science background or love of ice hockey to anyone who would listen. He also fiddled with everything, tidying up shelves or hanging our waders. We'd transitioned from using those bulky winter gloves to a more lightweight, mesh version that we usually clipped to a clothesline to dry overnight. Every morning, Will's first order of business was to organize the gloves. He'd pull them off the line, pair them up by size, and lay them out on the deck to dry in the sun. No one ever asked this of him; it was just something he did, day after day. It quickly became a habit, like a nervous tick.

In spite of our garrulous new crewmember's quirks, we were all grateful for the extra set of hands. The monotony of culling, counting, and bagging had drawn out for weeks but summer was almost here and things were about to really pick up.

One morning, Skip called a meeting on the float. He rarely gathered us all in one spot formally like this; he usually chose to raise issues casually, like when we were out picking oysters by hand or standing across the table from each other culling. His tone was always casual, in fact. It was hard to see him a boss at all, more like a fun uncle who happened to sign our paychecks. He'd been spending more time out on the float the last few weeks. When Will arrived, he played the "What would you do with this one?" game (Will responded by laughing, examining the oyster for several minutes, then shouting out a definitive "Select!"; Skip replied that it was actually a three).

But that morning, he was here to discuss official business. I set down my three-inch ring and motioned for A2 and Will to do the same. Berg was in the middle of unloading crates off the boat and stopped what he was doing to focus on our boss. The seed was about to arrive, Skip explained. The summer crew would start trickling in soon. He wanted to outline specific leadership roles for each of us before things got too busy. As his year-round crew members, we had the privilege of being the authorities, and now it was time to delegate. Berg would manage the crew, a task he already had a handle on, while A2 would carry on as the float manager to oversee our bag count, the cull, and supplies on the float. Will was to organize the crew's forays out to the lease during low tides—our oyster-picking manager.

"We'll have a ton of picking tides during the summer and I want everyone on the crew out there working," Skip said. "You'll need to make sure they've got enough crates, gloves, buckets. And you need to keep everyone in line," he stressed. "Think you can handle it?"

Will laughed nervously before flashing an overconfident smile.

Skip turned to me. "E-Rock, I want you to be in charge of seed. You're responsible for making sure the seed gets washed every day, that it's graded when it needs to be; then you'll coordinate with Berg once it's time to get it out to the lease." He paused, adding, "You'll be our seed mama."

I grinned.

"Seed girl, huh?" Berg mocked. "Does this mean she's the mother of your babies, Skip?"

"Yup," Skip said confidently.

"Way to go, Pain. You're Skip's mama-seeda," A2 cracked.

Running the seed program was one of the biggest jobs on the crew. Every year, the farm's production was determined by how successful a seed crop was. The latter provided Skip a year's worth of product, keeping him, the wholesale team, and our entire crew afloat for almost two full harvest cycles. In some cases, the seed could make or break the fate of a farmer, even the whole company. It was the future of Island Creek.

But, you know . . . No pressure.

First, I had to figure out what a seed was.

A few days later, I found one of the farm's growers, Mike George, lying facedown on one of the Maritime School docks, the upper half of his body submerged inside a rectangular pit that was cut in the center of the wooden dock. He heard me approach and pulled himself up to reveal a clenched, dripping fist.

"Got my babies today," he grinned proudly. He opened his fingers cautiously, revealing a palm full of what looked like beige pepper flakes. Mike was one of Island Creek's youngest growers, a former University of Massachusetts football star who had left the corporate world to work for the farm. He'd started out driving Island Creek's delivery truck, then worked as a farmhand for Skip until he was able to secure his own lease and become one of the farm's growers. Standing there on the dock, he looked like a proud, nervous new father.

He reached out his hand to give me a closer look.

I was surprised to see that each oyster seed, which looked like little more than a fleck of shell, was actually a fully formed oyster in miniature. I picked a few up with my forefinger and thumb and squinted at the specimens. They were fragile, their edges thin like ash, but with a firm bead at the center: the belly. Only two and a half millimeters in length, each would eventually grow into full-size oysters like I'd been used to handling. Up close, I could see that each shell varied in color from darkish brown to jet black.

"Careful with those," Mike said, pointing to the flakes adhered to my fingertip. "That's about three dozen there."

This seed was just six weeks old and had been delivered, like ours would be, by FedEx, packed in a Styrofoam cooler, which sat open by his feet.

I knew nothing about the seed and therefore nothing about the very beginning of this whole process. But seeing that little tuft of belly meat was enough to make me curious. Island Creek, I would learn, sources its oyster seed from two different shellfish hatcheries (commercial aquaculture facilities that spawn and raise shellfish), one up in Muscongus Bay, Maine, and the other on Cape Cod, called Aquaculture Research Corporation, or ARC. Dick Kraus, who started ARC in the 1960s, was one of Skip's first contacts in the aquaculture industry; he was the guy who sold Skip his first batch of clam seed—and later became a mentor.

I got to meet Dick when I tagged along on Skip's next visit to the hatchery specialist's Cape Cod facility. The Aquaculture Research Corporation is set on an undeveloped swath of the northern shore of the Cape. It's a modest site, made up of a couple of small warehouses that sit beside a saltwater inlet. Skip led us into one of the buildings, eager to hunt down Dick. We found the tall, tanned, salt-and-pepper-haired man deep in conversation with one of the hatchery technicians, but he broke away long enough to greet Skip with a warm handshake. The two swapped industry news like old friends. Dick was experimenting with triploids; there was an outbreak of MS-X, an oyster virus, on the Cape; Skip was having some good success with last year's broodstock—could he get that one again? Flummoxed by this new vocabulary, I wondered what the hell they were talking about.

A woman named Sue, one of the hatchery experts, walked me through the facility, and in the process, gave me a brief lesson on oysters and sex. All oysters are sequentially hermaphroditic, she explained, meaning they can change sex by becoming male or female based on the needs of their particular environment (if there are too many males around, an oyster will switch to female and vice versa). Both in the wild and when farmed, Eastern oysters (the species that Island Creek grows) reproduce externally, meaning the males release sperm into the water at the same time that the females release eggs (females can produce up to 100 million eggs at one time). The sperm meets the egg, and voila: fertilization. The process is called spawning and only happens in warm water, usually over seventy degrees. In New England a spawn might occur in the wild from late May through September, but inside a hatchery, ARC specifically, specialists manipulate water temperature and force a spawn to occur in a controlled environment. First, they fatten up the adult oysters, which are chosen specifically for their lineage (as with all animal husbandry, breeding plays a large role in how they grow) by placing them in a tank and pumping it with water filled with phytoplankton, an oyster's food source, which comes from algae. They then place the well-fed oysters in temperature-controlled breeding tanks. As the temperature rises, the oysters act like they do in the wild, releasing eggs and sperm. Once there's a spawn, the fertilized seed (of which there might be millions) grows quickly, each forming its own thin shell, which will continue to grow throughout its lifetime. The seed is then collected and put into a separate control tank where the newborns are pumped continuously with fresh seawater until they've grown large enough to be shipped safely to oyster farms like Island Creek—in our case, that would get them to about two and a half millimeters or six weeks old.

Under a microscope, Sue showed me the oysters we would be getting in a few short weeks. Magnified a couple thousand times their size, the microscopic organisms looked just like their adult selves: hard shells with bulging round bellies. They were moving slightly, pumping water in and out of their tiny bodies. Somewhere, deep inside me, a motherly instinct kicked in. I thought they were adorable.

As we made our way back to Duxbury, I pummeled Skip with questions about the process. When would we get our seed? How was I supposed to take care of it? What was an upweller and how did it work? Who would help me on the crew? And when could we start?

Tickled by my newfound excitement, Skip told me to be patient. "You have no idea what's in store," he said. "But we still have plenty of time. We've got to get the upwellers in place, get our pumps running. We need the rest of the crew to get here," he offered.

"Plus," he added, eyeing me with a grin, "we still have to get through Nantucket."

Skip wasn't born into oyster farming. But oyster farming, it turned out, was what he was born to do. He grew up on the bay, digging clams and catching lobsters with his dad, Billy, who was a commercial lobsterman for years. Back then, Duxbury was still a small, off-the-beaten-path town known mostly for its stunning barrier beach and beautiful old ship-captain mansions (it had been a ship-building hub in the 1800s). Skip grew up a few miles from the water, next door to what is now the farm's headquarters, in an area of town called Island Creek, named for the crick of water that runs through it. He spent all his time in high school playing ice hockey, running around with a group of guys from the neighborhood, or out on the water in his dad's boat. He went away to Merrimack College to get himself a finance degree but came back home every summer to make extra money digging clams. After graduation, he intended to look for a finance job to go with his new degree, but first he came home to do some lobstering.

Billy, a hardworking lobsterman, had shown him the ropes as a kid, teaching him how to take care of his traps, what bait to use, and which lobsters to keep and which to throw back. Spending all that time on the water with his father taught Skip what it meant to have a work ethic as well as how to be a steward for the bay and everything in it. Billy taught him to take pride in his catch.

That summer after college, Skip caught the fishing bug, bad. Lobstering became a competitive sport between him and his father as they tried to outdo each other in their catch numbers—but it also became Skip's primary source of income. He used his commercial license to sell lobsters to a local fish market, where the fishmonger asked if he could bring in steamers and razor clams, too. Pretty soon, he'd given up on the idea of finding a desk job. He was too busy making a living on the water.

He'd heard about some guys who were farming clams down on the Cape using aquaculture, a method of farming the ocean. It was just getting off the ground in New England, chronicled in a *Boston* magazine article Skip read about Pat Woodbury, a clam farmer in Wellfleet. After a bit more digging, Skip learned that Duxbury was starting to offer grants by the acre and that residents could lease those for commercial shellfishing. He applied for one with the thought of farming clams.

It was a rocky start. Skip struggled through by selling lobsters and razor clams on the side. But to get his clam business off the ground, what he really needed was capital. Through Dick, he learned about a small research group that was interested in collecting horseshoe crabs for medical research. The 400-million-year-old species contained an incredibly rare blue-colored blood, a coagulate, that researchers were able to extract from the horseshoe crab's tail without harming the animal. Skip and Dick worked out a deal: Since Duxbury Bay was teeming with the ancient softshells, which would flock to the bay during their mating season every spring, Skip agreed to harvest them, pack them into totes, and drive them down to ARC. Dick would pay him for the crabs, which Skip would pick up after the blood had been extracted and release back into the bay. This partnership went on for a few years, during which time Skip earned enough funding to buy his first batch of quahog clam seed.

For about three years, Skip diligently watched over his clams, investing money in new equipment when he could. But timing and bad luck eventually tripped him up. In 1995, weather conditions were just right for a disease called QPX—quahog parasite unknown—to flourish in the bay. The single-celled organism existed just about everywhere clams were farmed, but every now and then it reared up in unhealthy numbers, wiping out entire crops, similar to a tomato blight.

With all of his money already poured into clam equipment, Skip's only other option was to use the equipment to grow another type of shellfish. He'd heard about guys growing oysters in other parts of New England, so he called Dick at ARC and asked for his mentor's thoughts. Dick told him he was crazy and that he'd be going from bad to worse. Skip reluctantly brushed him off. He desperately needed something, anything, to keep himself going—he was almost thirty years old, had no real job, and no other source of income. What else could he do?

Oysters had never been known to grow wild in Duxbury Bay and there was no proof that a farmed variety would do well there. Not to mention, oysters weren't known to have selling power just yet. But Skip took a chance and purchased oyster seed from a nursery in Maine. There were enough similarities between clams and oysters (they were mollusks that needed very little maintenance once they were planted) that he could use most of the same equipment until he figured out what worked and what didn't. He put the oysters into clam seed trays and spent the summer watching, cleaning, waiting, and fretting. He found moral support from the guys who ran the nursery he purchased his seed from. Called Chance Along Farm, the nursery was run by a couple of brothers who bought seed from a hatchery, where another brother, Christian, worked. Skip got to know them all, including Christian, whom he became friendly with. Eventually, Chance Along had a falling-out with the hatchery and Christian was left with a pile of seed. He and Skip started talking and Skip offered Christian space on his lease in Duxbury. In 1997, Christian brought some seed down to Skip's farm and the two started a loose partnership, growing both of their seed on the Skip's small acreage of the bay. Together, the pair started cobbling together bags of oysters and selling them to a local wholesale company. At first, they sold under Billy's fish market license, Bennett Lobster and Seafood. But slowly and surely, Duxbury oysters started to make their way into the marketplace through the seafood wholesalers Skip sold to.

Christian eventually got his own lease and the two spent their days harvesting oysters, which they would bag up and deliver to wholesalers. After a sale, they'd rush back to the bay, clean and grade their seed by hand, then head out on the tide, sometimes racing to beat the sunset, to dig razor clams, which they sold by the pound for extra cash. At the end of the day they'd regroup over beers at a nearby watering hole, the Winsor House, and hash out the day's challenges—and successes. There was a huge opportunity for the taking—they just needed time and patience. What if they could grow a million oysters, they wondered? And how quickly could they get there?

In 1999, the Duxbury Bay Maritime School, still a young institution set in an aging facility, installed several stunning new docks directly beside the town boat launch. The docks would house the school's rowing shells, but Skip, ever the opportunist, took note of the space underneath. He'd heard about a guy growing oysters in Rhode Island who was using a floating upweller system, or a "flupsy," to grow out his seed. Skip asked the folks who ran the Maritime School if he could rent dock space from them, but glossed over the part where he would need to cut huge holes in their brand-new dock to make it work. They agreed to the arrangement and Skip, despite his minimal knowledge of carpentry, got busy building his first upweller (he covered the holes with undetectable but easy-to-open doors). He installed it that spring and, on a whim and a prayer, placed a batch of two-and-a-half-millimeter seed into the system. Within three weeks, it quadrupled in size.

The flupsy acted as an incubator, holding and protecting the seed while giving it access to a natural food source. A small electric motor pumped water over the seed continuously, force-feeding them into fattened, hearty specimens that could be planted directly on the bay floor.

By 2001, the hardscrabble team was producing a couple hundred thousand oysters a year. And then, September 11 hit, followed by a crippling recession for the restaurant industry. The wholesale business dried up and orders stopped coming in. Suddenly, Skip and Christian were sitting on a pile of oysters and had nowhere to send them. That's when Skip, ever industrious, and antsy to keep his fledgling business afloat, started knocking on restaurant doors. Chris Schlesinger became a customer, as did a few other Boston chefs. But Skip still had a ton of product, so he started researching oyster bars in other parts of the country, especially New York. Because he didn't have time to trek down to Manhattan in person, he decided to make some cold calls. One of them would change his future forever.

Sandy Ingber was the head chef and seafood buyer at the Grand Central Oyster Bar, Manhattan's oyster mecca. Skip had read about the bar's prominence and called the restaurant directly; Sandy Ingber answered.

"Are you the grower?" Ingber barked after listening to Skip's spiel about Duxbury-grown oysters. Yes, he was the grower, Skip replied.

"Well, what do you call them?" Ingber asked.

"Um, Duxbury oysters?" Skip replied, uncertain of what he meant.

"No, what do you call them? You gotta give them a name," Ingber demanded. "It's how you market the oysters. Think of something around there, a landmark or identifier, and give them a name."

A lightbulb went off. "I live in an area called Island Creek," Skip said.

"I like it," Ingber announced. "Send me some of those Island Creeks."

And so, the brand was born.

"That was the holy-shit moment," Skip says now. "That was when I knew that this thing might actually take off."

Island Creek's annual pilgrimage to the Nantucket Wine Festival had become a highly anticipated farm tradition. The four-day food and wine event was attended by a high-class clientele decked out in seersucker suits and Nantucket reds. Skip and the guys went down each year to shuck oysters, hang out with their chef friends, and spend the weekend downing magnums of wine. It was their kick-off to the long, hard summer season.

Skip first hit the festival shortly after he'd established the Island Creek brand. A friend in the seafood wholesale business suggested he go down and shuck oysters at one of the wine-focused events. It didn't take long for Skip to see the benefit. All these well-heeled food and wine fans loved his oysters. And they wanted to get to know the attractive, sun-kissed guy in flip-flops who grew them. They asked questions, tried the oysters, and continuously refilled his wineglass. It was in Nantucket where he first understood the similarity between wine and oysters. Tasting them side by side, he experienced his first co-branding experience as wine experts fought to put their bottles next to his oysters. He wound up staying an extra night and returned to Duxbury with a handful of new customers. The long weekend became an instant Island Creek tradition.

Skip put his dutiful and industrious young director of business development, Shore, in charge of organizing the annual road trip. While most of the team saw the weekend as a time to play, Shore saw an opportunity to get Island Creek's brand in front of as many eyes as possible. That year, he invited my whole crew to tag along and even offered us a place to stay—with the stipulation that we shuck behind the farm's traveling raw bar all weekend.

I can't remember the first time I ate an Island Creek. They were ubiquitous on restaurant menus when I was eating my way through the city as a food writer. But I distinctly recall the first time I saw, and sidled up to, their raw bar. I found the hollow-bottom six-foot wooden boat with Island Creek's logo stenciled across the front, filled with ice and covered with glistening half shells, at a new restaurant's opening party. Neither the restaurant nor the party were memorable, but I just couldn't forget the raw bar. Behind it stood three scruffy but good-looking guys who chatted up everyone in sight. I stopped by the raw bar a couple times that night, slurping back oysters and listening to the informal company spiel. Everyone in the room seemed to be buzzing about those guys from Island Creek.

The combination of disarming swagger, freshly shucked oysters, and that humble little boat might have been a scraped-together look but it was actually a killer marketing ploy. The boat's battered wooden rail and simple logo decal went perfectly with the handsome guys behind it. Together, they were eye-catching, especially when placed at an event where everyone else in the room wore ties and high heels.

On Nantucket, the boat and the boys were legendary.

The "oyster guys" would carry the boat through town from one event to the next, shucking anywhere between three thousand to four thousand oysters over the course of four days. Year after year, they fed thousands of tipsy revelers who would all go home and Google the words "Island+Creek+Oysters." The guys would spend the weekend collecting phone numbers from pretty girls and making memories of their own.

I decided the offer of a weekend on Nantucket and a free place to stay was all the bribing I needed. Berg, Will, and I flew out to the island together, anxious for a mini-break from our farmwork. I invited Dave to join us but he turned me down, claiming he couldn't get his bartending shifts covered.

"You go out with your farm buddies and have a good time," he said grudgingly. I was pushing it by going off to an island to eat and drink with my all-male work buddies for a weekend. But he stubbornly acknowledged that I deserved the time off.

We landed on Nantucket on Friday afternoon and found Shore, Skip, and the raw bar boat set up under a tent on the lawn of the White Elephant hotel. Skip was about to do a cooking demo and Shore needed help shucking. Skip looked nervously around the tent as it filled with strange faces. Despite his evolution from a simple oyster farmer to a representative of his brand, Skip was still slightly uncomfortable speaking in front of audiences. He was, after all, at his most comfortable when he was out on a boat, zooming around the harbor, not mingling and socializing with hundreds of strangers. He watched longingly from his perch near the stage as Berg, Will, and Shore stood behind the raw bar boat, shucking enough oysters to feed the crowd. (Still a beginner, I stood to the side with Skip and let the pros handle the shucking—I would get my own lesson later.) The demo also featured winemaker Jim Clendenen of Napa Valley's Au Bon Climat winery. Jim was a sweet, long-haired, aging hippie who, along with a creamy white wine called Hildegard, eventually set Skip at ease. The two got up in front of the audience and entertained the crowd while we stood to the side sneaking glasses of Jim's wine.

Afterward, with Skip's official duties wrapped up for the day, he was able to relax and return to his casual, fun-loving self. He mixed up a batch of Dark and Stormy cock-tails, which he poured into a plastic cup and carried up to the roof of his condo and drank looking out over Nantucket Harbor. Being on the island brought out Skip's carefree side: no daughters, no oyster farm logistics, no responsibility. With that frame of mind he took on the role of festivities leader, making dinner plans for the group and ultimately setting us up for a wild night out.

There was a gang of farm folk in attendance: Matthew from the office along with his wife, Kate; CJ, our truck driver; office manager Lisa; grower Mike George; a couple of Shore's Duxbury High School friends, Will and Gard-ner; and Skip's neighbor Peter. We weren't going to find a table for that crowd easily but Skip had a plan. Over the years, he'd become close friends with Seth and Angela Raynor, an easy-spirited couple who owned two of the is-land's best restaurants, the Pearl and the Boarding House. Seth was a spiky-haired surfer and award-winning chef.

Angela was a raven-haired mama bear with stunning blue eyes and a ringing voice. She was the ultimate hostess, pouring glasses of Laurent-Perrier rosé champagne for her friends like it was water. They both adored Skip and had been loyal fans from the beginning, so when he arrived with an entire crew from the farm on the Friday night of Wine Fest, Angela found a way to oblige.

"You guys want to sit in the private dining room at the Pearl?" Skip asked as we plowed through a round of beers at the Boarding House bar. While we looked perfectly comfortable in sweatshirts and jeans inside a tavern, the Pearl, which sat directly next door, was fine dining.

"So what?" he responded, waltzing us past the modernist dining room in our grubby gear. We trudged up the stairs to the second floor, where we found a small, bubble-gum-pink room with a large square table set directly in the middle. Tucked away from the restaurant's more appropriately dressed diners, we could get as rowdy as we wanted, which was exactly what Skip intended.

Our host made quick work of the wine list, ordering a magnum of Zinfandel for the table. Angela handled the menu, picking out a handful of the restaurant's signature dishes. A parade of Seth's seafood-heavy, Asian-inspired food arrived on family-style platters: martini glasses filled with pearls of tuna and tobiko; pork-filled lettuce wraps topped with slivers of mint; a salt-and-pepper-crusted wok-fried lobster served over chunky udon noodles; a quick-seared steak under foie gras jus. We ate dish after dish in wide-eyed wonder. I'd heard about the Pearl's menu but was floored to find every dish so exquisitely balanced. Each individual flavor held its own before melting into a salty, citrusy pop where the freshness of the fish and Asian spices and sauces worked in harmony. At first, I tried savoring every nuance, but with a table full of jokers, I eventually gave up and let the ocean of new flavors wash over me in a blur. Berg sat beside me, moaning with every bite.

"Pain, I don't think I've ever eaten this well," he sighed after demolishing a papaya salad. Besides me, he seemed to be the only one at the table savoring the food. Across from us, Mike George was cracking up the room with funny accents and quips about jumping on the "scotch train," followed by his impersonation of a train whistle. Skip's neighbor Peter pulled up some music on his iPhone, unleashing a short-lived but highly entertaining dance party between Lisa and Matthew's wife, Kate. We were halfway through the second magnum of wine and well on our way to oblivion when Skip, from the other end of the table, gave me a huge Cheshire cat grin.

"To Nantucket," he toasted, before diving into a plate of glassy noodles.

The night degenerated into a romping rove through the island's most notable dives. Along the way, women flocked toward the crowd of handsome guys, giving Berg, Will, Skip, and Shore no shortage of flirtatious energy. Sensing that I might have been a hindrance to their success, I stuck close to Lisa, who had left her boyfriend at home for the weekend. We eventually found ourselves at the Chicken Box, where a U2 cover band called the Joshua Tree won Berg's heart (he was a die-hard Bono fan) and got Lisa and me slam dancing in front of the stage. It was four A.M. before she and I stumbled home arm in arm, falling into our two twin beds with the lights still on.

I woke up the next morning to a dense, chewy fog that hinted of rain. My cell phone beeped at me with a text message from Will: *I was abducted last night. Lost my contacts (and dignity) so I can't see signs and am somewhere downtown. Where are we staying?*

Taking full advantage of his newfound freedom from the real world (and therefore all of life's dull regulations), Will had succeeded in finding a female cohort for the night. She'd convinced him to get a hotel room, which at three o'clock in the morning proved harder than he expected. They took a cab all over the island, stopping at swanky hotel after swanky hotel, finally landing at the Jared Coffin House, where the amused desk staff offered Will a discount, "because he only needed it for a few hours."

He regaled Berg and me with the tale while we scarfed down bagels smeared with bluefish pâté at a handsome little sandwich shop called Provisions, trying to fortify ourselves for a marathon day of shucking ahead of us. It wouldn't be the last time we heard stories like this—from Will or some of the other guys.

The wine festival itself was set at the tony Nantucket Yacht Club and had drawn hundreds of wine lovers from up and down the East Coast as well as winemakers from around the world. Our table and boat were set up on the yacht club lawn, a bit removed from the crowds of the main tasting room. Next to our boat, Angela and Seth had set up a grill and were ready to smother our oysters in a melted five-chile butter. Their third restaurant, a ceviche bar called Corazón del Mar, was opening a few blocks from the Boarding House later that summer, and they were eager to experiment with—and market—their upcoming menu. The raw bar itself was decked out with several of Seth's sauces, as well as a few Mexican wrestling masks and sombreros in honor of the new restaurant. The sauces were outstanding. There was fiery heat in the tomato red salsa; a tomatillo salsa gelée gave the oysters sweetness; and the leafy-green thai-lime cilantro sauce was downright perfect. Something earthy stayed on my tongue while the lime and cilantro danced around the meat of the oyster. It was lip-smacking and sour but utterly addictive. Like liquid crack.

"Angela calls it green love." Seth smiled, watching me heap the stuff over another oyster. I wanted to dump the squeeze bottle straight down my gullet but held myself back; the guests had descended on our station. We were there to work, Shore reminded me. He handed me a knife.

I'd shucked a few oysters in the past. But the wine festival was for professionals. If I didn't know what I was doing, I'd get crushed, the guys warned. I jumped behind the boat with my knife and looked around for someone to give me a lesson. Skip was nearby and handed me a lightweight kitchen towel, showing me how to fold it up and wrap it loosely around my hand for padding. We used blue-handled knives made in France; the blade shot out of the top into a pointy, triangular tip. They were deadly if jabbed the wrong direction, especially when pointed toward the fat, fleshy base of a thumb.

The trick, he explained, wasn't force but light pressure and a strong wrist.

"Once you get the knife in there, they just pop open," he said. His knife slid into the shell effortlessly, releasing the hinge. He slid the knife against the bottom of the top shell, cutting the meat away from it.

"It comes off like this," he said, peeling back the top to reveal the perfectly intact oyster meat within. Holding the cupped shell in one hand, he neatly tucked the knife under the meat to release the other adductor muscle from the bottom shell, a courtesy to our slurpers.

"Then, if you really want to make it look good, you can flip the meat over," he said, using the tip of his knife to nudge the meat around in its watery bed. Not a drop of briny broth, the oyster liquor, had spilled from the shell. He went through a few more with me until I felt comfortable taking the knife. A handful of onlookers had gathered, waiting patiently for me to produce the same delicious results.

I concentrated on my knife, careful not to let it slip one way or the other. It wasn't long, though, before I nicked my hand on one of the shells. The paper-thin edge sliced my top layer of skin so gracefully, I hardly noticed. I felt the sting a moment later when I picked up a lemon wedge. A small trickle of blood had crept down to the base of my finger. "Such a rookie!" the guys teased as I ran off to find Band-Aids.

I soon resumed my post but still took my time, careful to let each oyster tell me how far to put the knife in. I found it easier to rest the oyster on the edge of the boat than hold it in my hand, ensuring less opportunity to shove the knife through my palm.

I kept thinking back to a conversation I'd had with Jody Adams, the chef-owner of Rialto, an elegant Italian restaurant in Cambridge. She was one of Boston's most beloved chefs and she'd known Skip for years, having used his oysters at her restaurant almost since the beginning.

Jody and I originally met during an interview, and over the years got to know each other more personally. Lately, she'd taken to inviting me to Rialto to try out new menu items and catch up over glasses of wine. During our last tasting together, I announced my plans to work for the Duxbury oyster farm and she hugged me like a proud mom. It launched us into a long, winding conversation about farming and oysters during which she revealed an anxiety about shucking.

"Oysters always put up a fight," she said emphatically. "More so than any other food, they really fight you, making it so difficult to eat them. And that struggle makes them one of the most wonderful foods. I think that fight is what makes them taste so good. Everyone should know how to open oysters. Well, everyone who eats them, anyway. I can open them but I'm terrible at doing it in front of other people. It's a challenge to do it well . . . and fast."

As I stood before the growing crowd, I could feel her words—her anxiety—rising up inside me. There was a line of people waiting for our oysters. The raw bar was turning into a free-for-all with guests grabbing for shells before we even set them on the ice. I tried shucking faster.

"Where are these from?" one kindly older gentleman asked.

"We grow them in Duxbury, just south of Boston," I offered.

"Oh, Duxbury! I went to summer camp there as a kid. Beautiful bay," he said, lighting up. He was downing his third Island Creek.

"They're harvested right in the middle of the bay," I answered, delighted to have something helpful to share.

"My, they taste just like Duxbury, don't they?" he said, taking down his fifth and sixth in the process.

Our fans treated the oyster boat like a regular bar, leaning on it to share stories about eating their first oyster or to ask questions about how to shuck. One couple spent an hour in front of us, casually slurping and sipping their wine while a line of people waited patiently behind them. Still others came to the raw bar looking for the cute group of guys they'd seen out the night before. Fans snapped photos with Skip, and chefs and winemakers came over to shake his hand. It was like hanging out with celebrities.

Meanwhile, I just tried to keep my knife steady. Over the course of the weekend, I would learn that shucking for an audience required an appreciation for the art of service. A good shucker had people skills, oyster knowledge, and a deft hand with the knife. I watched my comrades carefully to see how they fared. Skip and Shore were laissez-faire, stepping away from the raw bar frequently to get another glass of wine or have their picture taken. Berg treated it like a job, shucking as fast as he could without looking up. CJ took his time, carefully fondling each oyster before opening it. Will was a natural. He was engaging and funny. He could shuck quickly and tell a good joke while doing it. I, meanwhile, felt ill-equipped and slow, only engaging in short conversations when my knife wasn't in use. Otherwise, I probably would have sent myself to the hospital.

I probably logged about a dozen shucking hours that weekend, opening hundreds, if not thousands of oysters over the course of four days. By the time we reached our final event on the patio at the Boarding House, my hands were mangled. My fingers were covered in stinging cuts, nails caked in grime. The muscles in both hands and forearms ached from my perma-grip on the knife. Skip laughed when I showed him my battered paws.

"You'll be on the competition shucking circuit in no time," he teased. I was still an amateur.

The subsequent achiness in my forearms and wrists lasted for days after we returned. I struggled to lift crates again and work felt like a drag after so many highs from the weekend. But there wasn't time to loaf. We had new crewmates to welcome, starting with Maggie Ogden. A ten-year veteran of the farm, she was on summer break from Brandeis University, where she was getting her master's degree in painting. She had feathery hair, a cherubic smile, porcelain skin, and she dressed like an artist, always in ragged flannels, leggings, and mud boots. I liked Maggie immediately. She had a calming, steady presence and a strong, independent spirit. She reminded me of the women I'd met and become close friends with when I was in college at Syracuse University. There were twelve of us, a band of women who'd met as sorority sisters but grown into a tightly knit, eternally supportive clan. I'd watched those women grow from a group of party girls into talented, successful, and powerful peers, ones who inspired me with their strength every day. Maggie would have fit right in.

It was nice to finally have another female on the float, especially one who could hold a conversation. She tossed out commentary about Kanye West's latest album (A2 was instantly smitten) as easily as she opined about the current state of our country's education system. She'd worked in the magazine world in New York, held a dozen odd jobs, and had a deep, throaty laugh. Above all else, she loved to argue about the cull.

We'd been culling as a pretty cohesive unit since Will arrived. Our threes all looked about the same, meaning we were filling bag after bag with consistent sets of oysters. Plus, both Will and I were now confident in our ability to pick out Per Se's, which A2 loved taking credit for. But Maggie showed up and things shifted. She had worked at the farm longer than some of the growers, starting back in high school on Don Merry's crew. He'd originally hired her at his Back River Fish Market; when he decided to sell the business and go into oyster farming, he convinced her to tag along. Later, she worked with Christian Horne, a well-known stickler for culling perfection, before joining Skip's crew. Besides a brief hiatus to live in New York, she'd spent almost every summer of the last decade culling oysters. She was a pro.

A2 wasn't sure how to handle this confident, fully educated new team member. Her sarcasm rivaled his so instead of caving to his playful teasing, she dealt it right back. So while A2 was charged with managing the summer crew, Maggie, it seemed, was more interested in managing things herself. The cull had already changed slightly since my first day on the farm; we were harvesting a different section of Skip's lease and because of it, we were wrist deep in snail eggs. The tiny, super-sticky balls looked like fuzz-covered caviar and attached themselves to our oysters; they had to be scrubbed off with metal brushes. On top of which, the oysters were starting to show new growth (like flower buds, new growth unfurled from the shell's outermost edges) so some of them were brittle with new edging. A2 had taken his duty as float manager seriously, inspecting bags after we'd counted them. He'd seen almost every oyster that passed through the float in the last few weeks. Maggie had not.

On her first day, Maggie set up her station, grabbed a full crate of oysters, and dumped them onto the table. A2 stood across from her, waiting for the opportunity to teach her something.

"We're running a little thin these days," he told her as she picked away at the pile. "We're a little more generous on the cull than you probably were last summer."

Maggie eyed him cautiously. "So, you're saying we're throwing crap in there?" she said, pointing to a crate of threes.

"It's not *crap*," he balked. "I'm just saying . . . we've got to be more liberal, you know? Let the smaller stuff get through now and then."

"Riiiiiight," she drawled. "So, we're putting in smaller

stuff, the runts basically, and you're telling me that's okay? Because I don't think it's okay. It's like selling seventy-five amazing oysters and twenty-five pieces of shit. Look at this!" she said, pulling out a pathetic, boomerang-shaped shell. "You'd really sell this?"

A2 fired back. "No! You're not listening. Look, just cull like you would normally cull. I'll go through your returns afterward."

"You'll go through my returns? What is this, a *regime*? I'll cull the way I want to cull and we'll bag them and they'll be perfect. The end," she said, eyes flickering. She was fired up, but I could see the corners of her mouth creeping upward. Will and I watched in awe as our unflappable float manager got the ego knocked out of him. Maggie cracked a smile.

"What?" A2 said, trying not to laugh himself. "What do you think, you invented culling or something?"

"Yes! I *invented* culling," she shouted, giggling as she leaned over to dangle her ultrathin specimen in front of his face.

"Sure you did. So cull already." A2 shrugged, smirking. He'd met his match. Eventually, after arguing over a few more crates, the two relaxed into a conversation about their only common ground, music.

Another crewmate, Quinn, arrived a few days later. He'd just finished his junior year at Indiana University and was home for the summer, his second working for Island Creek. He was smart but painfully shy that first day. Our longest conversation involved a few fun facts he'd picked up from last night's episode of *Jeopardy*.

I enjoyed my new crewmates as well as the extra bodies. We flew through our tasks while the new personalities injected life into our tired conversations. We were dissecting a million new topics like books, movies, music, food, and of course, the cull. The float was starting to feel like a party, a place where we gathered to hang out for the day—and, oh yeah, get some work done, too. Summer had officially arrived.

Seth Raynor's Grilled Littleneck Clams "Smooth Hummocks Style"

Seth and Angela Raynor not only fed us insanely well in Nantucket, they opened their arms like family. Their relationship with Island Creek started long before I arrived, which means they've shared countless meals—and bottles of wine—with Skip on the Boarding House patio. This recipe was named for an area of the island where Angela's parents own a beach house and has become one of the Raynors' most well-used family treasures.

> *60 fresh littleneck clams*
> *1/2 cup sea salt*
> *2 gallons water*
> *10 ounces unsalted butter*
> *2 garlic cloves, minced*

2 shallots, finely minced

2 tablespoons flat-leaf parsley, chopped

1 tablespoon thyme leaves, chopped

3 tablespoons chives, finely chopped

1 tablespoon tarragon, finely chopped

1 tablespoon lemon verbena, finely chopped

2 tablespoons lemon zest, micro-planed

2 tablespoons lemon juice

Sriracha hot sauce, as desired

Scrub littlenecks. In a large bowl, dissolve salt in the water. Add clams and let purge for a few hours or overnight. Meanwhile, mix butter with garlic, shallots, parsley, thyme, chives, tarragon, lemon verbena, lemon zest, and juice. Refrigerate until ready to use.

When you're ready to grill, remove the clams from the brine and rinse them off. Prepare grill with charcoal until coals are very hot (if using a gas grill, turn heat up to medium high). Melt herbed butter in a stainless steel bowl over the grill, adding Sriracha hot sauce if using.

Gently place the clams on the grill and cover (do this in batches if your grill isn't big enough to hold them all at once). Cook for 1 minute, at which point clams should just be starting to open.

As soon as the clams open, transfer them to a large bowl (try not to lose any liquor) and drizzle the clams with the melted butter. Serve with slices of grilled baguette and dig in.

Serves 6

CHAPTER FIVE

SEED GIRLS

The seed was set to arrive any day: It was time for the upwellers to go in. I watched Skip and Mark Bouthillier, who occasionally helped Skip with carpentry projects like this, install the mammoth boxes and troughs, bolting them into place underneath the dock's wooden planks. The Maritime School, that massive building that had been under construction at the water's edge all spring, was finished and had finally opened, leaving us with a gleaming glass-steel-and-shingled structure to work around. Their docks, which went into the water at the start of every summer and held the rectangular frames of our precious upwellers, had gone into the water, too. The bay now felt like a bustling harbor with boating families and Maritime School students buzzing around us all day long.

On the docks, with all of the pieces laid out in the open, the upweller looked like nothing more than a few cobbled-together wooden boxes. There was nothing scary about their engineering but as soon as the guys put piece after piece into the water, bolting them into place, and then turned on the water pump that churned darkened water through the system, it became a living, beastly thing. I stood over it, peering in, waiting for a tongue to lash out.

The upwellers and I had a love-hate relationship. Skip had three upwellers that summer (two on one dock, the third on a neighboring dock) and like it or not, I needed each of their snarling and grunting bodies to get my job done. Skip, who knew the upwellers intimately, danced his way around the edges, hopping across the beams with an agility that came from years of practice. The system was simple—in fact, with a few updates and modifications, these were just like the first handmade one he'd installed years earlier. Each upweller had a large wooden trough running length-wise down a rectangular hole cut out of the middle of the dock. It was sunk about three-quarters of the way into the water (Mark stood inside one to demonstrate—the water came up to his knees) and on the outside of it, also sub-merged in the water, eight wooden boxes (four on each side) were secured into place with bolted wing nuts. The boxes, around two and a half feet tall and two feet across, could be removed and pulled out of the water individually with two rope handles secured across the top. Each box was called a "silo" and weighed about forty pounds dry; sixty to eighty when they were wet and full of seed. They were awk-ward to carry like a dead body might be: clumsy, unevenly distributed, and something you immediately want to put down.

Skip was giddy the day the final upweller went in. His seed was being hand-delivered, so he kept checking his phone for signs of its arrival. With three upwellers in place that season, we'd eventually have twenty-four hulking silos full of baby oyster seed. Mark gave me a lesson on how to pull a silo out of the water. First, you manually unscrew the wing nuts from the bolts and hide them in a strategic spot so they don't get knocked off the dock, he instructed. Next, you jimmy the silo loose from the trough, being sure to hold on to the box's rope handles so it doesn't sink. Then, squatting slightly and using your back and shoulders, you hoist the box out of the water to lift it up slowly.

He pointed out the tightly woven mesh screens on the bottom of the box, then paused to rest his elbows on his knees while water drained out of the screen. Finally, he pulled the box all the way up onto the dock, using the edge of the upweller as leverage.

"Easy, right?" he said, panting lightly.

I tried the next one. To unscrew the wing nuts, I had to kneel down and stick my head halfway into one of the boxes. Pulling myself up to my feet, I hefted the box up with the ropes. Mark's strategy took the strain off my back as I rested my elbows on my knees, then I leaned back and dragged the box up before lowering it flat onto the dock. My hands burned from the nylon rope and I was sweating.

Skip came barreling down the dock a minute later, dropping to his knees next to one of the upwellers. He placed a Styrofoam box on the planks beside him and ripped off the lid, revealing two plastic bags inside. Each one held a thin blue cloth filled with seed. He held one of the bags up in the air.

"The babies!" he proclaimed.

Kneeling in front of the upweller, whose pump had been shut down so that water no longer churned through it, he lowered one of the cloth packs into a submerged silo, carefully unwrapping it layer by layer. At the core, packed into a bricklike bundle, were 500,000 baby oysters, each smaller than a pepper flake. He carefully dipped the cloth into the water, releasing the seed. The flakes flurried down into the watery abyss, settling like dust on the bottom screen, which was too tight to let the little flakes pass through. Skip rinsed the cloth off, getting every last animal into the water, before pulling himself up. He looked up at me expectantly.

"Want to do the other one?" he asked.

By now, we'd drawn an audience as Christian Horne (Skip's original partner) and a few other growers gathered around the upweller. My crew had just come off the water and stood at one end of the dock, watching quietly. This was a sacred ritual for the farmers, who treated the group of baby oysters like actual newborns. My hands trembled as I unwrapped the second packet over the water. Skip leaned in close to me, instructing me to be very careful. I dipped the cloth into the inky saltwater, shaking it gently to release the seed into the darkness. One by one, they floated down, softer than snowflakes. I carefully rinsed and re-rinsed the cloth making sure I got every last seed into the water as Skip patted me on the shoulder. He leaned over the silo one last time and whispered, "Now grow, little oysters."

I looked up at the group watching us.

"That was kind of spiritual," I muttered to Skip. The group chuckled.

"More like nerve-racking," Christian cracked, doubling my crew over in laughter.

But he was right. Those two packets of seed actually constituted a pretty big portion of Skip's future livelihood— a several-thousand-dollar investment that would potentially yield a few hundred thousand oysters. One gust of wind and we all would have been screwed.

I started making it a habit to check the upwellers a few times a day. It was essential that the pumps ran continuously—if the oysters sat for too many hours in stagnant water, they could foul themselves to death. I would lift the upweller's doors every morning, peeking in to see if the pumps were running and how the oysters looked. I liked to stir them up with my hand, reaching all the way to the bottom of the boxes and mixing them up slowly.

Oysters, I would learn, can eat and eat and never get full. Every single one filters up to forty gallons of water each day, stripping phytoplankton as it courses through their meaty middles. The phytoplankton is turned into energy and glucose, which fattens them up, while carbon from the water is sequestered inside their ever-growing shells. The upweller, which pulls gallons of the bay's ever-flowing, plankton-rich water over them every second, force-feeds them, providing an endless flow of fresh nutrients, filling their gullets with a microscopic diet; oysters were like the foie gras geese of the ocean.

In the process of filtering, though, oysters do a great

service to the rest of the environment by removing impurities from the atmosphere, like nitrogen and carbon, gases that end up in the water thanks to runoff from fertilizers and other man-made chemicals. Shore's tidbit about the bay being filtered out every nine days suddenly hit home for me; as we placed several million seed into the upweller, we were adding more filter feeders to that particular environment and therefore, contributing to a massive environmental cleanup. Oyster farming is one of the most sustainable types of food farming on the planet.

After filtration, oysters have to eject whatever impurities they come across and the result is released into the water as a brownish, sludgelike pellet, which the growers call "fouling." I call it oyster poop. And like any babies, oyster seed pooped a lot. The "poop" is actually mucus-encased solids, the nonnutrient matter that oysters filter. In both wild and farmed oyster environments, the poop sinks to the bottom and lands in the mud, where a special denitrification bacteria occurs naturally on the ocean floor. Once the nitrogen is processed by the bacteria, it's diffused into the atmosphere as nitrogen gas, thereby creating a more conducive habitat for other plant and fish life. Oysters and their poop are miraculous in that way.

To me, it was just poop: A sticky, sour-smelling sludge that clung fiercely to the oysters and everything else it came into contact with. It was disgusting, but it would soon become my life.

One morning, I arrived to find a tall, waify brunette lifting up the door of one of the upwellers—after receiving more seed day after day, we now had two of Skip's three upwellers mostly full of oysters. She lowered the door as she heard me approach, smiling nervously.

"Sorry! Just checking on the babies," she offered. I knew instantly that this was my new crewmate Catie. Both Berg and Maggie had prepared me for her arrival.

"She's obsessed with the seed," Berg told me. "Not sure how she'll feel about you taking her throne with the seed, so maybe just go easy on her."

"She's a really good worker," Maggie offered. "But she and I have some, uh, fundamental differences."

"Like what?" I asked, fascinated.

"I dunno," Maggie said, smiling vaguely. "Just politics and stuff."

I introduced myself to my new crewmate, studying her for clues to her true personality. She was a Duxbury girl who'd worked on Skip's crew every summer for four years; she'd been in charge of seed for two of them. She'd just graduated from Colgate University and was on the lookout for a "real" job as an environmental consultant. She was endlessly fascinated by things like the erosion of Duxbury Beach and the reemergence of a sand shark migration in the bay—two things I'd never thought twice about. And despite possessing a classic, all-American beauty, she was a tomboy who cursed a lot and shotgunned beers (she dulled one of her incisors doing it during college). Catie was a tireless worker. Too tireless, in fact. Berg told me that the previous summer, she rarely asked for help with anything, including lifting the beastly silos—and that her intensity for a strong group work ethic would oftentimes push others on the crew to a point of exhaustion.

Frankly, I wasn't sure how I felt about working with such an intense personality for the summer. But she seemed nice enough to me and whatever potentially anal work habits she harbored were masked by a cute freckled face and a chirping, high-pitched voice.

Skip was on the dock a few minutes later to welcome her and announce that now that Catie was here, he hoped the two of us could work with the seed together. Today we would start washing the silos. He started rattling off instructions in some code that I couldn't pin down.

"Make sure the Muscongus Bay are on window screen. I want eighteen to be free. Let's get the ARC seed moved over to the twenties later this week," he said. Did he just say "window screen"? And what were all those numbers? My confidence deflated. Catie just nodded, assuredly.

"Sure, Skip, we'll take care of it," she said.

"We need to get a bible," he added. He didn't mean a holy book but a waterproof notebook where we would track the seed for the summer.

"I'll grab one tonight, Skip! No worries!" Catie replied, fumbling in her bag for a pen. I could feel the excitement pulsing out of her. She was eager to please her boss.

"Oh, Catie, I've been meaning to tell you." Skip looked at her nervously. "We're going to pass the torch to Erin. She's going to be our seed girl this year," he added hesitantly.

Catie's smile froze.

"Oh! Okay," she said with wide eyes. I smiled back.

"I'm really hoping you can help me out," I offered guiltily. "I have no idea what I'm doing."

"Of course!" she chirped, her megawatt smile shining back at me. All I could see were her impossibly white teeth. All I could think about was her youth.

The age gap had only tripped me up a few times so far. A2 and Berg were in their early twenties and I'd gotten a kick out of listening to their stories about entering adulthood, like when A2 had to detach himself from his parents' insurance or Berg lost his college e-mail account. It hadn't been *that* long since I'd been through the transition to adulthood myself.

The biggest difference between me and everyone else on my crew wasn't age at all. It was that I was married. Having a husband marked me as "An Adult." To them, my being married put me in the category of nearly ancient.

Catie was a new kind of youth for me. She was a cutout doll for what I assumed was a generation of twenty-year-olds marching into the workforce with alarming self-confidence and sense of entitlement. I doubted she'd ever heard or recognized the word "no."

I felt bad for robbing her of a title but it was Skip's decision, so here we were. She had to teach an old married woman how to do a job she'd already mastered. And I had to swallow my pride and take lessons from a confident, brash little vixen who was cuter, smarter, and stronger. It made both of us uncomfortable.

We set to work executing Skip's tasks. We needed to clean the seed and move some of the seed batches around so that there would be space for another seed delivery later that week. While we worked, Catie explained her system for keeping track of everything.

Each of the three upwellers was numbered per a system Skip had put into place long ago: the Teens, the Twenties, and the Thirties, she said, pointing each of them out. (The Thirties lived on the neighboring dock.) She then numbered each silo by its position, starting with the first one on the left. Looking down the length of the Teens, she called them 11, 12, 13, 14, 15, 16, 17, and 18. Odd numbers on the left, even numbers on the right. The same thing followed for the Twenties: 21, 22, 23, and so on. Simple, she declared.

I stood there visualizing the numbers, trying to memorize each position, but quickly lost track of what was what. Catie had already moved on. The seed, which we called either ARC or Muscongus Bay (based on which hatchery it was from) stayed in their respective groups. Several silos now had seed in them, but a few were still empty. Thinking back, I deduced that we'd dropped about a million Muscongus Bay across two silos in the Teens upweller a few days before.

Now, Catie instructed, we were going to pull them out to clean them. She showed me how to lift the doors off and where to stash them while we worked (usually to the side of the dock; the narrow space was jumbled with rowing boats and other equipment so our space was limited), then gave me the same lesson Mark had, lifting the silos out using her knees, her back, and the dock for support.

"We line them up in order, just like they sit in the upweller. That way we don't lose track," she offered. We started pulling silos one at a time. Mine came out slowly as I danced around the edges to keep from falling in. Catie pulled hers out quickly, like it was a race. After everything was pulled, Catie looked over at my row of silos. I looked over at hers. Mine sat errantly to the side of the upweller; hers were in a perfectly straight line. Her face turned serious for a minute before she walked over to my set of silos and with pursed lips, pushed each of the boxes into one straight line. I stood to the side, not sure whether to help her or stay out of her way. When the silos were all neatly placed side by side, she stood up straight and smiled at me. "There! Now they're all organized," she declared. I smiled stiffly, wondering what it would feel like to punch her square in the cute button nose. Her actions spoke volumes: Do it my way or I'll be forced to do it for you. I shook the urge to throw a hissy fit just because she knew more than I did. I had to. Whatever competitiveness was rising up between us was not going to work if we were going to spend the whole summer working side by side.

Once the silos were pulled, she tilted one up on its edge to show me the plastic mesh screen on the bottom. Depending on how small the oysters were, we would transition them from boxes lined with the tightly woven, micromesh screen to ones lined with a looser woven window screen. The micromesh was a tighter weave, so while it kept all the tiniest babies from falling through, it also held back water flow. The goal was to get the seed moved onto bigger screen as quickly as we could—within a few days (oysters grew quickly once they were inside the upweller). And we could only do that if we kept them clean. Catie demonstrated with the hose.

"You want to spray all the poop off. You really need to

pummel them, breaking them up and getting every single seed cleaned off. The water chips their shells, which makes them grow back stronger," she said, tipping the box to one side so she could get the hose nozzle all the way down to the bottom. The screens were filthy from the fouling, and as she sprayed, brown sludge poured out of the bottom.

"You try," she said, handing me the hose.

Holding the box at an angle with one hand, I used the other to maneuver the hose. I reached inside the box, filling my head with the muddy stink of oyster poop. As I sprayed down the sides of the box and then turned the hose on the babies themselves, I could see the oysters glimmering in the sunlight. I took my time, removing every last speck of poop from the colorfully mottled shells. A few minutes later, once I was certain the poop was entirely gone, I pulled my head out and straightened up, wrenching my lower back.

"Yeah, it's not the most comfortable position, but you get used to it," Catie replied cheerfully to my scrunched-up face. She looked inside my box, then took the hose from me and gave it an additional spray. "Make sure you get *every last bit*," she chirped forcefully. I rolled my eyes. We had fifteen more silos to do. There was no time to argue.

"The last few years we've done this, the other seed girls and I usually came up with a system," she said as I turned my hose to the next box. "If you want, I can be the one to pull and drop the silos and you can wash. Does that work?"

I could feel Catie wanting to take control of our shared project—if pulling and dropping silos would give her that, I was all too happy to oblige. Washing the seed was therapeutic, I realized as I watched the brownish trickle of water creep along the dock. She, meanwhile, seemed happy to jump in and out of the trough, fastening the boxes back into place. It gave her the power to set the pace for the entire process—but it also meant that I didn't have to lift the damn things. The arrangement suited me just fine.

It took us two hours to get all of the silos in both upwellers clean, but I finally pulled the doors shut with a sense of accomplishment. As I rolled the hose up at the top of the dock, Catie walked over with a smirk on her face. I looked down at myself. My legs and arms were caked in drying brown goo. I was covered in oyster poop.

"Good job for your first day on the seed!" she sang a little too cheerfully. It wasn't a mocking tone but I took it as one. Instead of betraying my waning enthusiasm, I smiled back and bared my teeth as we walked up to Frenchie's together for a mid-morning coffee. I kept thinking back to our new task. Standing bent over for hours, sliding those goddamn boxes around, not having a clue how I'd keep letters and numbers straight, and all under the watchful eye of an overachiever who knew more than I did. This job was starting to suck.

Like it or not, I needed to find a rhythm with Catie. We washed seed every morning, usually in stages. She would pull the silos one by one while I followed behind her with my hose, spraying down the boxes. Instead of spending every day on the float, I now started my days on the docks with Catie. It bummed me out to watch the crew board the Bateau and make their way out to the float each morning. We'd wave them off as we got to work pulling silos. But I felt like I'd been shunned from the cool kids' table.

On the docks we were surrounded by a new set of faces and I was determined to learn everything I could about the seed. Christian, whose upweller was set right next to ours, became a regular fixture to our morning routine, working alongside us for hours at a time. He was a wry, sarcastic Mainer with white hair and a muscular build. Occasionally, he'd give me progress reports on the seed.

"Just wait, they'll really start to grow once the water hits sixty degrees," the former hatchery expert told me one morning. He'd been around oysters his entire life so I did my best to soak up whatever bits of knowledge he was handing out. "It's always during the second week in June. Coming up next week. We have these late-afternoon tides plus warmer weather, which warms the water right up. You'll see. They'll really start growing then."

Sure enough, that second week in June produced a pop of growth. After each wash, they normally doubled in size, gaining a few millimeters each time, but that week produced a spurt so huge, the volume on one of the silos tripled in just two days. Catie and I stood gawping into the box like proud mamas.

"The babies!" she sighed, grabbing a fistful of tiny shells. They were becoming shapely, with a deep, smooth, fingernail-sized cup. I admired the layers of poop. It was a good barometer, I'd learned. The more they fouled, the larger they grew.

As the weeks passed, we filled all twenty-four silos with seed (Skip received it in batches so he could spread out the growth) and Catie and I worked like machines. Pulling, spraying, organizing, dropping. We learned how to dance around each other gracefully. We'd found we had a few things in common (it wasn't sand sharks or beach erosion, but I loved a good drinking story and we both had plenty of those). She helped me master the beam walk, making the upwellers feel much less scary. We bonded over the tasks themselves, complaining about the weight of a box or our calloused hands. And our favorite thing to do was curse at the bolts that attached the silos to the trough. Unscrewing and rescrewing the wing nuts was brutal on our hands, especially as they started to rust over from the salty water. We'd attack them barehanded, scraping our knuckles around the wood as we twisted them tighter or looser, all the while unleashing a stream of obscenities into the morning air.

"Shitfuckmotherlovinasshole, fuck you, bitch!" Catie screamed one morning, just as a group of Duxbury moms arrived on the docks for a rowing class. She was standing inside one of the upwellers while I hosed down the silos on a neighboring dock. The moms froze, mid-conversation, as her torrent echoed across the glassy water. I caught her eye and smiled.

"Sorry!" she squeaked before tumbling over in laughter. Catie grew on me, in her own charming way. I came to see her controlling nature for what it was—raw ambition. Newly out of college, not quite ready to tackle the real world, she was priming herself for a lifelong fight to the top. She had been a rower through high school and part of college and had coached a rowing crew for the Maritime School for a few summers. She was a competitor who truly honored the competition.

She also gave wonderful encouragement because of it, throwing out quips like "great job washing today!" or "I'm so proud of you for pulling all those silos yourself!" I eventually learned that she wasn't mocking at all—that overt enthusiasm was genuine.

As she slowly let go of any residual frustration from not having her old job back and I warmed up to my partner's enthusiasm, we both realized that her demotion came with perks. She was no longer in charge of the seed or the upwellers and therefore no longer to blame when things weren't done the way Skip wanted them done. Instead, Skip had put the responsibility on my shoulders. Every day, he stopped by the docks with some specific orders, like moving one batch of seed to another upweller or splitting up one of the groups to minimize the volume that each silo held. I came to understand the language of seed so that when he said he wanted to move the ARC in the Teens to window screen, I knew exactly what he meant. But, when things went wrong, he came down on me.

One morning, he called me with some basic instructions— wash as much of the seed as we could before running out to the float to help Berg and the crew wash and bag some adult oysters (for now, we were splitting our time to spend half the day on the docks for seed work and half the day out on the float). Catie and I got through two upwellers but didn't have time to wash the silos in the third so I decided to leave it until the following morning. But the next morning he was on the dock before I was, freaking out over the amount of poop on the oysters in that upweller. Another time, I didn't secure the pipes properly before a big storm blew through, and found out later he'd done it himself.

Then, one night during a much-needed outing with some old coworkers, I was two glasses of wine deep at a bar in the city when I got a phone call from him.

"The upwellers aren't running very well. Did you clean them today?" he asked sternly.

"Yes, of course we did, Skip. What's wrong with them?" I stammered, my mind racing through the events of the day.

"They're running slow. I think something got caught in the pump. Did you guys pull them all at once and leave them out or did you pull one silo at a time, clean it, then put it back in?" he asked.

"We pulled them all at once, like we've been doing," I said, starting to panic.

"Okay. Well, maybe just do them one at a time from now on," he stressed. "You know how important it is that those upwellers are running, right? If they're not, the oysters could die. That's how serious this is."

I was fully freaking out at this point. Faulty upwellers. Dead oysters. My responsibility. I wanted to cry.

"Okay, Skip, I'm so sorry. I didn't realize we shouldn't be washing them that way. We'll do it however you want us to do it," I choked out, trying hard to make it right.

Skip backed off. "It's fine. Just be more careful, okay?" He hung up before I could respond.

It was a slap in the face. We'd been following his instructions to the letter for weeks. I'd checked the upwellers before leaving that day and they were running just fine. I wanted to call him back and plead forgiveness or just defend myself but it would have been pointless. Instead I called Berg for reassurance.

"Ah yes, the freakout phone call," he said sympathetically. "I get them a lot. You shouldn't worry about it. He gets worked up when he sees something that wasn't done the way he would do it. But if you did what you were supposed to do, then he can't fault you. And he won't. I guarantee he'll be over it by tomorrow."

He was right. Skip came down to the docks the next morning and apologized for the call.

"I just stress about it, that's all," he explained sheepishly. Clearly he felt bad. But I could see that seed stressed him out more than anything else on the farm. While he handed the everyday management of his oyster lease and harvesting to Berg and the crew, he kept a diligent eye on the seed. He not only watched it more carefully than we did, he sensed when things weren't right. I discovered later that during big storms he often slept in his truck by the docks overnight, just so he could check on the upwellers every hour.

The weather had become a problem. It was still late June but temperatures hovered below sixty degrees for weeks and rain fell constantly. Every day that we washed, it rained. And no matter how many layers I tossed on or which waterproof gear I chose, my skin remained swollen with moisture, permanently amphibious.

We'd gained a few more hands on the farm, including Eva, who was a student at Brown; Andy, a Duxbury high school graduate whom we called "Pops" (his last name was Puopolo); and Greg, a college kid and tuna-fishing fanatic. Together, we were nine strong, an energetic wolf pack with a strong collective work ethic. Every night, Berg gave us our start time for the following morning, and no matter how ungodly it was—4:45 A.M. some days—the entire crew was at the harbor at least ten minutes early, ready to work. We'd spend the day hustling to meet whatever deadline Berg had set for us, and when we got there, we'd relish the moment with fist bumps and long, heavy sighs. While Catie and I handled seed chores, the rest of the crew worked tirelessly on the float. The farm was operating at full speed: seed work, prepping the lease for the nursery, and of course, our bag count. We were putting in around 450 bags per week.

Skip also had us readying equipment for the nursery, a time-consuming chore that required pulling all of the nursery gear (hundreds of huge metal cages and thousands of bulky plastic mesh bags) out of winter storage, ordering new gear to replace anything that had been damaged the previous season, and repairing general wear and tear. But all of those tasks were put on pause when we had low tides. Summertime brought the longest low tides of the year, so we were out on the leases regularly to handpick oysters. As a group, we were especially efficient on the tide.

The way the timing worked, drainer tides usually occurred early in the morning, around sunrise, or late into the evening. The early-morning tides meant I had to be up two hours before our call time thanks to my commute, putting me in bed around eight P.M. the night before. I started to feel like the walking dead, but there was no way around it: I had to be at work. Once waking up at three A.M., I found Dave in the living room. He had just gotten home from a bar shift and shook his head as I walked out of the bedroom wearing my farm gear. It was the first time we'd seen each other in two days.

Because of my separation from him and the sheer exhaustion of waking up at ungodly hours, it was out on the tide where my emotions ran high. Frustration, exhilaration, exhaustion, a burst of energy. Despite what the calendar said, it was freezing out there in June, usually just barely reaching fifty degrees. I could cover myself in layers and keep my hands dry inside my gloves, but the chill and multiple hours of hunched-over work stiffened me.

I could have complained, but once we were out there, the work went by quickly. Spread out over the football field–sized lease, the crew would get to work quietly, each of us shaking off whatever sleepiness or hangover we were struggling through. Someone would throw out a hypothetical question: What would you eat for your last meal on earth? As others shouted out answers, we would start to migrate closer together until we were clustered within a few yards of one another, where a discussion might ensue. How many courses? What type of cuisine could we choose from? Would there be dessert? Before we knew it, our voices would drown out the sound of oysters hitting the bottom of a bucket and our crates would be full. Occasionally, when we spent too much time standing up to gesture or hammer home a point, Berg would scold us, like a mindful teacher.

"Back to work, Pain," he'd prod, head down in focused concentration.

We usually brought the radio out to listen to classic rock—the only station we could all agree on—and sing along to Journey or U2 (which always put Berg in a better mood). The crates would pile up and just like that, the tide would be rippling back in just as quickly as it had left.

Loading up the boat at the end of a tide always invited more discussions of food and we would focus on breakfast. We'd imagine heaping platters of pancakes, some with fruit, others with chocolate chips, alongside fried-egg sandwiches, red flannel hash, greasy piles of bacon and sausage, and endless cups of coffee. The tide made us ravenous and usually ended with all of us standing in front of the pastry display at Frenchie's ordering a smorgasbord of doughnuts, flaky croissants, sausage-and-egg sandwiches, and éclairs. It helped carry me through—and kept me from thinking about all of the meals I was missing at home.

One early morning in late June, Skip announced that it was time to set up the nursery system for the season. Our equipment was all prepped and ready to go out to the lease. First, we needed to set up a system of cages on a designated section of the oyster fields; the cages were part of a rack-and-bag system that created a nursery area for the oyster seed once it was removed from the upwellers. Each cage held six or eight stiff plastic mesh bags, made up of either three-sixteenths- or three-eighths-inch weave—the weave was tight enough to hold quarter-inch-large oysters. The bags were then secured on each end with PVC pipes. They held around 1,200 oyster seeds each.

The setup, Skip explained as we lifted cages out of the boat and onto the drying lease, was similar to a vineyard trellis system, or the fencing that helps train grapevines to grow in a specific way. He instructed us to set the cages about six feet apart in rows of ten, all facing southeast, and to stagger the rows slightly—their weight (around thirty pounds each, empty) would keep them from moving once they were set on the mud. It created an even water flow between the cages, allowing the oysters maximum exposure to their food source.

It took us several tides to get all three hundred cages in place. Will, Maggie, and I worked with two six-foot-long plastic pipes to measure the distance between each cage like a massive human protractor while the rest of the crew worked ahead of us, dragging the still-empty cages from the boat to the field. Racing the tide to get the cages set was exhilarating, if tedious. With so many hands, the work was easy but still took hours to complete. Skip came up beside me one morning while we dragged cages across the lease.

"I can't believe I used to do this by myself," he said, huffing as he pulled.

When we eventually finished, days later, my crew looked proudly over the oyster field. The cages covered an area the size of a football field, marking the territory where we would raise the seed until it was ready to be planted. We were now prepped for what would be months of nurturing the babies in this protective nursery state. It was a time-consuming and rewarding accomplishment (one that eventually had a consequence, but I wouldn't discover it until much later in the year). It was finally time to celebrate.

That night, Will invited the crew over for a barbecue. He was renting the guesthouse of a prominent Duxbury family named the Hales. The tiny, one-bedroom cottage was actually one that Skip once rented when he was just starting out as an oyster farmer; it was located about a quarter mile from the Island Creek headquarters, close to where Skip had grown up. The guesthouse sat just off the Hales' main property, tucked at the end of a private way overlooking the southern reaches of Duxbury Bay. That night, we gathered on Will's porch, still bundled up against the early-summer chill, and turned on the grill.

This being an oyster crew, we were impressively flush with oyster recipes. Berg showed us how he baked them, Rockefeller-style, with bits of spinach and Parmesan cheese, while Will offered a recipe for fried oysters served on Triscuits. The girls and I happily munched on our oyster appetizers while the guys pulled together a feast of grilled zucchini slices, sweet Italian sausages, potato salad, and chicken kabobs.

After dinner, the party moved over to Catie's house, a waterfront cottage her family was renting for the summer. A2 and Berg invited a few friends, putting our party around a dozen strong. The music raged, the guys played cards, and we drank Budweisers like they were water. It wasn't long after our first six-pack that Catie and I found ourselves on the covered porch, rehashing our teenage youth.

"This is exactly what we used to do in high school," Catie chirped, her voice becoming squeakier with every sip of beer. It felt so nostalgically similar to my own high school years that I momentarily blocked out all those feelings of angst and rebellion I'd actually felt as a teenager.

"We used to hang out in fields, guzzling wine coolers and bribing my best friend's older brother to buy us beer," I confessed. Back then, I had no idea who I was or what I wanted in life. I just cared about what my friends were doing. As I blabbered to Catie about my past, it occurred to me that little had changed in fifteen years. In my hazy, booze-induced stupor, I felt like a kid again. Dave flashed through my head briefly and I wondered if I should call him before I completely lost track of the night.

Right about then, Catie suggested we go skinny-dipping.

Leaning in toward my comrade dramatically, I whispered, "I've never been skinny-dipping."

That was all Catie needed. She popped out of her chair, pulling me up by the arm. "Let's go," she instructed, leading me out the back door.

We ran down the street in the rain, pulling our clothes off along the way. We arrived at the water's edge, a pitch-black hole surrounded by the grayish edges of a marsh. I couldn't see a thing but the house lights reflecting in the water. Catie was already down to her underwear, pulling her bottoms off awkwardly as she tiptoed toward the edge. The tide was out, giving us a long stretch of muddy beach to cross before we reached the lapping waves. I tossed my clothes in a pile on what looked like a rock and slid my flip-flops off, feeling the mud and tiny pebbles squish between my toes. Cold pelting rain fell around us, electrifying my nerves. Catie's pale body disappeared headfirst into the shallow water before she came up gasping with a scream. "It's freezing!" she shouted before diving back under.

I followed her into the icy abyss, diving without thought. It knocked the wind out of me and I came up heaving for air. I wanted to scream but nothing came out. I settled my feet into the swampy mud and stood briefly before discovering that the air was colder than my blanket of water. I relaxed, sinking down to float just below the surface as Catie swam in circles around me, kicking up water with her feet. I flailed nervously, trying to avoid the muddy bottom, livid with pleasure and fear, as a trail of sobering thoughts poked through my clouded brain. *What night creatures are we stirring up? Is this safe? Is anyone watching? How will we get back without towels? What will Dave think?*

My reverie was broken by the sound of whoops and hollers coming from the house. The rest of the party had figured out where we were and were heading down to the water at a breakneck speed. Catie and I abandoned the water and ran up the beach, collecting our clothes. I used mine as a shield, running past the descending crew, who called out "Cowards!" as we ran back to the house in the dark. Teeth chattering, we ransacked the closets for towels and dry clothes.

Huddled under blankets, Catie and I later laughed over our naked escapade.

"It's amazing, isn't it?" Catie whispered, still shivering in her skin. "It makes you feel so alive."

Alive, I thought. Nakedly and utterly alive.

Confessing my silly escapade to Dave was not nearly as thrilling as the act itself. Retelling it almost made me feel guilty, especially when, after I'd recapped my night, I received silence in return.

"You went skinny-dipping?" he finally replied. I'd hoped he would see the humor in it, see how silly it was to jump into a freezing cold body of water after a few beers, to feel like a kid again. Everyone did it at some point, right? My whole crew had done it the night before, I joked.

"That's just it," he said somberly. "You're married and you're out there taking your clothes off in front of other people?" It was gruff and accusatory and it immediately made my hackles go up. "How do I know that's all that happened last night? What aren't you telling me?"

He was being unreasonable, I argued. I hadn't done anything *wrong*. No, of course nothing else happened. We were just having stupid fun, I said, fuming. His jealousy seemed completely unwarranted.

"It's not even that other people were there. You've never once gone skinny-dipping with me," he finally conceded.

Dave was sore for days, but his initial anger quickly faded to sadness. I apologized for hurting him but not for the act itself. I had no regrets.

· · ·

After a week of super-long early-morning drainer tides during which we hardly saw each other or spoke, Dave and I drove up to Portland, Maine, where we were scheduled to celebrate his birthday. It was a trip we'd planned months ago, so despite our lingering frustrations with each other, our reservations awaited. Dave was still nursing his wounds and my pride was keeping me from feeling remorse. But we had dinner at one of our favorite spots, Fore Street, a cozy, brick-walled restaurant in the heart of Portland where, at the bar, we tucked into a plate of fragrant, wood-roasted mussels, and I proposed a truce. I felt more distant from him than ever before and I wanted to move past it. He admitted that his pride had been hurt and that he was reaching uncomfortable heights of jealousy both for my connection to the farm and for the time this job was taking away from our lives together.

I would never go skinny-dipping without him again, I agreed. He apologized for losing his cool about something that, admittedly, was really nothing. It had hurt both of us but it wasn't a deal-breaker. As we lapped up the mussels' aromatic broth with slice after slice of the restaurant's legendary rustic country bread he leaned in to my side and said he was sorry, too. "I didn't know it would be this hard," he admitted. And neither had I.

At work, the clouds only strengthened. I felt saturated, like a sopping sponge, as my skin soaked with sweat, saltwater, oyster poop, and rain. Nothing, not dry towels, multiple layers, sweatshirts, or air-conditioning made me comfortable anymore. I was a swamp thing.

On the first day of July we were driven off the water by an afternoon thunderstorm that came screaming in from the west. My fascination for thunderstorms had been fueled as a kid when my sister, Shannon, would lay me down on the living room floor on dark, stormy nights. We'd prop our feet against the sliding glass door that led out to the patio and watch lightning bolts dazzle across the darkness. We always counted the seconds until the thunder boomed from the sky.

But on the oyster farm July thunderstorms were a nuisance, the lightning and rain a threat to us as we worked outdoors in the elements and to our seed, which could get blown around in the upwellers under high winds.

A story was circulating about a clam digger who had been struck by lightning in Pleasant Bay off Cape Cod. He'd been out digging and was on his boat returning home with a haul of clams when a zap of lighting struck and killed him. Another man, standing onshore, saw the whole thing and was so startled he had a heart attack. Thankfully, that man survived.

"We always see big storms these few weeks at the end of June, early July," Christian assured me as I passed him on the dock one morning. The seed crew and I had a long day of washing and moving seed ahead of us. Catie and I had recruited Eva, who had a tall, long-limbed frame and easygoing demeanor, to join the seed crew. As the three of us got busy pulling silos, I nervously checked the skies.

Halfway through the morning, the three of us were drenched but it was the seed I worried about. It wasn't supposed to sit in freshwater—if it sat too long, the oysters would open and die. When the rain started falling in buckets,

I told the girls to stop what they were doing and get things covered up. Then Berg came running down the ramp, clattering the metal and all of our nerves.

"Get out of here!" he shouted, waving his arms. "Get under cover. It's about to get bad."

I told the girls to drop everything and go. Catie was in the process of lifting one of the silos and looked up at me helplessly. I ordered her to drop it on the dock and get under cover. Christian was on the dock, too, hastily pushing his silos together to keep them protected. In the distance, I saw Billy's crew, his grandson Joe and fellow crewmate Steve, out on Billy's float, stacking crates and hustling to get off the water. I waved them in and they waved back—they were on their way.

I glanced at the ramp, wondering if this would be the wrong moment to come into contact with a massive metal object, but took my chances and sprinted to the top. I took cover inside the wood shed, where the rest of my crew was standing stiffly in the dark. Looking up, it occurred to me that we were standing under a tin roof.

"It's okay, as long as we're not touching the walls," Will reassured me. We were standing on concrete. I hunched down beside Catie, who was hiding behind an upturned sailboat. We listened as the rain pelted the roof like a jackhammer.

Out of nowhere, a thunderous boom crackled through the air near our heads, sending everyone to the ground. I felt the concrete vibrate beneath me and looked up just in time to catch a flash of pink light up the door frame. Catie screamed and cowered behind a chair. Maggie was on her knees covering her head. Eva ducked under a table. Will and I both stood up stick straight, staring upward at the roof. I couldn't move.

It hadn't hit our building, but from the smell of burning plastic, I knew lightning had touched down nearby. Will was mesmerized. "That was *friggin' awesome!*" he yelped. I looked over at Catie—she was sobbing.

I asked if anybody had seen Berg. No, he never made it back in, Maggie reported. I thought about Christian and the guys on Billy's float. The minutes passed as we waited for something to happen. All we could hear was a wind-gushing rain and Catie's muffled sobs.

Finally, the door swung open with a bang and Berg and Christian came flying into the room, both wild-eyed.

"I saw it!" Christian shrieked. "It hit the *Windswept,* a sailboat about fifteen yards from the dock. Right behind Billy's float—it hit the mast." His arms flailed as he described the scene.

"Steve was in his rowboat, paddling like a crazy person to get in. He had his back to shore so we both saw it. I was standing on the dock when all of a sudden the sky turned pink. I could feel it coming. I could practically smell it," Christian said, catching his breath.

The door flung open again, this time bringing our bedraggled rower Steve. He looked petrified, mouth agape, his eyes zipping around their sockets. He'd been about ten feet from the boat when it was struck, he said with a whisper. The lightning had raced down the length of the mast and shot out through the back of the boat.

"All I could do was paddle," he stammered, shaking.

When the storm finally passed, we stumbled out toward

the water to survey the damage. The silos were still covered—our seed had not drowned. But the sailboat sat smoking in the harbor, reminding us of just how close our friends had come to dodging death.

The dramatic retelling of the story lasted for days. Our group, one of the few that watched from the front lines, swapped stories with everyone we saw, giving more re-markable details every time. It was all we could talk about leading up to the highly anticipated long weekend. Battle-weary, broken, and spent, my crew limped anxiously to-ward the Fourth of July.

Berg's Baked Oysters

Berg's off-the-cuff cooking methods came in handy a number of times that summer. This is his riff on the classic Rockefeller; it can be pulled together in minutes flat. Though Oysters Rockefeller might seem like the first course to some staid sit-down dinner, these are best eaten outside, on someone's deck, under the fading sum-mertime sun—preferably near the water.

> *2 dozen Island Creeks*
> *1 cup baby spinach, chopped*
> *3 tablespoons minced garlic*
> *3 tablespoons butter*
> *Couple handfuls of shredded Parmesan*

Preheat oven to 375°. Shuck the oysters, making sure to separate the bottom muscle but keep the meat intact in the shell. Top the meat with a couple pinches of spinach, ¼ teaspoon garlic, a small pat of butter, and a couple pinches of Parmesan. Arrange on a baking sheet and bake for about 5 minutes or until Parmesan is melted.

SERVES 6

CHAPTER SIX

E-ROCK

uxbury has to be one of the absolute best places in America to celebrate our country's birthday. With a history spanning back to the arrival of the Pilgrims (it was founded right after Plymouth), the town still boasts residents who claim ancestry to folks who came over on the *Mayflower* (Skip's mom is one of them). The entire town takes enormous pride in the flag-waving Fourth, capping every bobbing sailboat and white clapboard house with an American flag.

That summer, like every summer, a parade of fanciful, handmade floats hosted by high school and community groups marched down the length of Washington Street, passing the stretch of Norman Rockwellian houses that line up behind airbrushed green lawns and white picket fences. Don Merry lives along Washington Street in an updated Cape house and invites everyone from the farm to camp out in lawn chairs and bring their own picnics (and traveling wet bars) to watch the parade. Afterward, the party moves out to the water, where Skip and a few of the other growers pull their floats together, creating one giant party barge where, from a safe distance, the revelers watch as the town's amateur arsonists set off thousands of dollars in fireworks.

It's a display they brag about and cherish, like the national pastime that it is.

Unfortunately, that summer, the crew's plans conflicted with my own long-standing tradition of vegging out on a Cape Cod beach with Dave and a small group of his old college buddies, drinking cans of beer and cooking out under the stars. I considered trying to convince Dave to spend the weekend in Duxbury—I'd been hearing about the festivities for weeks and wanted to see firsthand what all the fuss was about. But I could tell he was still smarting and had no interest in spending time with my farm crew just yet. Instead, we stuck to our tradition and watched the fireworks over Chatham that year.

I returned to the farm after the holiday and found Skip on the dock with his head in an upweller.

"Did you hear about Berg?" he shouted over the sound of the pump. He sat up as I got close enough to hear him. "He got hit by a car," he said solemnly.

Walking home from the beach late Friday night, Berg had been on his cell phone when a Cadillac, going thirty-five miles an hour, clipped his legs from behind. His body was thrown upward and landed on the hood of the car, smashing the windshield. The driver said she never saw him in the dark. Miraculously, he only suffered a hairline fracture in his leg and some severe bruising. But he was in a cast and would be out of work for a week.

The news stunned me—I'd only been away from the crew for a few days and came back, it seemed, to chaos. Everyone was in a funk. Without our gentle leader, we felt lost. Berg had his eye on everything from the seed crew's moves to how many bags were going into the cooler each week. He was our main line to Skip and our director. But more than that, we were worried about him being holed up in his house for a week. He was a water nut who felt more comfortable outside than under any roof. This much time indoors would crush his spirits.

Catie was devastated. She and Berg had developed a solid, somewhat flirtatious friendship, so the news left her both worried and sad. Eager to help out in his absence, she suggested that the seed crew start arriving an hour earlier than everyone else so we could hammer out our duties and join the crew on the float much sooner. Both Eva and I agreed despite the earlier-than-ever wake-up time. The crew needed a hand and it was the only way we could get it all done.

Of course, the extra hours and added workload crippled my energy level, so I turned to caffeine, in the form of massive iced coffees from Frenchie's, as a daily savior. As a result, between coffee runs and bathroom breaks, I actually became pretty skilled at driving the boat. Aside from parking (i.e., slamming into the side of the dock) I'd become comfortable enough to shuttle myself from the float to land with minimal boat damage.

One morning on the Oyster Plex, desperate for a coffee jolt, I set off on one of our skiffs (we now had two), the Carolina, for a quick coffee run. She (all of our boats were women) was a finicky little skiff, often requiring a couple of gentle key turns before sputtering to life. But this time she started up immediately, though only carried me about ten yards from the float before the engine died. I turned the key but the engine didn't budge. I tried again. Nothing.

The boat and I were drifting at a nice clip by this point, as the wind pushed us south and out toward the far end of the bay. I was too far away from the float to toss a line and shouted to my crew for help but my voice disappeared on the breeze. Trying desperately not to panic, I jumped to the back of the boat to check the fuel line. It could have been anything, I thought. A dead battery. Empty gas tank. How did I know? I checked them all, tried the key again, and still nothing happened. A2, who now stood on the edge of the float watching me drift, called my cell phone.

"Pain! Is the boat in neutral?" he said, stifling a laugh.

"Yes, godammit! *It's in neutral!*" I turned, double-checking to make sure it was in neutral.

"Oh, shit. Is it the battery? Do you have gas?" A2 stammered, not sure how to help me.

"I have gas. No idea about the battery. It just won't turn. What do I do?" I was walking in circles, trying to determine my next move.

"Look, look—there's a boat behind you, you're coming right up to it, attached to that mooring there. Grab it and hold on," he instructed. I dropped the phone and dove out to grab hold of a small, eighteen-foot sailboat coming up beside me, wrapping my hand around the boat's narrow railing. I fumbled around for a rope, finding one crammed under my foot, and pulled myself toward the back of the sailboat. My shaky hands managed to tie the rope up to one of the cleats, giving me enough slack to keep from bumping the sailboat's outboard motor. I had no idea who owned the boat but silently thanked them for not using it on such a beautiful windy day. My phone was sitting in a puddle on the deck but I could still hear A2 shouting through it.

"Pain! I'm calling Skip. Sit tight, okay?"

I waited on the boat for something, anything, to happen. What had I done wrong? I tried the engine again but no luck. Feeling utterly helpless, I kept checking my rope to make sure I'd tied it tight enough. I looked up to see my crew all gathered at the edge of the Oyster Plex, watching me. Will waved at me awkwardly.

What felt like an eternity later, Mark Bouthillier came motoring out toward me, pulling his boat next to mine with a smug look on his face.

"So, did you put it in neutral?" He smirked.

"Yeah," I responded, unamused. "I think the battery died."

Mark pulled out a pair of jumper cables and motioned for me to get my battery prepped. He tried jumping it three times before giving up. "Guess it's not the battery," he declared.

Another grower, Scott Doyle, pulled up to the other side of me, curious about why Skip's boat was hanging off the back of a sailboat.

"What, d'you run out of gas?" he asked with a laugh. At least these guys could laugh about it. I smiled stiffly as the guys conferred over what could be wrong. Mark finally concluded that he should tow me in.

As we made our way to the dock, tied together side by side, Mark nodded over at me. "Hey, way to be a good mariner out there, kiddo. You got yourself tied to a boat. That was good thinking, E-Rock."

I smiled meekly at the praise—and the nickname. A good mariner, I thought. I hadn't wound up stranded in the middle of the bay, miles away from shore. I hadn't gotten hurt. But I was terrified that I had somehow killed Skip's boat.

My boss appeared on the dock as we approached and asked me all the same questions I'd been asking myself. He fiddled with the electrical panel only to discover that something was wrong with the wiring. It would need to go to the shop, he said. I sighed—thankfully it wasn't my fault. But when I saw Skip's face, I realized that this was most definitely a problem. Our crew would be down to one boat for several weeks while this one got fixed. One boat for shuttling nine people to and from the float, for harvesting, for getting our daily work done. This would slow everything on Skip's farm down to a crawl.

After we pulled the boat from the water and onto a trailer attached to his truck, Skip and I stood in the parking lot. His brow was furrowed.

"This sucks. The boat's dead. The weather's been shit. We have a shitload of seed to plant. This will push us back for weeks," he vented. "And Berg got hit by a car."

I'd come to learn that Skip tended to dramatize the negative . . . but only for a minute. Like the seed phone call I'd gotten earlier that summer, this was a moment of sheer frustration that came out in a spurt of anger. He was typically an even-keeled guy who rarely freaked out about the minor emergencies that came with a life spent working on the water. But occasionally there were flares, like this. Eventually, though, Skip's saner, more pragmatic self would return to reason his way out of the frustration. By the time I saw him the next day, he had snapped out of it.

Meanwhile, the seed girls and I were smack in the middle of grading season—a process during which we sifted the seed to sort it by size. The sun had returned, giving us a string of gorgeous days, and the seed was as excited about it as we were. In warmer waters, they started to pop with growth, doubling at least once each day, and a lot of the seed was getting close to reaching a quarter inch, about as long and shapely as a pinky-sized fingernail.

Seed grows at different speeds, and we needed to separate out the larger pieces in order to give the smaller ones more space to grow. It was survival of the fittest inside the upweller; a seed could live toward the top of the pile for weeks, getting more food and growing faster than its brothers. We called those seeds the heroes. They simply outate everyone else in their class. Oysters that grew slower or sat closer to the bottom might take a few more days, or even weeks, to reach the same size as the heroes.

Once the seed reached a quarter inch (we called those quarters) they went out to the nursery—the system of three hundred cages we'd set out earlier in the summer. We'd drop them into those sturdy black mesh bags whose weave was tight enough that the oysters couldn't float out, and leave them there for a few months until they were large enough (around two full inches) to be planted directly on the muddy bottom.

Grading, or sorting the seed, was a slow process—one scoop at a time—and all done by hand. It wasn't exactly efficient or cost-effective since it required several able, hourly-wage bodies, but it was the method Skip had used since the beginning. More important, it was a method that worked.

Unfortunately, it was also a method that involved heavy lifting and a six-handed effort from Catie, Eva, and me. Thanks to Catie's expertise and a little practice, we devised a system, learning how to pull silos out in unison, working together to lift eighty pounds of seed off the ground. It was like one of those trust-building games where you make the other person hold all your weight—only, if you failed, the other person might smash a toe or go crashing into the bowels of the churning upweller. It usually ended with all of us cursing wildly.

To grade, we first had to transfer the seed from those large upweller boxes into plastic totes or bins. We did this by carefully lifting a box over a tote and pouring out the contents, then spraying the box down with a hose to get all of the babies—and clumps of adhered poop—unstuck from the corners. If we weren't careful, we'd end up with oyster seed all over the dock, which we did a few times on our first few tries, causing Catie to freak out. (Seeing baby oysters slip through the cracks of the dock as we tried to pick them up was like watching change fall down the drain). But once we got a system in place, two of us could dump the seed into totes while the third person set up our grading stations; each station was set about waist high and made up of a tote filled with seawater and a floating wood-rimmed metal screen called a grader. Then, for hours, we would stand there scooping oyster seed onto the graders and slowly sift the oysters out over the water. The smaller seeds would float through the metal screen to the bottom, leaving the quarters (too big to fit through the screen) on top. Once all of the small seeds had floated through, we'd dump the quarters from our graders into an empty tote and scoop again.

It took us hours to get through a single tote of seed. No matter how many times I scooped, shook, flipped, and scooped again, the pile never seemed to shrink. It took Catie several arguments to get Eva and me to realize that, contrary to what seemed logical, smaller scoops could be shaken faster, and therefore make the whole project go more quickly.

But standing across from two women for that many hours in a day was like therapy. Once we pulled out our graders, lathered on the sunscreen, and doused ourselves in bug spray, we were married to the job—and one another. We often dissected the details of each other's lives, starting with what we ate for dinner the night before and transitioning into what songs we'd listened to on the way to work, what our roommates (or, in my case, my husband) had done to make us laugh, and what we all wanted to be when we grew up. Would we have kids? Would Eva ever get married?

What movie would we see that weekend? Would Catie date that guy who'd been calling her? Would Berg ever come back to work? Why were those rowers so rude? Who owned that boat over there? Did we believe in God? And who was our first kiss?

We bitched, we laughed, we gossiped, we cursed, and we became intimate with the local wildlife, naming a silky black cormorant Gustav and personifying a family of pigeons who nested on a railing above us. We gave them French voices and a dramatic, soap opera storyline. As we talked, I would run my hands across the seed, feeling the smoothness of the shells as they bumped and scurried along the edges of the grading screen. Tote after tote, we stood in a cluster, talking and clucking, shaking and stretching as entire days melded together into one ever-lengthening conversation.

Occasionally, we stared down into our watery stations and questioned the very miracle that turned these fragile, teardrop shells into fully grown oysters. They were showing off vibrant new colors now, so instead of being the brown and black flakes I'd seen when they arrived, the shells popped with creamy beige, rusty orange, and plummy merlot. Some had bold black stripes running down the middle or on either edge. That was a design element, Skip told me one day. The hatcheries chose a broodstock that specifically produced those stripes, which they used as an identifier; ARC seed had brazen black stripes zipping down the creamy-beige shells, while Muscongus Bay produced more solid-color seed that took on hues of inky purple and red. It took me weeks to identify one from the other but as they grew, the colors became more solid, giving me more confidence.

Grading required an arsenal of weaponry that included bug spray, hats, graders, stacks of bulky totes, a hose, dustpans, a wooden mallet, sunscreen, and wing nuts. Depending on which batch of seed we needed to grade, we would transition from one dock to the next, sometimes up to three times a day, carrying our artillery around in buckets or backpacks, like nomads. The army-green messenger bag I carried became a repository for sunglasses, water bottles, snacks, and bolts. The bible became my actual Bible. I would sit on the docks each morning studying our progress as we tracked it religiously. In it, I kept notes on what seed groups were moving where, what groups were in each upweller at the end of the day, and how much seed we had graded. I sometimes recorded the weather or notes about the color of the seed. Christian would see me taking notes and update me with his own reports.

"The seed's really bright this year, brighter than other years. It must be all this rain," he reasoned. "All that freshwater can really affect what they're eating." Slowly, I was gaining an understanding of how delicate the oysters were, to be so strongly affected by the simplest of changes.

We were grading at a rapid clip and all for the purpose of getting the seed from the upweller to the nursery. The babies didn't wait, they just continued to grow. And the longer they stayed in the upwellers, the more Skip stressed. Each day was a race to see how much seed we could move.

We were beholden to the tides. It was Berg's job (he was happily back at work but hobbling around in a plastic

My first day on the tide, with acres of oysters around me.

The three-inch ring (attached to a small buoy) is used to measure the oysters; the screwdriver is for jimmying the oysters apart when their shells have grown together; our bulky, blue astronaut gloves.

My crewmate Andy Seraika surrounded by orange crates culling in the rain behind the Shop.

The Bateau, or Bat for short, is our oyster skiff— my favorite boat to drive.

Corydon Wyman (left) and Andy Yberg make their way out to the Oyster Plex.

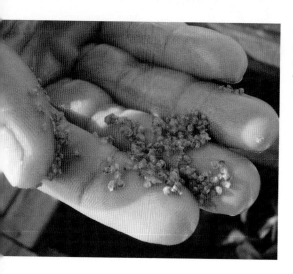

Baby oysters, or seed, at about two and a half millimeters in size. This is how small they are when they arrive at the farm in the spring.

The orange crates are made of a durable plastic and are built specifically for oyster farming. When full, they stack atop one another so as not to crush what's inside—and they weigh around fifty pounds each.

The upweller, set inside a rectangular hole in the dock, is a system of screened boxes attached to a trough that runs down the middle (I'm standing inside the trough). Skip is about to put seed into one of the silos; a whole "pulled" silo sits on the dock to the right.

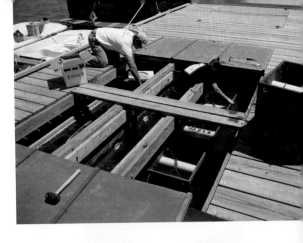

Oyster poop, or "fouling," blankets the seed inside one of our silos. The sticky brown substance needs to be washed off the oysters almost daily; otherwise it will continue to multiply and eventually suffocate the oyster seed.

My boss, Skip, on the Oyster Plex around sunset.

A far cry from my days in heels, this was my uniform of choice on freezing, wet days: waterproof pants, Hunter boots, a hoodie, my blue grunden jacket, and a baseball cap.

By the middle of the summer, the seed has popped to about a quarter-inch in length, at which point it's ready to grade.

By September, the seed has grown to two full inches and is now ready to plant. We dump the seed from their plastic mesh bags directly into the boat. From here, Skip will shovel the oysters onto the lease.

The Oyster Plex in full swing farmhands Will Heward (left) and Dana Hale wash oysters, while inside, the rest of the crew counts oysters int hundred-piece bags.

BELOW: *Mornings on the Ba are quiet and still before the rush of oyster work begins.*

Occasionally we plant oysters by hand by scattering them directly on to the Bay floor from stiff, black plastic mesh bags. Those mesh bags are the same ones that sit in the cages on the lease and go through the power-washing process each winter.

Once the oysters are counted into these yellow mesh bags, they're delivered to the Shop, where they'll be shipped off to restaurants around the country.

We receive our seed from a few different hatcheries that spawn oysters from specific broodstocks (parents). The result, in some cases, creates coloring or stripes on the oyster shell, which allows oyster farmers to differentiate one hatchery's seed from another's.

In the summertime, the Bay is filled with sailboats and pleasure cruisers as well as a handful of oyster skiffs.

boot) to get the seed from one spot to the next, which meant that the minute we had a tote full of graded quarters to give him, he was prepping the float crew to distribute the seed among bags and get the bags out to the nursery. It was a project he could do only on low tides, putting us in an even tighter spot. The seed couldn't sit out in the sun for longer than a few hours before the oysters started to die, so we were forced to either grade it all in time for the tide or sink the quarters back into the upweller. Every day became a juggling act that ended with me putting all of the puzzle pieces back into place.

I was mesmerized by the seed migration. Like a well-choreographed dance or an intricate machine, there were beats and minutes, pauses and twirls. It helped me tap into the idea that growing food was like practicing art. We were touching every oyster from the very start of their lives. Everything we applied to the process, from the water in the hose to the stringlike edges of the metal graders, added something to the growth process. Each shell we chipped grew back stronger and fuller, like bonsai trees, contributing to that consistent shape. Each tumble through the grader ensured a sturdier, thicker shell and heartier meat. Even if we lost a few seeds to clumsiness or the wind, that helped the remaining oysters grow larger by giving them a teensy bit more space to grow. I started to understand how much our hands-on effort affected these little creatures.

And what's more, I was learning that these weren't ground-breaking new methods. They were time-tested by hundreds of oyster farmers before us. I started digging up research about oysters and the culture of farming when I got home at night, Googling certain terms or methods to learn more about this world. I discovered a book called *The Oysters of Locmariaquer,* written by Eleanor Clark, who wove a poetic and bewitching story about oyster farmers along the coast of Brittany, France. I was entranced by the community Clark captured, where oyster women outnumbered the men ten to one and the entire coastline participated in the industry. The rituals, the labor, even the spirit with which they celebrated the seasons resembled the world I'd stumbled into, giving me goose bumps as I considered the tiny place in oyster history that we actually occupied.

It made me consider every other food product I consumed, too. Specialty or not, almost everything I ate had started this same way, as a seed or an egg that was then nurtured and grown, in some capacity, by human hands like mine. Steps were repeated and improved year after year to produce one singular ingredient for someone in the world to consume. From carrots to caviar, every single piece of food that passed my lips (including the occasional Twinkie) had a valuable, hardworking live human behind it.

It was changing me. Not in any outward or noticeable way. And not even in a conscious way. I didn't get all reverent and spiritual every time I ate a sandwich or picked up a celery stalk. But something was opening in my world. An appreciation and respect for the work, perhaps. I saw the growers as more than just men and women trying to make a living on the water. They were stewards of the earth and of the sea. They were getting their hands dirty every day for the sole purpose of feeding people. And I finally felt like I was one of them.

On our way in from the tide late one afternoon, Skip turned to me while driving the boat and asked: "Can you imagine what it must be like for people who don't have this connection to oysters? Imagine eating oysters on the half shell in a restaurant, seeing them all nice and chilled on ice but not having any connection to this or how they're grown? Can you *imagine*?"

I stared at him. "That used to be me, Skip," I responded. He looked at me like he couldn't fathom it at first, and then his gaze softened. We both smiled and rode on to the dock in silence. I wondered if he realized how lucky I felt.

My connection to Skip was growing deeper. We'd established a close friendship and understanding. Working on seed together had us working in sync. I was learning how instinctual he was and how he reacted or responded to every gut feeling. He was completely in tune with his own emotions and the oysters themselves. I diligently studied his needs as he oversaw the grading system. I checked in with him before putting seed anywhere, careful not to leave totes in a place where he couldn't find them or put seed into silos where he didn't want them. The more I learned, the more I felt his trust. He was revealing what was burrowed so deeply inside of him: his love for the seed and the animals that they would become. Like a dutiful charge, he felt responsible for their safety and their growth. The more I touched the seed, the more I felt it, too. For all the jokes that flew about me being the Mama Seeda, there was a root. Skip and I were parenting these babies along together. We were bonded by it.

The connection was deeply comforting to me. It was my first experience getting to know a boss on that level, making me feel valued both as an employee and as Skip's friend. And it drew me into the work in a way I'd never felt about a paying job before, which in turn gave me a deeper sense of satisfaction in life. It was as though what I was doing really mattered. To him, to the bay, to my crew, and to the rest of the planet. For the first time in my working life, I felt like I was truly giving something back.

Of course, my time on the farm wasn't all spiritual seed releases and soul-feeding reveries on the water. It was backbreaking, and much to my dismay, involved a lot of numbers and math. In high school, math used to make my eyes glaze over. But here I was, using fractions and percentages in a real-life setting. I had to pay attention.

One morning after we'd gotten the Carolina back from the shop, Skip informed me that we would take our quarters to the Back River, a freshwater river that ran into the bay from the north, where he had set up a floating nursery (the water there had enough salinity to make growing oysters viable). It was an area he leased from the town just like the one in the bay, but instead of cages that sat on the ground, this nursery floated on the surface, connected to a system of lines that were attached to mesh bags stuffed with Styrofoam. The Back River was a freshwater source that was rich with nutrients and a slightly different type of phytoplankton than what grew in the bay; this different food source would give the oysters an ever-so-slightly different flavor profile. Placing the baby oysters up there for a short while (about two or three months) was an experiment to see how it would affect the final flavor—it was where Skip got to play with the oysters' merroir—their sense of place.

The girls and I graded a batch of ARC seed first thing that morning, resulting in two full totes of quarters. Skip loaded them onto the boat and instructed Berg to meet us out in the river with the other boat, a stack of floating bags, and a crew of workers.

Skip helmed the Bateau, maneuvering her through the harbor's maze of moored sailboats before gunning it at top speed across a stretch of the bay. He steered us north, directly toward the old wooden bridge that connected the town to the long, spindly piece of land that created Duxbury's barrier beach. With his hair whipping off his forehead and his mouth slightly open in the wind, he reminded me of a dog hanging out a car window—purely and utterly happy. He leaned into the wind, willing the boat forward as fast as he could push it. As we approached the bridge he pulled down the throttle just in time to glide through the pilings and swing us toward the mouth of the river.

Marsh surrounded us on all sides, narrowing toward a bend where the waterway started to snake north. We slowed as we neared a large flat platform bobbing in the wake. A white sign perched on top with scrawled black lettering: CAUTION: SHELLFISH LEASE, TOWN OF DUXBURY.

A similar sign sat about fifty yards upstream, marking the other end of Skip's designated growing area. Between the two platforms lay a dozen rows of heavy-duty system lines that were secured to the ground by moorings and floated to the surface with huge orange buoys. Skip pulled us in between two of the lines, tying one onto the boat, then examined the totes of seed we'd brought with us.

"Each tote holds about sixty liters when it's full. I usually count out one hundred milliliters' worth of seed, then multiply it out to figure out how many seeds are in the tote," he said, dropping a handful of oysters into a measuring cup. Once he'd filled it to the one hundred milliliter mark, he dumped the contents onto the bow and with a penknife, counted the seeds out one by one. He reminded me of a pharmacist counting pills. The oysters were wet and clung to each other, making the task tedious, but he pulled them apart and counted them into piles of one hundred. He ended up with around 540 seeds.

"That's around fifty-four hundred per thousand, and by the looks of it, our tote is about two-thirds full, I'd say around forty liters. That puts the number around two hundred and sixteen thousand, give or take," he said. He eyeballed the second tote. "Between the two, we're probably around four hundred thousand."

I looked at the totes and back at Skip, wondering how he had wrapped his mind around the numbers so quickly. All I saw was a pile of seed.

Berg pulled up on the Carolina with the rest of the crew and a huge pile of empty mesh bags. With the two boats secured to the line, we set up an assembly line. Maggie and I each grabbed measuring cups and set up shop next to a pile of empty bags. Skip showed us how to fill the cups to just over the brim, another eyeball method that put about 1,200 oysters in each scoop. We poured the contents into the bags, which were already holding sheets of Styrofoam, then handed them over to Will and Pops, who sealed them shut with PVC pipes. Quinn, Catie, and Skip stood in the water in waders and secured the bags to the line with metal ring hooks (Berg supervised in order to keep his leg dry). Maggie and I set the pace but Skip encouraged us to move quickly so we could finish before the tide turned. With so many hands to do the work, we had 400,000 seeds set in the nursery in less than two hours.

It would take me a while to get used to the counting process. Skip's eyeball method was simple enough when we were out on the tide with bags to fill. But there was a lot more pressure on me to count accurately when it came to handling his side business: selling seed.

For the past several years, Skip had raised seed not only for himself but for a handful of other growers, too. He usually purchased a few million more than he would need each season, grew it all out in his upwellers, then sold it to other growers for a small markup to cover his costs. Running upwellers was expensive: there was an initial investment of seed, paying a staff to run it, and keeping it powered all summer long. It was a cost that not every grower could afford. Skip did it both as a service to them and for a small profit.

I didn't know Skip to have any serious vices. He didn't do drugs. He drank but usually just to enjoy the drink itself, whether it be a warm Budweiser or an expensive bottle of wine. His only addiction, from what I could tell, was buying seed. I think it fed some desire to gamble, only instead of chips and cards, he played with nature. He bought seed to see how much he could get out of it.

Three upwellers and several million oyster seed could add up to a hefty wager. When he started using upwellers back in 2000, he quickly latched on to their powers, understanding that having the ability to feed hundreds of thousands of a single species in a controlled environment could net big results. There were losses, of course: He could only really count on 40 percent of his oysters coming to market size. That's 400,000 for every million he bought. The loss factored in everything from human clumsiness to weather, meaning at least 600,000 babies would never see a shucking knife. Each year, Skip worked hard to nudge that loss down. The more seed he bought, the more room he had to play.

The seed sales were a small part of Skip's overall business, but it quickly became my top priority to make sure his customers (aka: his dad, his fellow growers, his friends) were getting their money's worth. Orders came in by the piece, with one grower wanting 150,000, while another requested 600,000. Skip walked me through the steps of counting out each piece, nudging the ornery seeds away from each other to make sure I was accounting for every one. I started by carefully measuring out one hundred milliliters and counting that number before multiplying it out. I also did precise volume counts on each tote, diligently counting it out by liters one scoop at a time. I usually did both counts twice for reassurance—I couldn't stomach the idea of under- or over-selling seed to somebody as important as Billy Bennett.

Billy was Skip's biggest customer and therefore, Skip's biggest priority. I could always tell when it was Billy's day to pick up seed by how fidgety Skip would act. He wanted to please his father by giving him a good grade and delivering it precisely when his dad needed it. I saw it one day when Billy pulled up to the dock in his boxy, blue-bottomed skiff, his baseball hat perched high up on his forehead.

"Hey, Skip, you gonna have seed for me today?" he shouted over the motor. With his thick New England accent, it sounded to me like: *Ya gahnna have seed foh meh to-deh?*

"Hey, Dad," Skip answered. "I'm doing counts on it right now. Do you need it right away?"

"Not right this minute, Skip. Tide's not till later. Maybe in an hour or so?" Billy responded dropping his smile for a minute to concentrate on Skip's hands as they worked.

"Okay, Dad. We'll leave it here on the dock for you," Skip replied, eager to get the work done in time. As Billy pulled away, Skip set to the task of counting in serious concentration. Such conversations were casual, but the message was stern: Billy needed seed by the tide and Skip would deliver.

Once he trusted that I was up to the task, Skip let me do counts on my own. It was a responsibility I took very seriously. If I were to screw up on a hundred-milliliter count, I could set the whole tote backward or forward by thousands of seeds. And that translated into dollars. Whenever Skip asked me to do counts, I could sense him buzzing around the docks, hovering and tossing questions as he passed.

"What was the count for this tote?" he said, picking up a corner of it to check the weight.

"Forty-four liters?" I said, trying not to make it sound like a question. I'd counted it once but hadn't had time to get a second count.

"It feels lighter than that," he said. "Want to get another count, just in case?" His intuition for these things was always spot-on—he could read me instantly. Those questions weren't meant to alarm or make me second-guess but they always made my heart beat a little faster. I had to be on my game at all times.

I started getting approached by his customers on the dock, wondering when they could pick up their orders. Catie and Eva laughed the first time one of his customers, Bob, came down looking for seed. The sturdy, stubbled grower looked like someone trying to score drugs. He hung around the top of the dock for about ten minutes before slinking nervously down the ramp.

"Hey, you're Erin, right? Skip said I should see you about some seed," he said, peering into the tote as though he were peeking behind the curtain.

"Yeah, I can help you. How much do you need?" I responded, grabbing a pen and the bible.

"Uh, I think we asked for two hundred thousand. Can we get a hundred today and the rest tomorrow?" he answered, playing with his fingers nervously.

"Sure. We'll finish up this grade and see what we can do," I said. Bob scuttled away, mumbling that he'd check in with us later.

Those encounters happened a few times a day; we'd reached peak seed deployment season, meaning all of the growers were putting quarter-inch seed into their nurseries. A string of blue-sky days and warm water took us to the third week in July, which was packed with several double-tide days; crews could hit low tide in the morning and at night before the sun set, getting seed out to the nurseries en masse. I started doing counts after every single grade, pulling the totes over to a quiet corner of the dock where I could sit and concentrate on the numbers.

My writerly brain was shifting gears—I was counting a little faster each day as some ancient, unused portion of it creaked back to life. And then, just like that, once I turned the faucet on, it wouldn't turn off. I became Rain Man, counting every mile marker on my way home, every bite of sandwich it took me to finish the whole thing, every blister on my worn-out feet, every board on the docks. Between the seed counts and counting out oysters into bags after the cull (we were now putting in up to 450 per week) I was becoming a human spreadsheet.

My motivation for counting came down to the up-wellers. By counting, recounting, then bagging up the seed to hand off to someone else or deploy onto our own lease, we were slowly emptying our silos. I'd grudgingly gotten used to living with an endless throb in my lower back from lifting the boxes, which were all fattened up to about eighty pounds. Despite Catie's insistence that she could lift them on her own (we'd take to calling her "The Hero" for her superhuman desire to do all of the work herself), I begged Berg for some help lifting silos each morning. He conceded and offered a few of the guys to help. Watching Will and

Quinn, who had both been bulking up on farmwork all summer, struggle to pull the bulging boxes out of the water made Catie realize that she was simply being stubborn.

But despite my lower-back ache, I felt strong and remarkably healthy. After a string of hot days, I had the sun-kissed look of a lifeguard. My wardrobe had been whittled down to a pair of worn-out khaki shorts, a tank top, flip-flops, and a baseball hat. The few times Dave and I made it to the beach that summer, he snickered when I finally unveiled my bathing suit—I had an honest-to-goodness farmer's tan, down to the white stripes that crisscrossed my feet from my flip-flops. No matter how much sunscreen I slathered on, I couldn't avoid those lines.

I was also more fit than I'd been in years. My arms were chiseled, I'd probably lost fifteen pounds since starting on the farm, and everything I wore fit in all the right places. The girls and I took to wearing bathing suits under our clothes while we worked. Instead of coffee breaks, we would go for a swim, often jumping in fully dressed just so we could stand under the sweltering sun and dry out. Berg had mastered the float push, too.

"Hey, Pain, can I borrow your cell phone?" went the joke. As soon as I handed it over, someone would hipcheck me over the side. It always ended with me sputtering to the surface with a laugh. Everyone got a taste except for A2, who just stood there like a brick wall when someone tried to push him in. Catie tried almost daily, pushing all hundred pounds of her scrawny frame into his back, but he hardly budged.

Finally, we'd reached summer. It was what I'd been

waiting months to see—the sunshine glistening off the bay, the oyster lease operating at full speed, the crew in good spirits. We were putting in ten to twelve hours a day without blinking. The crew was working as a unit. We could read each others' movements and worked in sync. We felt like a family, and each day brought another excuse to hang out in the sunshine, go for a swim, grab an ice cream cone at lunch. It was the very best time of year to be an oyster farmer.

Around us, the bay had reached full capacity, too. We were passed by a parade of sailboats, motorboats, fishing charters, and leisure cruisers. The Maritime School ran sailing and rowing classes every day, which meant the docks now swarmed with small children. Standing at our grading station, we felt like zoo creatures on display as students filed past, staring into our totes.

Out on the lease, the cages were filling up with bags. The cage system itself had become a life force where we discovered horseshoe crabs and baby lobsters hiding out under the wiry frames. Some cages acted as sanctuaries for the millions of green crabs that scuttled around the bay. They'd come pouring out of the bottom of the cages whenever we approached; the cages themselves were a breeding ground for warm-weather organisms like the slimy, alien-like substance we called "sponge." It grew on the wire frames of the cages as well as on the bags themselves, coating everything in a thick layer of Day-Glo sludge. The colors might have been pretty but the sponge was like a bloodsucker, suffocating the oysters by blocking water and nutrient flow. Armed with sturdy, steel-bristled brushes, we marched out to the tide a few times a week to shake and scrub down the bags, rotating them through the different slots to kill off the nasty sponge and give the oysters better access to water and sunlight.

Along with all that scrubbing we were out there to hand-pick, too. During a week of lengthy double drainers, we arrived at the farm for a five A.M. tide, well before the sun was up, and made our way silently out to the lease under a blanket of stars. Sleepy and silent, my crew diligently scrubbed bags, watching the sun creep cautiously up to the edge of the horizon. Once it appeared, we all came to life, suddenly finding our voices and some laughter. With hours to go before we would make it back to land, Berg asked us all to grab buckets and get to work picking.

For the first time in weeks, I realized that the ground near where our cages sat was almost completely void of oysters. It was the field Skip had planted two years ago, and we'd been hitting it hard for months. I asked Berg about what that meant for our supply.

"We're trying to clear this section, to get as many oysters off of it as we can before moving over to that part of the lease," he said, motioning toward a swath of land that was exposed to our north. I looked over to see hundreds of thousands of jagged oyster shells scattered across the mud there.

"We rotate the fields, just like a vegetable farmer would," he explained. We were emptying this field so that we had a place to plant all of the seed that currently sat in our nursery and upwellers. I surveyed the two football fields of mud we were centered between. The crew was picking around the outermost reaches, from east to west, meaning we'd reached the very last of this crop. Berg looked back over at the oyster-laden field.

"Hope we can get this one to last a few more weeks before we jump into that one," he said, sounding stressed. "I'm not supposed to drag it until September. It was all the seed we planted last summer and it's almost ready. Just need to give it a few more weeks."

Berg had his eye on the oysters every day, diligently studying the fields during every tide to gauge how long we could go until we dipped into the new crop. When Skip was on the lease, the two would walk together, Luke and Obi Wan, heads bowed in concentration. I was impressed with the amount of responsibility Skip handed to Berg. The fresh young college grad not only ran Skip's farm and managed a ten-person crew, he protected Skip's future.

To celebrate the height of the season, Skip and Shore, who was still mostly holed up in the office despite the beautiful weather, invited their close friend, Chef Jeremy Sewall, and his entire restaurant team out to the farm for a float party. Jeremy was the chef-owner of a Brookline restaurant called Lineage, which boasted a huge wood-burning oven and served some of the heartiest New England cuisine I'd ever tasted. Dave and I loved Lineage (which was close to our condo) both as a cozy wintertime escape and a special-occasion spot where we liked to bring our parents whenever they visited. I'd interviewed Jeremy in the past, so we'd gotten to know each other pretty well. He had a round, perpetually youthful face and a dry, clever sense of humor. He was one of my favorite chefs in Boston.

Jeremy had a long and deep connection to the farm—he was actually the first chef ever to visit Island Creek. A native of Upstate New York, he'd moved to Boston after several years on the West Coast to helm a new seafood-focused spot called Great Bay. In an attempt to get to know his local purveyors, he requested a visit to the farm. At the time Skip was still in his infancy as an oyster farmer and couldn't believe a world-class chef, newly arrived from California, wanted to see his operation. Nervous at first, Skip relaxed once he and Jeremy got out on the water, and the two quickly bonded over their mutual love of lobstering and fishing. They became fast friends and every year since, Jeremy made it a point to get to the farm at least once during the summer.

So, on a sparkling, late-July afternoon, he continued the tradition, bringing twenty staff members from both Lineage and Eastern Standard, where he was a consulting chef, along with his wife and two sons, down to the farm for a tour and dinner on the float.

I invited Dave to come too. It would be a comfortable gathering with people he knew—not just me and the farm crew—and it would be a great way to introduce him to the farm itself. Dave had admitted to me over the July Fourth weekend that part of what was irking him so much about my new life was that he had no connection to it. Maybe all he needed, he said, was to see where I worked and get to know what I did all day. I completely agreed, grateful that he'd been the one to make the suggestion. While the world had become distinctly my own, an escape from my "real" life up in Boston, it was also one that I wanted to share. Dave had always been innately woven into the social fabric of my life—from the circle of friends I'd made through work to my tightly connected group of girlfriends from college, he was a constant and familiar participant. This was the first time since we'd met that I was forging friendships that didn't involve him; it was the one part of me that he didn't know. While I knew it was important for me to maintain those friendships even without him, I didn't want to leave him out. I wanted to be able to share the stupid jokes and banter with him, to be able to explain my day to him without getting a blank look in return. A summer night out on the float, having dinner and drinking beers with Skip, Shore, and Jeremy, was exactly what would help him understand this world.

Dave arrived in time to find a minibus full of restaurant staffers unloading in the parking lot. I still had some work to finish up with the seed, so I sent him off with the restaurant group for a tour of the lease with Skip, Shore, and Don Merry. I watched from the dock as the three tour boats navigated the channel and settled themselves near the exposed lease. Dave was the first one in the water, barefoot and shuffling around in the mud while Skip filled the group in on the basics of oyster farming.

I got out to the float just in time for the tour's return and found Dave and one of the Lineage bartenders swapping war stories. He had a goofy grin on his face and I could see, immediately, that he'd caught a glimpse of the world I had fallen in love with. I grabbed him a beer, then went to help Skip, who was kneeling down, trying to light the burner of his steamer kettle.

Dinner on the float was a rare treat since it gave Skip the opportunity to show off his second-most prized catch: lobsters. He'd brought his grill and kettle out and covered our culling tables with a red-checkered cloth, surrounding them with stacks of overturned crates for seats. He'd also spent the day digging baskets of steamers and emptying out his lobster traps to collect enough food to feed the voracious crew. He and Shore, his sous chef for the night, were having a hard time getting the fire started.

"Hey, Bug, can you get some rockweed for me?" Skip asked, calling Shore by his familiar nickname from childhood (when he was a kid, Shore's mom called him "Shorey Bug"—the name stuck).

"I'm on it," Shore responded, grabbing one of the boats for a trip to the rocky wall along the outer edges of the harbor to collect a basket of stringy bulbous weed; it would sit atop the lobsters as they steamed.

Skip got busy filling the huge kettle pot with ocean water. He was jumpy, trying to get the timing right while entertaining his guests, too. He eventually gave up on the banter and just focused on lighting his fire. The restaurant crew came over to examine his catch, picking up the banded lobsters to watch them flop around. Seeing this world through their eyes made me smile. It was magical to be on the water on nights like this.

The clams went into the steamer kettle first, sitting in just a few inches of water. A minute later Skip was handing massive bowls of steamed clams and vats of butter to the group, who had rolled up their sleeves in anticipation. Jeremy dove in first, grabbing a steamer and chucking the shell off the side of the float before dunking the whole meaty body into butter. He popped it into his mouth like candy, letting the butter drip down his chin. He closed his eyes.

"Oh my God. Skip, what did you do to those?" he sighed. The staff leaned in after him, digging into the piping-hot bowl with timid fingers. One after another, they slurped back their clam bellies, tasting the sweet, rich, and oozy flavors of fat mixing with sea. Dave ate one, then a few more before shaking his head in awe. "Unbelievable," he said.

The night went on like that, with platter after platter of shellfish reaching the tables straight out of the steam kettle or off the grill. More clams, then shucked oysters with lemon, then lobsters, then corn. Each simply prepared ingredient got rounds of applause and the *oohs* and *aahs* of a fireworks display. I sat with Dave on the edge of the Bat, our feet dangling into the water as we tore into our lobsters, picking out every last morsel of meat. We hadn't been this happy or relaxed in months. I tried the tomalley, the guts of the lobster, after an urging from Jeremy, who explained that's where the flavor was. It was earthy and salty, like mushrooms out of the ocean. After a few bites, Dave leaned in and wiped a bit of stray tomalley off my cheek, then kissed me on that spot.

"This is so cool," he whispered.

After dinner, Skip and Shore tempted a few folks onto the boat to go tubing, a Duxbury Bay tradition. They zoomed off, leaving the float rocking in their wake as the rest of us started to clean up—it involved little more than dumping the lobster shells in the water and tossing our plates into a garbage bag. From across the glassy bay, I could hear Shore's high-pitched *whoop!* every time they took a tight turn, then the belly laughs of everyone on the boat as someone flew off the tube. Skip came careening back into the float, like that dog hanging out the window, his mouth open in a wide grin. This was summertime at its peak for him.

The restaurant crew eventually made its way back to land. The sun was going down and with it the temperature, causing them to shiver in their dripping wet clothes. Jeremy, wrapped up in a towel after being thrown into the water by a couple of his cooks, gave each of us a hug and told us we'd better do it again next year.

Dave and I stayed on the float, picking up the extra beer bottles and breaking down the cooking station until Skip, Shore, and Don returned for one final beer and to watch the sun go down. We sat together on the floor of the float, talking about the summer and how it was going in comparison to years past. It was the first time I'd seen Dave interact with Skip or Shore like this in a quiet setting. Dave had very little in common with my new work friends—a Southern boy with roots in rock and roll next to a couple of weathered, New England watermen—but they all had the same wry wit and swapped jokes casually.

Don Merry, having been one of the first to join Skip on his oystering endeavors, rehashed some of his stories from old days as we watched the sun drop down below the horizon. He and Skip laughed as they recounted their first few years as growers when it was just a handful of guys working on makeshift, rickety barges (both men now had garages on their floats and large crews running their farms).

Their big excitement back then was selling ten bags a week, Don admitted.

"Look at us now," Skip laughed, slapping Don on the back.

The night ended at the Winsor House, an ancient inn and pub that sat less than a mile from the harbor. The dark, low-ceilinged space was full of old stories and ghosts but we filled it with laughter as we told more stories and sucked back Don's favorite drink: vodka with a splash of soda and a drop of cranberry juice. He called it the Don Merry.

We would host another dinner on the float later that summer for the Hale family, Skip's neighbors and close friends who had won the dinner as an auction item, a prize Island Creek donated to only a few charities each year. That dinner ran more formally than the Lineage one, as a sit-down, course-by-course event with plenty of wine and fanciful dishes like dill-laced razor clam chowder and a striped bass ceviche. Skip made lobsters and steamers and this time, grilled up a few strip steaks.

The night ended with the stars on full display and our twenty-one guests singing along to the Pointer Sisters. Shore, Catie, and I, whom Skip had recruited to help out, listened from the back of the float, swinging our feet in the inky black water as our toes ignited tiny waves of neon-blue luminescence. Once the crowd was safely back on land, after we'd struggled to clean up the float under dimly lit gas lanterns, we sat in folding chairs, enjoying the last of the party's beers under a star-filled night.

"We should probably tell them," Skip said to Shore mischievously once we'd all sat down and relaxed. "Don't you think it's time?" Catie and I looked at them curiously, wondering what kind of secret they were keeping.

"By all means, you definitely should," Shore replied, grinning. Whatever the two were holding back was making them giddy with excitement.

"Okay, then. Girls: We have news," Skip said with his Cheshire grin.

"We're opening a restaurant in Boston," he gushed. "And Jeremy's going to be the chef."

I couldn't believe it. These guys, this little place, opening a restaurant? I jumped up to give both of them hugs, congratulating them on such a big move. I wanted to know every detail, getting more excited as they divulged. It was still around a year away but the paperwork had been signed. And the name of it, I asked?

"The Island Creek Oyster Bar," Skip replied.

Just like that, summer started to fade. It happened so subtly, we hardly had time to notice. In early August, we graded our very last quarter-inch seed and sent it out to the nursery. We still had some seed in the upwellers, but it had reached half an inch in length and was past the point of grading. We spent the last few weeks of the summer doing what we'd done at the beginning—washing, washing, and more washing.

After that final quarter-inch grade, I asked Skip what we should do with the half a silo's worth of seed we still had left over: the runts of the litter. Instead of putting them back in the upweller, he told me to dump them out into the water. I was shocked and stricken that we would just toss all that tiny seed, the ones that would never quite make it into fully grown, sellable oysters. My heart fluttered as they cascaded out of the tote to the bottom of the bay.

"It's all good," Skip assured me. "I've got the yield I expected and then some. You girls did a great job this summer. Consider this a small sacrifice to the oyster gods."

It was time for the summer crew to break up as Quinn, Eva, and Pops left to head back to college while Maggie launched an apartment hunt in Boston for her last year at graduate school. Catie was on her way into the real world, having landed her coveted job as an environmental consultant for a firm just north of Boston. She, too, was moving to the city but was reluctant to let go of the oyster world she loved so dearly.

On one of her final days on the farm, Catie and I watched as the guys shut down the upweller to pull the now season-worn system, trough and all, out of the water. We had one final grade to complete to get some quarter-inch seed separated from a batch of half-inch seed (we called those the "fiddies," short for fifty-cent pieces) so we stood to the side, quietly grading as the guys worked.

Pulling the troughs out was a pretty bum deal. Now that they were soaked through with water and covered in muck, sponge, mussel seed, and seaweed, each one probably weighed a full ton. The once-gleaming wooden silos were also a wreck, now caked with sponge and crusty oyster poop. The screens were broken and the wire mesh was falling off, making them look as worn-out and broken as we all felt after a grueling season of effort. They would need a lot of work before next summer. But, Berg assured me, we had all winter for projects like that. I watched as the guys loaded the trough onto the farm truck, feeling a weight of responsibility pour off me. The churning, massive old beast, my summertime enemy, was actually, now, a familiar old friend. It was back to lying on the dock, nothing more than a wooden box and a bunch of rusty bolts. I'd survived an entire summer dancing around the mouth of the thing, ripping my hands to shreds on those nylon ropes. It might have battered me, but the blisters would eventually slough off and my muscles would one day loosen. The upweller had taught me a lot about my own abilities. It had toughened and strengthened me. It had turned me into one of those female oyster farmers I'd been so enamored with just a year before. I felt like I'd survived a battle. Good-bye, silos, I said silently as the guys carried them off. Good-bye and thanks for everything.

With the upweller put away for the season, we wrapped up our final grade quickly with an anticlimactic finish but I took a mental note. The last shake of the grader, the last flip, the final pile of seed.

In a snap, all my summertime suffering came to an end. No more lying in bed with a throbbing back. No more hefting and pushing and stressing about timing. No more standing on the dock for hours. I actually felt momentarily sad about it, like I was leaving summer camp. Catie and I gathered with the rest of the crew on Will's back deck after work for a plate of his pan-fried oysters. Over a cheap bottle of Champagne, she and I toasted our success.

"Here's to not fucking it up," she announced noncha-
lantly.

"To not fucking up," I replied before downing the entire bubble-filled glass.

Will's Pan-Fried Island Creek Oysters

Will swears by a few specific ingredients for this
recipe, including the Kultrun chile oil, which he
picked up along his travels, as well as the Fireman Fred's
chili mix, which he discovered while living in Saratoga,
New York. The heat can be intense with heavy doses of
both—use sparingly so you can still taste the meat of
the oyster.

> *2 dozen shucked Island Creeks;*
> *reserve ¼ cup liquor*
> *Kultrun chile olive oil (or any standard*
> *chile oil)*
> *Extra-virgin olive oil*
> *4 farm-fresh eggs, minus 1 egg white*
> *1 cup buttermilk*
> *4 tablespoons flour, divided*
> *2 cups Panko bread crumb flakes*
> *Fireman Fred's Flaming 3 Alarm Chili*
> *Mix (or substitute standard chili*
> *powder mix)*
> *1 teaspoon paprika*

Pinch of cinnamon
Triscuit crackers
4 slices of pepper-jack cheese, quartered

Preheat oven to 375°. Place a deep skillet over medium-high heat and fill it halfway with chile oil and olive oil (half and half). In a large bowl, whisk eggs, then whisk in buttermilk, oyster liquor, and 2 tablespoons of flour. In a second bowl, combine remaining flour with bread crumbs, chili mix, paprika, and cinnamon. Dip the oyster meat in the egg mixture, then roll in the bread crumb mixture to cover completely. Fry the oysters for 2 to 3 minutes on each side, until the batter is just golden and crunchy.

Place fried oysters atop Triscuits, then cover with small slice of pepper-jack cheese. Arrange prepared oysters on baking sheet and bake for about 3 minutes, or just long enough to melt the cheese.

Serves 6

CHAPTER SEVEN

OYSTER FEST

The Island Creek Oyster Festival is the farm's annual end-of-the-season celebration, a wild beer-and-bivalve party set on a thin stretch of Duxbury Beach. All that revelry has a greater purpose, too: raising money for the farm's nonprofit arm, the Island Creek Oysters Foundation. Originally, the party started as a down-and-dirty celebration, a keg party in the parking lot behind the Winsor House. When I got to the farm, it was still considered down-and-dirty by some accounts (lots of beer and rabble-rousing), but over the past two years it had also grown into something the farmers never expected: a fund-raising powerhouse.

The foundation is the farm's way of giving back, both locally and to other communities. Skip, Shore, and most of the other growers have traveled extensively and been exposed to places all over the world that need money, support, and food. It was a powerful moment when they realized that the oyster festival could generate enough money to help one of those communities directly.

Shore played a large role in helping Skip create the foundation. He'd landed at the farm full-time shortly after graduating from Trinity College. Like so many of Island Creek's seasonal employees (he'd worked on Skip's summer crew), Shore was drawn to the allure of working in an anticorporate setting, one that was focused on the people it employed more than its own bottom line. He and Skip became good buddies when he worked on the farm—so close, in fact, that right after graduation, as Shore made plans to travel the world with his best friend and crewmate, Gardner, Skip asked if he could tag along. The three made an unlikely set of travel companions but spent several weeks traipsing through South America together. It was somewhere between Argentina and Chile, after too many glasses of red wine, where Skip asked Shore if he would consider running the business arm of Island Creek. Anxious to avoid the dreaded "real world," Shore agreed. After a few more stops around the globe, he eventually returned to the States and settled in as Island Creek's director of business development.

Little did he and Skip know that Shore's first few months in the office would help shape the farm's corporate culture. It was trial by fire for the twenty-two-year-old, who spent his first year incorporating the company, developing a solid sales structure, and cementing the company's cobbled-together marketing program. He executed Skip's ideas, weighed in with a few of his own, and before he knew it, he was running a million-dollar oyster business.

After incorporating the company, Shore quickly set to the task of creating the Island Creek Oysters Foundation, which came about the same time the festival graduated from the Winsor House parking lot to a tent on the beach. The foundation's mission, Shore and Skip decided, was to raise money to help feed people in malnourished regions through hands-on education. A small amount of money would go to local charities but they also wanted to fund a large-scale project in another part of the world, something Skip oversaw personally. By the time I arrived, they were considering a partnership project with the Woods Hole Oceanographic Institution that would take them to Zanzibar, a tiny island off the coast of Tanzania, to incorporate a shellfish farming program into that community. They wanted to build a shellfish hatchery that would help the natives establish a much-needed and sustainable food source.

And so, the fourth-annual Oyster Fest was set to take place on Saturday, September 12, with about three thousand people expected to attend. Shore and Skip had enlisted me and twenty or so Duxbury locals and farm friends to serve on a volunteer committee and help execute the now massive undertaking. It was a jolly group of do-gooders who all brought expertise to the table: Shore's mom, Elizabeth, who ran merchandise, Skip's mom, Nancy, who decorated, a few of the growers' wives, and other friends. I was in charge of press outreach and managing the festival's food program—two jobs that required a hefty time commitment. I offloaded our press efforts to a close friend and publicist named Nicole whose small but mighty PR firm, All Heart PR, was willing to take on a pro bono client, and dedicated my time to managing the festival's food situation.

The festival was, first and foremost, a party dedicated to the oyster. There would be a forty-foot raw bar holding thousands of oysters, which would be shucked by dozens of volunteers. The oysters themselves—40,000 total—were all donated by the Island Creek growers in support of the Foundation, which was a massive and generous feat that required more than a week's worth of free labor from each of them. But the event also had the reputation of being a booze fest with local brewer, Harpoon Brewery, bringing down dozens of kegs of their potent, high-alcohol brews. (Their Munich Dark was a perfect match for the briny sweetness of our Island Creeks.) There were also bands, kids' activities, and a tent for VIP ticket holders. And the volunteer committee was in charge of it all.

While the thousands of ticket payers came mostly to load up on oysters and frothy beer, we also needed a substantial amount of *real* food. I was tasked with wrangling an army of chefs to feed the ravenous crowd, so Shore drew up a list of restaurant folks who were all connected to Island Creek as customers or friends, including a who's who of Boston's culinary superpowers like Jody Adams of Rialto, Chris Schlesinger of East Coast Grill, Jasper White of Summer Shack, and young guns Tony Maws of Craigie on Main, Jamie Bissonnette of Toro, and of course, our friend Jeremy Sewall.

Asking a chef to take a Saturday night off from his restaurant and trek down to the South Shore with a contingent of staff was a pretty demanding request, one we tried to offset by offering each chef access to a selection of local, donated ingredients like scallops, oysters, striped bass, and tuna. We also decided to raise our own pigs. Island Creek, like any other farm, should have crop diversity, Skip thought. Why not take on other niche products, like pigs, in the name of fund-raising? Named Gourmet and Midnight, the piglets arrived at the farm in early June and were penned up at an old pigpen at a neighbor's house. By the end of August, after months of eating pig slop and day-old pastries from French Memories, they were a fat, happy pair weighing in at over a hundred pounds each. One would go to chef Chris Schlesinger of Cambridge's famed East Coast Grill, who would set up a pig-roasting box right on the beach; the other found its way to Jamie Bissonnette, the chef at Toro and a well-established nose-to-tail cook, who would serve as many parts of the pig as could be transformed into food.

Between sourcing thousands of pounds of local ingredients, watching over (i.e., cooing at and hand-feeding) the pigs, and communicating with our chefs, my festival planning time began to cut dangerously into my time on the farm. Berg, of course, noticed any and every thing that took my attention away from what he considered "real" work and made it a point to call me out when he felt like I was slacking.

But there was an understanding between us. It was the foundation that had drawn Berg to Island Creek in the first place; the Zanzibar project kept him there. He'd studied aquaculture at the University of Rhode Island, and wrote his senior thesis on the theory of aquaponics—the simultaneous cultivation of vegetation and aquatic life. A relentless idealist, he stood behind the "teach a man to fish" mantra and left school in search of a job where he might build aquaculture programs in other parts of the world. His interview at Island Creek ended with Berg explaining to Skip that he wanted to help feed people in other countries through aquaculture. Skip was sold. As plans for the Zanzibar project unfolded, Skip kept Berg tightly in the loop—they both hoped that Berg would be able to work in Africa on behalf of the foundation.

So despite his public admonishment (he took to calling me "Part-Time Pain" to the crew) privately I knew he approved of me volunteering my time. Then, in August, right before festival plans kicked into high gear, the foundation's board of directors settled on funding the Zanzibar project—and they wanted Berg involved. He, Skip, Shore, and a few others would take an exploratory trip to Tanzania that fall and, during the winter, they would send Berg back there for two months to oversee the hatchery build-out. His lifelong dream of working overseas was about to become a reality—and the festival was going to get him there. When he heard the news, his attitude toward me instantly warmed up.

A week before the festival, the farm was buzzing with party-planning excitement. Yet all anyone could talk about was the weather, which had continued to rage unpredictably into September. The second of two hurricanes, this one named Danny, screamed up the coast just eight days before our beach party. Five inches of rain fell in two days, enough to make the state shut down all farm operations until they could test the waters for any potential shellfish impurities.

Rain closures are atypical and crippling for the farm, since no product can be harvested during that time period. This one lasted three days, a devastating blow right before we needed to get our hands on 40,000 oysters. Shellfish farming in Massachusetts is overseen by the Division of Marine Fisheries, a government group that watches the farm's processing procedures carefully, strictly monitoring the water for any potential contamination. Oysters are, after all, a delicate food product, and safety measures are taken seriously.

The state reopened the farm on Wednesday, giving growers just two days to harvest, cull, and bag their donations. In the meantime, we spent three days idly looking for projects to keep ourselves occupied.

The morning of the festival I woke up to the sound of pelting rain. Dave and I had crashed at our friends Matt and Meghan's house in nearby Kingston and he rolled over grudgingly as my alarm chirped its early-morning wake-up call. The rain was a terrible sign. I bundled up in layers and pulled on my Wellie boots, packing two extra pairs of clothes just in case.

I'd spent the night before rushing around with the rest of the committee, setting up tables and hanging signs before meeting up with my parents, who had flown up from Houston to attend the festival. When I initially told them that I was going to work on an oyster farm, my mom's first question was: When can we come see it? They were pros at soaking up culture: When they first moved to Texas, they immediately made their way to the Houston Rodeo just so they could get acclimated to their new home state. They were here to see what a New England oyster festival was all about—and to support their daughter, of course. They called me as I made my way to the festival site that morning, wondering if the weather would affect the party plans. I reassured them that we had plenty of tent coverage—but encouraged them to dress warmly.

I stopped by French Memories on my way to the beach to pick up several bags of freshly baked baguettes, which would be used for one of the chefs' dishes. Inhaling the fragrant loaves, I drove over the Powder Point Bridge at a snail's pace, trying to take in the sight ahead of me. Framed by a steely gray sky, our tents looked shockingly white and out of place. The largest was the size of a circus tent, complete with multiple spokes topped with flags flapping in the breeze. Behind it, the ocean churned. I inched off the bridge and into the parking lot, willing the clouds to break, wondering whether anyone was crazy enough to eat oysters in the rain.

The morning flew as I worked with the other committee members to finish setting up the site. Everything about it felt haphazard, almost thrown together at the last minute. Having never planned a party this large, I found myself panicking about details large and small. And judging by the faces of everyone else on our fledgling committee, I wasn't the only one.

The chefs started arriving around the same time that the

beer trucks pulled in. I did my best to guide the chefs and their teams of assistants around the small lagoons that had puddled throughout the tents but a few of them eyed the space and their equipment warily. They were used to working indoors under heat lamps, not in a maelstrom in the mud.

Eventually, Chris from East Coast Grill and his sous chef Eric arrived with the Caja China, their roasting box, now stuffed with Gourmet. When I'd called Chef Schlesinger with the news that his pig weighed in at 125 pounds fully dressed, he chuckled and said they'd need her to be delivered to the restaurant early.

"We want to get to know her a little, if you know what I mean," he explained. La Caja China, the Cuban-style, steel-lined roaster that he was bringing down to the beach, was only built for a ninety-pound pig. It would take some finagling to get Gourmet into the box, he said. They set it up outside the VIP tent and immediately fired up the charcoal, letting off the belly-rumbling aroma of roasting meat. Within minutes, chef Jamie Bissonnette from Toro and Jay Murray from Grill 23 were gathered around it like they were taking in a backyard barbecue.

At three o'clock on the nose, the floodgates opened and the crowds started arriving in droves. Despite my concerns, the weather hadn't deterred the three thousand ticket holders from showing up, who came wearing every possible form of waterproof gear: checkered rubber rain boots, hooded parkas, ponchos. Kids ran from tent to tent, splooshing through puddles and flinging mud. It felt like an underwater carnival.

People descended on the raw bar, where an army of

volunteer shuckers made up of growers and farmhands stood at the ready. As the rain jackhammered the tent above, folks crowded up to the bar, taking plate after plate of freshly shucked oysters. The raw bar's melting ice water mingled with the rain, causing a small river to cascade through the tent. Within an hour, the raw bar was covered in bits of shell grit and the shuckers were having a hard time keeping up. But the crowds just bellied up to the tables, patient to watch the army work. One by one, they went through almost all 40,000 bivalves in one single night.

The chefs, meanwhile, had filled the tent with the irresistible smell of grilled meat. I walked through the tent around four-thirty to find lines already forming at a few of the tables. Tony Maws, a young, curly-haired chef, was anxious to fire his pork belly and scallop dish and started the frenzy by handing out plates. From there, guests descended upon the tables as if it were the last food to be found on earth. The menu was outstanding, from Jasper White's simple razor clam chowder to an elaborate torched oyster dish that chef Jay Murray fired off *à la minute,* melting a sliver of wagyu beef fat over oysters for every guest. Mary Dumont from the restaurant Harvest in Cambridge had a fragrant summer gazpacho that she was serving both with and without shots of vodka.

I spent the afternoon ducking through the masses, trying to avoid the river that now divided the tent down the middle. I passed my parents, who were headed into the main tent in search of food. My dad held a plastic cup of beer in his hand (a poor sign, considering my dad is a scotch man) while my mom smiled meekly from under her hooded jacket. Their Houston countenance had finally caught up with them.

I stayed with them until the sun set and the lights illuminated the tent from the inside, giving it a hazy glow. Around us, people darted in between the tents, splashing water as they ran and shouting with laughter. Despite the pouring rain, the cold, and epic lines for food, the guests seemed to be having a ball. The beer tent, especially, was rollicking. At one point I watched A2 run through the rain with a bottle of vodka under each arm.

"For the oyster ice luge!" He grinned, darting past me.

My parents and I found a table where we sank into the folding chairs. It was the first time I'd sat down all day.

"Great party, honey," my mom cheered.

"How can you guys possibly be having fun?" I wondered, resting my chin in my hand. My feet felt like lead.

"We're fine," my dad assured me, rubbing my back. "It's been a great event. In spite of the weather."

They were calling it a night, so I walked them toward the front gate to give them a hug and thank them profusely for making the quick but appreciated trip.

I made my way through the crowd (the vibe had turned from family fun to a wild, pulsating dance party) up to the stage, where I found Shore, Skip, and a few of the growers hanging out on the sidelines.

"Have you had a beer yet, E-Rock?" Skip asked, handing me his. "I think it's time." I looked at my watch—nine P.M. I broke down and took a swig.

The band was still raging when Dave and our friend Nicole made their way up to meet me near the stage. The three of us danced around in the mud alongside the rest of the growers until the band wrapped up with its final set, then watched as the security guards led all three thousand guests slowly out of the tents.

Once the tents were empty, Dave and I joined Shore and Skip, who were standing in front of the stage surveying the damage. The floor of the tent resembled a battlefield. Flip-flops poked out of the mud along with umbrellas and ponchos. We spotted jackets, sunglasses, and even a bra amid the chaos.

"Looks like we threw a rager," Shore said, sounding pleased.

"I'm just glad it's over," Skip sighed, sipping a Dark and Stormy from a plastic cup he'd secured from the back of his own pickup truck. I toasted that statement with my own beer and took one final swig.

Shore looked over at me expectantly. "So, E. Think you'll be up for doing this again next year?" he asked.

I leaned against the stage and thought about it for a minute, trying to imagine reliving the experience from beginning to end all over again.

Skip let out a chuckle.

"You'll be back," he said. "You'll see."

The days after Oyster Fest were punctuated by a long, collective sigh. The weather cleared up within hours of the band's last song, making the subsequent cleanup slightly less painful than it might have been. After tallying up all the numbers, Shore announced that we'd raised about

$120,000 for the foundation, enough to get the Zanzibar project off the ground. That fall, Berg, Skip, and Shore would head to Africa while the rest of us would wind down from the zany but successful summer season.

Jasper White's Razor Clam Ceviche

One of the many Oyster Fest dishes that I tried—and loved—was Jasper White's no-fail ceviche:

Ceviche is a Latin-American dish (actually a genre of dishes) where raw seafood is cured in juice from limes, lemons, and/or other citrus, then flavored with onions, chiles, and other foods. It is such wonderful dish for our times . . . bursting with flavor, high in protein, low in fat, and very refreshing. It is as beautiful and dramatic as it is delicious and healthful.

Note: This recipe can be made several hours in advance as long as you don't mix the clams with the other ingredients until two hours before you serve them.

> *12 razor clams (or 16 top neck clams)*
> > *shucked and diced small, combined*
> > *with their natural juices*
> *Juice from 3 large limes*
> *2 jalapeño chiles, stemmed, seeded, and*
> > *finely diced*
> *1 medium ripe tomato, seeded and diced*

> ½ *medium red onion, diced*
> 8 *sprigs cilantro, coarsely chopped*
> *Freshly ground black pepper*
> *Lime wedges and cilantro sprigs for*
>   *garnish*
> *Clam juice as needed*

Prepare all ingredients and combine them in a glass bowl. If it isn't moist enough (liquid should just cover the clams) add a little clam juice. Season to taste with black pepper. Refrigerate for at least two hours before serving.

Before serving, check the seasoning—if you want it spicier add a little hot sauce. If you want it more acidic, add a little more lime. If it is dry add a little more clam juice.

To serve, spoon ceviche into chilled glass bowls and garnish with extra wedges of lime and sprigs of cilantro.

SERVES 4 AS AN APPETIZER

Adapted from Jasper White—*The Summer Shack Cookbook* © 2007

III

Filter Feeder

[The oyster] manages better than most
creatures to combine business with pleasure.

—M. F. K. Fisher

CHAPTER EIGHT

BOOTS

It's no coincidence that fall is every Island Creek grower's favorite season. It became mine, too, once I realized that the waning sun meant shorter days. We were now down to a skeleton crew—Berg, A2, Will, Greg, and me—and started our days around eight A.M. After a few good nights of rest, I realized just how off-kilter I'd been all summer. It was like getting off a roller coaster and standing at a dead halt.

All of the farmers felt it. The madness of the upweller season was behind us. And with fewer this-instant tasks to fill our days, my crew started the more leisurely process of preparing the farm for winter. Our crew was one of the only ones still out on the water—most had been dismantled after the summer rush.

Fall draped itself over Duxbury like a fine cloak: The town's cranberry bogs, one of which sat behind Bennett's General Store, were suddenly blanketed in the autumnal crimson of ripening berries. The coastal tree line had transitioned from lush, summery greens to burnt yellows and amber oranges. For the first time in years I sat up and paid attention to the changes. I became aware that I was watching it unfurl one day at a time instead of in spurts through a window. The beauty and slowness astounded me.

Once the festival was behind me, I made an effort to put in shorter days so I could actually devote some time to our Brighton condo. One afternoon, after a harsh wind scattered us from the float early, I returned home and found piles of unopened mail, a barren fridge, and clothes wrinkled up in a heap near my corner of the bedroom. Thinking back to the summer I realized I'd been using our bedroom like a gym locker, stashing my dirty clothes in piles until there was time to do laundry, then leaving clean clothes in an unfolded stack. Dave had tried pointing out my pathetic habits long ago but gave up once he realized I was never home long enough to do anything about it.

He'd changed since his visit to the farm in August. I suspected that his glimpse of my watery world—the gear, our culling tools, the plex—had given him a sense of what kind of work awaited me every day, and it softened him to my now regular absences. Even in the weeks leading up to the festival, he'd been attentive and understanding. I was all but living in Duxbury for some of them, leaving him at home alone to take care of the house and fill the empty time and space that his wife usually occupied. It wasn't until after the festival ended and the rush of executing a massive event was behind me that I noticed how hard he'd been trying.

I wanted to thank him, starting with fried oysters.

Throughout the summer, Dave would ask me to bring home oysters. Sometimes I did, but most of the time, I forgot. I usually got my fill of them during my days on the float and, frankly, opening them at home felt like a chore. But as I surveyed the scene of our neglected condo, I realized that it wouldn't hurt to fulfill my husband's simple request more frequently. Dave loved eating oysters on the half shell but also adored them fried; he'd order them whenever he found them on a menu. So, one night, I decided to try my hand at frying them at home.

I brought home a bag of jumbo oysters, the large four-inch-long, boulderlike specimens, which were good for frying and usually resulted in a big, meaty bite. Unfortunately, their unwieldy size and ancient barnacle-covered shells made them impossible to open without a wrestling match. Plus, the shells were rough and smelled kind of terrible, like wet mud mixed with ammonia. When Dave found me in the kitchen, wrestling with the shells, he reeled back from the smell.

"Did you kill something in here?" he asked, holding his arm over his nose.

"Sorry. It's the jumbos. It gets better, I promise," I reassured him, hoping my surprise would actually turn out to be the good kind.

I pulled out a kitchen towel and my sharpest shucking knife (I now had a respectable collection of three) while Dave pulled a stool up to our tiny, butcher-block island and watched as I started with the smallest. At the hinge, a thick layer of mud hid the oyster's sweet spot, which, after some digging, I found with my knife. Having shucked all those oysters in Nantucket and throughout the summer on the float, I'd learned that there's one minuscule vulnerability in the hinge of an oyster that, when the right amount of pressure is applied, allows the knife to slide through and pop the shells apart.

But this oyster felt impenetrable, as though all its years surviving on the ocean floor had strengthened it against every possible intrusion. I dug deeper and pried the knife around, sticking the tip as far as I thought it would go before breaking. Finally, I felt something shift under my weight. The groaning budge of a treasure chest door feeling its hinges for the first time in ages. After a little more urging from my knife, the hinge released to reveal a glimpse of meat within.

I separated the top shell from the adductor muscle and found a fistful of creamy, coffee-colored meat, loaded with glucose and protein. I almost felt bad for exposing this old, ornery bugger to the elements. It had likely survived battles with the dredge, perhaps bouts with the bay's green crab contingent. But here it was, open and innocent, bulging from its shell.

Dave looked on, mildly impressed.

"Are you sweating?" he teased.

I set about opening another one, this one more gnarly and mangled. The struggle ensued again as I used my weight to push on the knife. My jaw clamped shut and I realized I was holding my breath until I found the sweet spot and felt the top shell give way. As I twisted the knife to pop the top shell upward, I heard a moan. Was that an air pocket? Or was the oyster screaming for its own life?

I took my time opening the other ten, dancing around on my tiptoes and cursing under my breath. Rex stood beside me, his fuzzy brown nose reaching up toward the counter. Rex actually loved raw oysters; he'd tasted his first straight off our coffee table earlier that spring. I saved one of my sloppier shucking jobs just for him.

By the time I finished shucking all of the oysters, the sink was covered in seaweed and splattered with mud. My kitchen towel was stinky with oyster juice and barnacle remnants, and the trash overflowed with empty shells. The oyster meats swam in their liquor in a bowl. My arms were tired, I realized while reaching up to wipe my brow. Yes, I was actually sweating. I felt like I'd butchered a cow.

Dave took over as my sous chef (he'd watched gleefully as I exerted all this effort just for him) and dredged the oysters in a mixture of flour, bread crumbs, and red pepper flakes before handing them to me to lay in a skillet filled with an inch of oil. They fried up quickly, browning up with a thick, hearty crust in minutes. Once we'd fried all eleven (I'd fed the sloppy one to Rex), we waited just long enough to keep from scorching our tongues before biting into them. Dave closed his eyes and groaned. Inside each little flavor bomb, the oyster flesh was just warmed through, as soft as a mushroom cap, melting away with each bite.

"Why don't we do this more often?" Dave said, popping another into his mouth.

My wrestling match with the shucking knife was already a distant memory. "Not sure," I replied, leaning in to give him a crumb-covered kiss. "But we can do it whenever you want."

. . .

The end of summer (more significantly the removal of the upwellers) signaled Skip's travel season. He no longer needed to worry about whether the upwellers were running or if his seed would grow, which meant he now had time to get away and relax. Shortly after Oyster Fest, he was on a plane to Munich for a weeklong revelry at Oktoberfest.

That left the crew with a few options. We could a) plant the seed for him, which he encouraged us to do, or b) enjoy some much-needed downtime of our own and wait for him to get back. Berg, forever conscious of how the crew managed its time, went with option A.

He took us out on an afternoon tide shortly after Skip left. In sweatshirts and waders, we worked against the backdrop of a Technicolor blue sky. Unfortunately, the crew felt utterly unmotivated for the tide. We'd culled and bagged most of the day with only a quick break for lunch. Our energy level was zapped. But Berg pushed us out there and gave us a deadline: 150 bags planted by sunset. Then we could go home.

Planting was another one of the farm's long-term projects. To plant, we needed to take the seed (now about the size of a potato chip) out of the mesh bags (which were still in the cages) and plant each one individually on the bay floor. Because each seed was about two inches long and thin but sturdy, once we put them on the muddy bottom, they would stay put. There was no need to bury them in the mud, like a vegetable seed (oftentimes, the water shifted mud over them, but it didn't harm them) so all they needed was to be placed on the ground and given enough elbow room to grow, usually with just a few centimeters between

each one. The density of seed on the oyster lease was tight—
it had to be if we were putting a million on each acre. So in
some ways, planting was both an art and a science.

But removing the seeds from the bags was a chore; the
bags were filthy, covered with layers of seaweed, oyster poop,
and that alienlike sponge, and some of the oysters had clustered and stuck together in the corners of the bag. The only
way to thoroughly empty a bag was to get in there with a
gloved hand and gently pull stuck-on oysters from their
hiding spots.

Skip usually planted seed by flinging it off the boat
with a snow shovel. It wasn't scientific or graceful but it got
the job done efficiently and, usually, ended up with a fairly
even density. If the seed landed on top of each other or in
large clumps, he would go out on a low tide a few days later
and rake the seeds to distribute them more evenly. Like
everything else on the farm, the snow-shovel method was
low-tech and hands-on but it did the job.

That year, Skip had us try out a new method in his absence. Instead of shoveling large quantities of seed off the
side of the boat, he had us shake the bags directly onto the
muddy bottom by hand. No snow shovel and no boat meant
many hands could do the work at once. It was tedious but it
also meant we got to have a personal hand in planting.

As we pulled out onto the tide with Berg's deadline in
mind, I watched as a mountain of clouds gathered in the sky
to our west. The peaks and rims jagged up into the blue-
ness, and the sun, just a few inches from setting behind it,
sent brushstrokes of orange and yellow through the sky. The
colors washed the town in a hazy, magical light—working

against that backdrop made me feel farther away from old life than ever before.

A2 broke my reverie with a nudge. We needed to get to work. Slowly, we emptied the bags one by one, plodding backward with short, deliberate steps, scattering the seed out in long even rows.

As the seed cascaded down from the lip of the bag I was careful to keep them from landing on top of each other. Some landed vertically in the mud, while others lay flat. I tried to picture them, one year later, filled out and sturdy, still stuck in these same positions.

Thinking back to the piles of oysters we'd picked all spring and summer, I couldn't fathom how Skip had calculated his densities. The process of shaking seed out like this seemed so willy-nilly, yet the man had a keen sense of just how many oysters sat on each section of the lease. I could sense that this part of the process—planting—was just as important as grading had been. Both were integral parts of the overall growth process.

We shook out seed bags as the sun faded from view, finishing our last bag with a loud, collective *whoop* that echoed out over the now quiet bay. Berg agreed to buy us a round of beers and we got ourselves back to land just as the lights in the harbor parking lot flickered to life. For the first time in months, the lot was deserted aside from our own cars. The bay was officially shut down for the season.

Toward the end of September, I developed a miserable, unshakable head cold. We were back to our routine of culling, washing, and bagging, with the occasional planting tide mixed in. But the cold made it all seem unbearable, as did the float's continuous rocking—the wind had picked up dramatically since the calm days of August. During one of my weekly chats with Christian in the harbor parking lot, I asked him what the deal was with all the wind.

"Eh, it's just September. Now that the water's starting to cool off, any time we have a really warm day, the wind'll blow like heck," he said matter-of-factly. "From now until May, it may not be so bad in the mornings, but afternoons, it gets whipping."

We'd seen the best of our fall weather and were on the dismal descent into winter. It put all of us into a foul mood, A2 especially. One day, as we rattled up Washington Street in the farm truck, I asked my bearish partner what was bothering him.

"I dunno," he sighed before going quiet. "I'm not really into the whole oyster farming thing anymore," he finally offered.

He'd been struggling to figure out what to do with his future. His father worked as a land surveyor up in New Hampshire and suggested A2 move up there to help him start a more substantial business. Not only was it in line with what A2 studied (he'd graduated with a degree in landscape architecture), but it would get him closer to the landscaping job he was searching for. He would probably leave the farm that winter to get started, he confided.

Having logged innumerable hours with the big, kindly teddy bear, I was sad to hear he was moving on. We'd long ago settled into a little brother/big sister routine and I genuinely adored his clever off-the-cuff comebacks and big, goofy grin. It was hard to imagine life without him.

We were coming up on a lot of transition. I'd been considering a move into the office to take on a more administrative role, in fact. My plan, as unstructured as it had started, had morphed into a full-on apprenticeship with the company. And part of that process involved seeing what happened on the wholesale side of the business so that I could understand the sales and marketing process. It was the "to" in farm-to-table that I was ready to see firsthand.

After dropping some empty mesh bags up at their storage spot, we returned to the harbor with fresh coffee in our hands and found Berg pulling up to the boat launch in the Bat.

"Good. You guys are back. We're heading out to Saquish," he announced, and motioned for us to hop on.

Saquish Neck sits at the tail end of the six-mile ribbon that makes up Duxbury Beach on a stretch of land called Gurnet Point, named originally by English settlers. Along with Clark's Island, it was one of the first points of land reached by the Pilgrims and their *Mayflower,* but the settlers eventually moved farther into the bay to land, more permanently, at Plymouth. From the sky, Gurnet Point looks like a backward *L* jutting southwest into the bay, and Saquish Neck, the long stretch of sandy white beach at the bottom of the *L,* faces due south, coming to a curlicue tip called Saquish Point.

Reachable only by four-wheel drive or boat, Saquish is one of the most secluded spots along the overpopulated coast of Massachusetts—truly the end of the world. There are a handful of cottages on the point and a handful more built along Saquish Neck, but generally they're only used in the summertime and have been owned by the same families for generations.

On the interior stretch of Saquish Neck, one knuckle's worth of land called Rocky Point juts out toward Clark's Island and at the very tip sits a cottage owned by Billy Bennett. Propped on nothing more than a swatch of green grass and surrounded by rocky beaches, it is a humble closet of a house with southern-facing windows, a woodstove and tiny kitchen on the first floor, and a low-ceilinged second floor crammed tight with beds and mattresses. Originally built in 1903, it was now a summer cabin for the Bennett family.

It had been in the family since it was originally built except for a brief period when the family was forced to sell the place during a dry spell—it broke their hearts to let the property go. But Billy knew the man who bought it and after several years passed, and Billy's financial tides turned again, he ran into the owner and asked if he was interested in selling. The man shook his head apologetically, stating that he and his family loved the place. They weren't looking to sell.

It went on like that for years, with Billy running into the man or leaving a note on the door every now and then. Still heartbroken for his family's loss, he figured it was always worth a try. Twenty years later, the man finally conceded. He was ready to sell the house and Billy happily took it off his hands. Today, Skip's dad still drives the six-mile bumpy beach road out to Rocky Point every morning year-round to check in on the cabin before starting his day on the oyster farm.

Skip used the jut of land and its small beach for side projects like making clam nets (despite his first failed attempt at growing clams, he continued to try to grow them in Duxbury Bay, forever attempting to improve his methods), so we were dropping off a few nets and other gear that he would pick up there later.

It was my first time seeing the cottage and, despite the appearance of the rickety structure, I immediately had house envy. I imagined warm summer nights spent out there on the remote little parcel of land, having the beach and the seclusion all to myself. After all those years trying to get it back, I knew that both Billy and Skip appreciated their luck for having it now. Berg woke me up from my daydream announcing that we were on our way to the Back River to pull some bags out of the floating nursery. A2 and I groaned. There were still a few rows of seed bags up there, and the longer we left them, the more grueling the task to pull them out of the water.

As we approached the long lines of the nursery, I could see that the bags, now burdened with the overgrown seed, dipped down into the water, leaving their top corners poking out like shark fins. Pulling these bags required kneeling against the side of the boat, leaning over to unhook the bag from the line, and hauling it up onto the boat using nothing but shoulder strength. Now full of two-inch seed, the bags weighed around forty pounds each and were covered in a carpet of neon-green sea moss. It was like pulling up the carcass of a life-size Muppet.

Two bags into the job and I was sweating despite the chill. Having paid little attention to what I was wearing except for waders and a pair of gloves, I'd drenched my sleeves by pulling the bags up too high and letting water drip down my arms. So much for recovering from my cold, I thought.

We got a pile of bags loaded up on the boat and took them back to the float to start the gruesome process of emptying the seed onto one of the boats. Easily a contender for one of America's dirtiest jobs, the task left me covered in scum and seaweed bits, which had even found their way into my ears. On more than one occasion, bits of mud landed in my mouth, reminding me to keep it clamped shut. The mud, after all, was laced with oyster poop.

Skip came out to the float just as we were reaching the last of the pile. Rejuvenated from his Munich trip, he was eager to get back to work planting the seed we'd just emptied.

"So, E-Rock, I hear you're headed to the office this winter," he laid out casually. Berg and A2, who had been chatting mindlessly, now perked up to listen.

"Yeah, Shore and I talked about me starting up there in December or January," I said. Skip gave me an up-and-down glance.

"You might want to shower first," he teased softly. I looked like a swamp thing.

"Part-Time Pain, coming up," Berg tossed out sarcastically. The tension between the office team and the farm crew was palpable. Berg staunchly believed that no matter how much work the office team *said* they had to do, what they were *actually* doing involved cutting out early for a round of golf, socializing, and generally wasting time. Though he never said it out loud, it was obvious that Berg thought the "suits" were lazy and generally good for nothing.

He, on the other hand, being a "boot" and a hardworking hourly wager, rolled up his sleeves, had no problem getting his hands dirty, and toiled tirelessly so that the suits had something to do all day. He wore the chip on his shoulder as proudly as his dirt-caked fingernails. He was a boot, plain and simple, and my leaving the farm crew for a job with the suits made me a traitor.

"Yeah, Pain. Don't go getting a case of the fuckits now that you've got a warm, cozy office in your future," Skip continued, his lip curling up in jest.

I took their commentary in stride, knowing full well that this wouldn't be the end of it. Truthfully, I was looking forward to a change in scenery. The cooler weather had me back to doubling up on socks and extra layers. My stamina for the bitter cold had peaked back in March. So yeah, the thought of spending my days indoors during the dark depths of a New England winter was pretty appealing. But I kept that fact to myself.

My introduction to the wholesale process came early—a few weeks into October. Matthew, the farm's private but disarming sales guy, was headed to Chicago for some sales calls and his timing coincided with an oyster festival put on by the legendary Shaw's Crab House. "Royster with the Oyster" was a bawdy Chicago tradition that drew oyster fanatics from around the country for three days of revelry, culminating at a Friday-night tent party outside the restaurant. Shore, whom I'd been communing with more and more frequently in anticipation of my upcoming office stint, suggested I go with Matthew to experience one of the more entertaining traditions in our country's oyster culture and to check out Shaw's Crab House's legendary Oyster Hall of Fame Dinner.

The Shaw's Oyster Hall of Fame was a collection of oyster-loving personalities who all had a close relationship with the restaurant. Every year, a new inductee was chosen to take his or her place alongside the oyster elite; they were celebrated with an oyster reception and dinner on the first night of the restaurant's festival. Island Creek had been inducted; as had Vermont author Rowan Jacobsen, who penned *A Geography of Oysters;* and the team behind the West Coast's famed Hog Island Oyster Company. The dinner would be my opportunity to meet and greet some of the most notable characters in the oyster world.

Matthew and I arrived in Chicago on the morning of the dinner and made Shaw's our first stop. Tucked away on a shadowy, overpass-hidden street corner, Shaw's is one of those classic, stylized spaces punctuated by murals and chintzy crustacean décor. The oyster bar is a small, tiled annex with wooden tables and stools surrounding a massive central raw bar. Helmed by a crush of shuckers and bartenders, the raw bar is a lively, entertaining centerpiece where aficionados can take a front-row seat to the shucking show. When we arrived, we found it filled with a boisterous lunchtime crowd but managed to snag a table near the open kitchen.

Matthew pointed out a private dining room toward the back of the oyster bar, saying it housed the actual hall of fame, a showcase of photographs of all the inductees. I got up to poke my head in, finding it eerily dark and somber. Each photo represented some immortal element of the oyster world: growers, restaurant owners, and authors. Renowned food writer M. F. K. Fisher was placed on one wall, the hall's second inductee, with the simple words "Author, *Consider the Oyster*" printed on a plaque beneath her photo. It was her book that first ignited my literary curiosity for oysters with its attention-grabbing opener: "An oyster leads a dreadful but exciting life." Standing beneath her gaze gave me goose bumps.

Back in the noisy fray, Matthew and I fell in line with the lunchtime crowd and ordered a plate of oysters. Their oyster list was full of familiar names: Beavertails, Hog Islands, Cape Bretons, Dabob Bays, and of course, Island Creeks. We drank the locally brewed Goose Island beer and tucked in to the restaurant's legendary crab cake, a lumpy, golden brown disc packed with fresh crab meat and the faintest hint of breading.

Later that night, we returned to the more formal side of Shaw's for the annual hall of fame dinner celebrating that year's inductee, Rodney Clark, owner of Rodney's Oyster House in Toronto. Called Mister Oyster in his home country, the restaurateur is a colorful oyster educator with a wardrobe to match. Many of those attending had personal ties to Rodney or the Shaw's team; there were seafood buyers, seafood lovers, a handful of Shaw's regulars, and former hall of fame winners.

Walking into the room felt like raising the curtain on some noble order. Uncertain of who was who, I recognized a few faces from the oyster wall, including author and biographer Joan Reardon, who held court at one of the banquettes. The rest of the crowd, tweedy but jovial as they sipped at flutes of Champagne, mingled together like old college buddies. There was a sense of occasion as white-gloved servers glided about with tiered silver platters. Even the oysters glittered for the occasion like jewels against crystal beds of ice.

Rodney's twenty-five-year-old son, Eamon Clark, stood behind the oyster table, black curls framing his cherubic face, as he shucked steadily for approaching guests. Father and son both held Canadian Oyster Shucking Champion titles and had been to Galway, Ireland, for the oyster shucking world championships (I'd only recently learned there was such a thing). Rodney chose his three favorite oysters for the reception: Rod's Queens and Sand Dunes from Prince Edward Island; and ShanDaphs from Nova Scotia. The ShanDaphs, grown by a small producer named Philip Docker to the extreme north of Nova Scotia, stood out for their cold, plump meat and perfectly teardropped shells.

I'd tasted oysters from around the country at raw bars in Boston but this brought oyster tasting to a new level for me. These oysters all had a history, now. And while I didn't know each of the growers personally, I knew what went into pulling these specimens out of the water. I savored each oyster carefully, making sure to offer a silent "thank you" to the men and women who'd toiled to bring them to the table.

We eventually sat down to dinner, where we were entertained with toasts and speeches, Rodney's own being the most poetic. He had a short list of thank-yous, including one to his son, "for his stroke of the knife to the calcium."

After his speech others got up to read letters sent from former hall of famers and Rodney supporters, offering a further glimpse into the oysterman's notoriety. Eventually, Rodney came around to our table for an introduction. A woman sitting at a table nearby asked Rodney to share his most memorable shucking experience. He thought about it for a moment before recalling a story about a female customer who came in and asked for one single oyster.

"She asked if she could handle it before I shucked it, so I passed it to her. She was feeling the texture, asking me questions about the shell growth, and feeling the coldness. I shucked it for her and she felt the meat inside the shell when I handed it to her. And then she ate it and she slurped it back, sucking all of the juices out of the shell," he explained, his eyes gleaming as he spoke. "It turned out she was totally blind and I didn't realize it. It was the *best, best, best* interpretation of what an oyster should be because she didn't miss anything."

After we finished the meal and made it back to the hotel, I thought about Rodney's story and about how I'd been eating oysters my whole life. My first taste—which I still remember vividly—happened when I was living in Spartanburg, South Carolina. I was only about ten years old, and my uncle Jim, a close family friend who had earned his uncle status, served me an oyster on top of a saltine cracker that was covered in a dollop of cocktail sauce. That first taste had me hooked, and as I got older, I kept eating more, eventually building up the nerve to try one with just a squeeze of lemon or a dab of mignonette. I'd probably sucked down thousands in my lifetime—only a fraction of the number that Island Creek grew every year. But I could relate to the blind woman and her need to feel, smell, and truly taste an oyster every time I ate one. I had that experience every time I lifted a shell to my lips these days.

I felt honored to be included in that night's ritual. So many of those we'd dined with, like Rodney and Joan Reardon, spent their lifetimes cultivating their own oyster experiences, diving into the culture with a commitment to the product and the art. More than anything, I was pleased to know that there were hundreds of people, like me, who shared a common love for these tiny and fascinating creatures.

We returned to the Shaw's Oyster Bar for more Royster festivities on Friday. It was a grim and chilly Chicago day, so a horde of festivalgoers were crammed into the tiny bar, trying to warm up. Matthew and I arrived in time to catch part of the annual slurp-off competition, which had contestants lined up around the bar with a dozen oysters in front of them, which they had to eat straight from the shells without using their hands. The crowd cheered madly for the contestants, who egged everyone on before leaning facedown into their plate to suck and chew one dozen meats in seconds flat.

Afterward, we made our way to the tented party, which was held just outside the entrance of the restaurant, half covered by the overpass. The otherwise dingy, forgotten alley wound up being a wild but fitting setting for a raucous bivalve bash (it wasn't Duxbury Beach but it did give our Fest a run for its money). We staked out spaces near the stage to watch the final round of the slurping contest. The event announcer, a local radio DJ, commended the great Chicago tradition, explaining that in order to take home the championship the winner was required to have "the dexterity of a tongue master and the suction of a man who can suck a tennis ball through a rubber hose."

And suck they did, each of the contestants vacuuming up their oysters with alarming precision. The winner, a Chicagoan named Jon Ashby who just happened to be wearing an Island Creek T-shirt, hardly paused as he pecked up each juicy piece like a goose nibbling insects off the ground. It was a tight race but his hands were in the air seconds before the reigning champion, leaving the crowd chanting his name as he high-fived his competitors.

The night swirled on with the same rowdy exuberance. Lisa, the office manager, had joined us, having flown out that day to visit her Chicago-based sister, so we stood in a shivering circle, downing platefuls of oysters and frosty beers before deeming it too damn cold to be standing outside. We flagged down a few cabs and made our way to the Publican, a popular new warehouse-district spot featuring oysters and a heavenly selection of cured meats. Matthew and I had been in earlier that day on our round of sales calls and met the owner, Paul Kahan, a famed Chicago restaurateur who also owns Avec and Blackbird, as well as his flank of chefs. We'd spent almost an hour talking to the chefs about seafood, the oyster business, and a bit about how the Publican's menu came about. I salivated over the offerings: charcuterie plates, bone marrow, a half-dozen different types of oysters, and an impressive selection of hard-to-find beers (I stole a copy of the menu for Dave). Paul, it turned out, was also a huge fan of oysters. He was at the Publican that night and came over to have a beer with our crew. His love of oysters was one of the main reasons he opened this spot, he told us.

"Every night I stop by my other restaurants and stay through service but I always end up here to shuck some oysters and drink a cold beer," he said.

Our crowd eventually broke up, but Matthew and I stayed and sat down for dinner. We inhaled plates of aged ham, baked tripe, and smoked trout hash browns, eating as though we hadn't eaten all day (even though we had). We swooned over the sweetbreads, massive and drizzled with truffled vinaigrette, and sopped up the fat of our roasted marrow bones with thick slabs of sourdough. We didn't roll out of the dining room until well past midnight, with Matthew proclaiming it to be one of the best meals he'd ever eaten.

I returned to the farm with a new set of eyes and a bulging belly. Having experienced the glorified traditions of the hall of fame as well as the Falstaffian debauchery of the Royster, I was starting to understand the oyster's appeal as an everyman food, one that could transcend class, gender, status, and table all in one morsel of a bite.

What I had yet to experience was the oyster as a culinary

work of art, something that elevated both a dish and a chef. But, as I found out the day I returned from Chicago, I was about to get my opportunity. Skip, Shore, and I were heading down to New York to have dinner at Per Se.

Crispy Oysters with Fried Brussels Sprouts and Russian Dressing

Dinner at the Publican was one of the most memorable meals I had while I worked at Island Creek. This recipe, generously provided by the restaurant's Chef de Cuisine Brian Huston, Sous Chef Erling Wu-Bower, and Executive Chef Paul Kahan, shows just a hint of what you'd find on their palate-whopping menu.

Russian Dressing

> ¼ *cup ketchup*
> *1 cup aioli (or 1 cup mayonnaise mixed*
> *with 1 tablespoon minced garlic)*
> *1 tablespoon prepared horseradish*
> *The Publican's "secret ingredient": 1 tbsp.*
> *pickling juice from jarred pickles or*
> *olives—optional*

Whisk together the ketchup, aioli, horseradish, and pickling juice (if using). Set aside.

Fried Oysters

2 quarts canola or rice bran oil for frying
1 pound shucked oysters in their liquor
1 cup buttermilk
1 cup sea salt & vinegar potato chips,
     ground (3 cups whole chips crushed in
     a food processor should yield 1 cup
     ground)
1 cup Gold Medal Wondra flour
1/2 teaspoon cayenne pepper
1 pound brussels sprouts, washed and
     quartered with stem end intact
Juice of 1 lemon
3 tablespoons olive oil
Salt and pepper to taste
1/4 red onion, sliced
4 ounces spicy greens such as arugula or
     mustard greens
4 ounces Parmesan, shaved with a
     vegetable peeler
In a bowl, combine greens, onion, and
     Parmesan, set aside
In a smaller bowl, combine lemon juice,
     olive oil, salt and pepper, set aside

In a medium saucepan, heat oil to 350°. Strain the
oysters from their liquor; soak in buttermilk for 5 minutes (or up to 2 hours). Combine the ground potato
chips, Wondra flour, and cayenne in a shallow dish.

With mesh strainer, drain oysters from buttermilk, then dredge oysters in potato chip mixture and drop into the heated oil one at a time, working in batches (careful not to overcrowd the pan). Fry until golden brown, about 3 minutes. Drain on paper towels.

Using the same oil used for the oysters, fry the brussels sprouts in batches until golden brown, about 3 minutes. Drain on paper towels. (Note: You can fry oysters and Brussels sprouts together if using a larger pan.) Divide Russian dressing among four serving plates, spreading it on the bottom of each plate.

To make the salad, whisk together the lemon juice, olive oil, salt, and pepper. Toss the onion, greens, and Parmesan together, then mix with the lemon/olive oil mixture. To assemble, place the oysters and brussels sprouts on top of the Russian dressing, then place small tufts of the mixed greens atop the oyster-brussels sprouts mixture. Serve and enjoy.

SERVES 4

CHAPTER NINE

KITCHEN BITCH

I learned at an early age that good things in life usually come if you ask nicely. Great toys, the right job, engagement rings. No matter how hard you wish or hope or dream (which I do a lot anyway), you won't get what you want without a specific and targeted request. So while I wish this story started with "Thomas Keller invited us down to Per Se . . . ," instead, it starts with me asking for it.

Long before I arrived at Island Creek, I was obsessed with the idea of visiting Per Se. I'd heard of legendary meals enjoyed at Keller's Napa Valley restaurant, the French Laundry, and read every story in print about the superchef's historical rise, his precise, superlative skills at the stove, and his ability to turn purveyors into culinary icons simply by selecting their ingredient for his menu. He is a rock star, and like any dedicated groupie, all I wanted in the world was the opportunity to eat his food.

Once I joined Island Creek, it wasn't hard for me to fi-
nagle an opportunity, especially once I discovered just how
closely the farm was connected to his New York restaurant,
Per Se. It turned out all I had to *do* was ask.

Both Skip and Shore were equally fascinated by Keller,
or TK, as they called him. (His birthday, October 14, lives
on the ICO group calendar.) Although Keller wasn't the
one who directly discovered and sourced Island Creeks, as
creator of the dish that showcased them he was partly responsible for elevating this tiny little oyster farm's product
from a damn good New England oyster to a nationally renowned brand. Keller serves his signature dish, Oysters
and Pearls, at both the French Laundry and Per Se every
single night of service (despite the chef's legendarily adjusted nightly menu) and almost always does so using Island Creek Oysters. For this, Skip is tremendously grateful.

Early in my tenure, I casually asked Shore if he and
Skip were planning on visiting Per Se anytime soon, and if
so, could I tag along?

"Yes, absolutely," he replied without hesitating. They
were always anxious for opportunities to drop in on TK.
"Skip and I went down for dinner last fall. The meal was
absolutely epic."

Emboldened by his response, I took it one step further:
"I'm dying to eat there. But what I really want to do is get
into the kitchen to see how they make Oysters and Pearls."

Shore, a budding foodie and cook, perked up at the
thought. "Soooo, you want to spend a day in the kitchen?"

"I think it'll really help me see the full spectrum," I

continued, gaining confidence with his interest. "I'd like to see the final step, the 'table' part of how oysters get from farm to table."

"I like it," he replied enthusiastically. "Let's talk about it in the fall."

I waited out the rest of the summer patiently; once Oyster Fest was behind us, I brought it up again. Shore suggested we try for November. Then, the day I returned from Chicago, I learned that he'd gotten us a mid-November reservation at Per Se. More important, Jonathan Benno, Per Se's chef de cuisine, had agreed to let me do a daylong stage—a kitchen internship—on the canapé station, where I would watch one of the chefs put together Oysters and Pearls. I was elated and terrified. The closest I'd come to working in a professional kitchen was during my brief time at culinary school. But this wasn't any ordinary kitchen. It was Per Se! A temple to gastronomic perfection! A temple to cuisine! I would be entering, and working in, Thomas Keller's laboratory.

Meanwhile, my crew reminded me, I had oyster feces to attend to. Our day-to-day culling and bagging work had slowed back down to our pre-summer pace but there were more hands on the team, making us needy for extra chores. Berg decided we better get a jump on cleaning our equipment before winter set in. That included all of those gunked-up black mesh bags from the nursery.

Despite our best efforts to scrub the bags on every tide, they came out of the water overgrown with slick, sludgy sponge. We stashed the filthy lot in a pile behind the shop, where they sat, festering in the sun or freezing up with icicles, until we had time to power wash them. Finally, the day had come.

A2 and I pulled out Billy Bennett's squat, ancient power washer, a primitive-looking gas guzzler that belched and reeked of gasoline as it spewed water from its needle-nosed gun nozzle. I let A2 handle the machine while I took on the tedious task of moving each of the three-foot-tall bags in and out of the target area, five at a time. We used cages as a makeshift rack, leaning the bags up against them so that they stood side by side where A2 would spray the sponge off the front and back. I flipped the bags and then replaced them with dirty ones once they were clean.

Bag flipping quickly made it to the top of my most-hated farm job list (pulling nearly full silos ranked up there, too). Between the washer's fumes, the dust it kicked up, the errant spritzes that showered me in mud and grime, and the monotony of the work, I truly believed there was no other task in the world I would loathe as much as this.

I only made it worse by trying to calculate the number of bags we needed to clean. Would it be five hundred? A thousand? I timed how long it took for me to get through five bags. Eight minutes. Eight whole minutes times five, times . . . yes, this would take an eternity. Eventually, loopy from the gasoline and the math, I asked A2 if we could switch jobs. He handed me the gun reluctantly. Washing was just as repetitive as my job but at least he got to hold a big, vibrating gunlike toy.

He instructed me to hold the nose of the gun steady, which I did, before squeezing the trigger. The force of the water shot me backward a few steps, sending the spray up into the sky. A2 ducked for cover as water pelted him from above.

"Easy, Pain," he snickered. I tried again, this time widening my stance and keeping a tight grip on the long end of the sprayer. I held the trigger down and aimed. The buzz of the machine shimmied down my arms and legs as the water slammed into my mesh bag target, pulverizing the dried-on seaweed. My spray was remarkably precise despite all those bone-rattling vibrations. I tackled the row, feeling a deep sense of satisfaction as the caked-on mud and sea gunk melted away to reveal black plastic mesh that shimmered like new. A2 lined up another dirty row for me and I got to work again. I felt a renewed sense of purpose, like I could finish the bags in a day. I looked over at the pile. Did I say a thousand? Bah. Bring it on.

I kept at it, row after row, trying to keep track of how many we were moving through. I lost count after fifty bags. Finally, A2 motioned for me to stop. I couldn't hear anything over the buzz of the machine so I hadn't noticed Berg standing to my side, watching us work. He was laughing at me.

"Having fun?" he said, motioning for me to wipe something off my head. I lifted my hand up and felt clumps of mud adhered to my forehead and scalp. I'd forgotten to throw on a hat.

"Let's wrap it up for the day," he said as he shut down the power washer. The silence was deafening as the roar of the machine died down. I walked over to Berg with a look of smug satisfaction.

"Don't worry. The pile will still be here when you get

back," Berg reassured me. I was leaving for New York that night.

Skip, Shore, and I rode the train down together, all antsy to arrive in the big city. Skip admitted that he was something of a country mouse when it came to New York. "It makes me feel so small," he said with a bit of wonder.

We arrived late and immediately found a spot to eat dinner. This type of trip deserved a celebratory meal and Skip wanted to check out Craft, one of Tom Colicchio's restaurants. Host of TV's *Top Chef,* the prolific restaurateur was also a big Island Creek customer—our oysters were served at several Craft restaurants around the country.

We managed to secure one of the last tables inside the vast brick-and-copper dining room, and dove headfirst into the menu. We started with cocktails and oysters before moving on to a family-style feast of scallops, gnocchi, roasted duck, and a half-dozen side dishes served in tiny copper pots and cast-iron skillets. A bottle of big, saucy red wine and we were fully enamored with our New York experience so far.

Meanwhile, the guys unraveled the details of their previous meal at Per Se to me. It had totaled more than twenty courses and drawn out for almost five hours. Be prepared, they warned.

"I wouldn't eat much before tomorrow," Shore advised. Too late, I decided, and finished off the last bite of the duck dish. But the next morning I woke in a panic. Having spent the last few days struggling through farmwork, I hadn't actually prepared for the kitchen part of my visit—my stage. A stage was a chance for a young cook to trail more experienced chefs and was meant to educate the student as well as introduce the chef to new talent. I, of course, was not going there to secure a job at Per Se, but I did want to do well (i.e., not screw up). I'd meant to study a few of Keller's books, do some research on the kitchen hierarchy, maybe even reread *Service Included,* penned by a former Per Se server, which gives a tell-all account of Per Se's first few years in business. But I'd run out of time—and energy— and now felt completely unprepared for the day ahead of me. The reporter in me fumed.

What I did have were marching orders. I'd spoken to Chef Benno very briefly a few days before the trip. He'd told me what to wear (black pants, kitchen-quality black shoes, black socks, white shirt) and to bring a small set of knives, and if I liked, a camera and notebook. He was kind but stern on the phone, offering just a glimpse of his dry sense of humor with a joke about Skip bringing a Red Sox player to dinner. (Benno was a die-hard New York Yankees fan, a bitter Red Sox rival, and his team had just won the World Series. Again.) He informed me that I would work from noon until about 6:30 P.M., giving me a chance to fol- low the chef de partie on the canapé station before sitting in on a premeal meeting and then observing the first hour of dinner service. Our dinner reservation was set for eight P.M.

That morning, the guys came with me to the Time Warner Center, where we fueled up on grilled cheese sand- wiches at Keller's casual boulangerie, Bouchon Bakery. I tried very hard to remain calm while the guys peppered me with advice for the day.

"Don't cut yourself," Shore warned, only partly joking. "Seriously, though, you'll be great. I bet they'll try to impress you."

"Impress me? But I have no idea what I'm doing," I replied.

"But they know you're with us," Skip said with a cool-kid swagger. "They love Island Creek."

Earlier that summer, one of the cooks from Per Se had come to the farm for a two-day externship. He was a young kid from New Jersey who, as a new cook, had won a scholarship through the restaurant—it provided him access to a series of site visits to the restaurant's most notable purveyors. He spent both days on the float learning the cull with my crew, who naturally grilled him about what happens in the kitchen at Per Se. He was the first to describe Oysters and Pearls to me, going into detail about how the cooks who prepared the dish cut out the oyster bellies and used the trimmings for an oyster pudding. I remembered my crew being impressed to have such an important figure on our team for a few days. Maybe Shore was right.

The guys wished me luck, saying they'd see me at the pre-meal meeting, and waved me off. I rode the escalator up toward Per Se wondering what awaited me at the top. As I approached the door to the restaurant, I remembered Benno's instructions: Do not go through the main entrance. Go to the receiving door to the right of the main entrance to get into the kitchen. As I got closer, all I could see were the restaurant's signature sky-blue double doors, the main entrance, set with ornate brass doorknobs. What was it about those doors, I wondered? My eyes were so fixated on them that I never noticed a receiving entrance and instead walked directly toward the restaurant. To the side of the blue doors, a smoky gray glass door opened silently, revealing the restaurant's host stand and three people standing just beside it.

Oh shit! I've gone in the wrong entrance! But I couldn't stop myself. I was being gravitationally pulled toward the three faces standing in front of me. Two women and a man, all dressed in suits, stood smiling, holding trays of champagne flutes. They looked at me, and my kitchen clogs and ponytail, oddly.

"Welcome to Per Se," the man offered warmly.

"Um, I think I'm in the wrong place," I stammered. "I'm here to do a kitchen stage? I'm looking for receiving?"

One of the women subtly motioned for me to follow her and guided me around a darkened corner to a hidden door. "Right through there," she offered.

"Thank you, so sorry," I mumbled, mortified at my horrible timing. They were hosting a private luncheon and, clearly, I wasn't on the guest list.

I opened the door to a long, brightly lit hallway and a short, trim gentleman in a suit.

"Are you Erin? Perfect timing." He smiled before whisking me down the hall.

This was Gerald San Jose, the restaurant's culinary liaison, whom Benno had mentioned during our chat. "I'll get you set up and give you a tour," he offered.

We landed in a tiny office where he held a white chef's jacket out to me. I shimmied out of my own coat, uncertain of what to do with my things. He pointed to a spot where I could hang everything and waited while I got changed. Still discombobulated from my entrance, I dug through my bag wondering what I should bring. I pulled out my camera but—*double shit!*—my battery was dead. I tossed it back into the bag and grabbed for a notebook and pen. Gerald was starting to look impatient. I told him I was set and realized ten steps out of the office that I'd completely forgotten to grab my knife kit. But it was too late. We were on the move.

He walked me past the bakery and then the chocolate truffle room, where he opened the door for just a moment to let me catch a whiff of its sugary aroma. We stopped by dry storage, which was lined floor to ceiling with beautifully colored bottles. The pantry appeared to be about as large as my bedroom. Moving again, he guided me down a narrow hallway and stopped in front of one of the kitchen's eighteen reach-in refrigerators to point out how efficiently the kitchen was put together. Our final stop, after a peek inside the secondary kitchen, which was used mostly for private dining, was at the entrance of the main kitchen.

As we approached the entryway, I could feel my heart beating through my chest. This was it: Keller's Kitchen. The space was massive and my eyes were immediately drawn to the stunning centerpiece: a flat-surfaced cooking range that was covered with various pots, including a large vat of something fragrant and bubbling. Every tiled and stainless steel surface was spotless—a shock after so many days working among the messy, muddy enclave of the Oyster Plex. Gerald introduced me to a smiling, dark-haired, intricately tattooed man: Chef David Breeden. David was the sous chef in charge of the kitchen that day; he sang out a drawled hello and gave me a warm smile. I looked up to see a TV above one of the entrances: the famed interactive flat screen that linked this kitchen to the one at the French Laundry in Yountville, California. The screen was dark.

David beckoned for me to follow close behind him. He chuckled deeply, letting off a mischievous grin. I caught a smidge of a Southern accent; I later found out that he, like Dave, is from Tennessee. He walked me over to the stove to introduce me to Kenny, the canapé chef de partie.

"Kenny does O and P, Oysters and Pearls," David explained. Kenny was a gentle, round-faced guy with a constantly raised brow, as though he were staring in wonder at everything he saw. As a chef de partie, he sat a few rungs below Chef Benno in the hierarchy, but the canapé station had the immense pressure of creating a handful of daily specials, most of which would be offered to VIP guests. (Chef Thomas Keller seemed to have a soft spot for VIPs, giving them a taste of whatever rare, special ingredient the kitchen had access to that day.)

Kenny moved briskly at all times but with focused purpose. He familiarized me with his station quickly and explained that he was making the base for our dish, O & P. My training was under way.

I knew that the dish started with an oyster-infused tapioca sabayon, an egg-based pudding, which was topped with poached oyster bellies and a spoonful of caviar. What I didn't know was how much work went into those seemingly simple components—work that essentially reflected all of the effort we put in to growing the oysters on the farm. On the stove, he had a pot of cream and milk simmering away. From a small cooler that sat beneath his station, he pulled out a clear deli container that was full of oyster bits.

"The trimmings—the part we cut away from the oyster belly," he explained before dropping them into the milk mixture. I pulled out my notebook discreetly, hoping I wouldn't immediately need to use my hands.

"Now comes the tricky part," he said. He spoke quietly, directing his thoughts toward me, but really it was like he was speaking to himself, following an inner monologue that seemed to flow through his head as it spilled out of his mouth. He was ready to make the sabayon but needed to get his plates ready first. We headed into a small dish-washing room where he'd found extra counter space to stack several trays with a special type of dishware. I ran my fingers over the flat, wide rim of one tiny dish. It had a perfectly round bowl, about the size of a halved orange.

"Designed *specifically* for O and P," Kenny whispered, awed by his own statement. We were back in the kitchen at another counter space where Gerald joined us to stand and observe. Gerald explained that Keller had the saucers designed by Raynaud, a French porcelain tableware designer. They were touched with a gentle, white-on-white checked pattern that was meant to mimic the hound's-tooth of the classic chef's pant. These saucers were presented on the table atop similarly designed plates, creating concentric circles; the number of tiers was dictated by the status of the guest. Everyday diners received one or two plates; VVIPs, or the big dogs, received four plates.

It was time to start the sabayon, Kenny announced, guiding me back toward his station by the stove. He pulled out his *mise en place*: fourteen egg yolks, a deli container of oyster liquor. He poured both into a bowl resting in a bain-marie (a pan filled halfway with hot water), which sat toward the edge of the heated flat top, and started whisking methodically.

"It's a classic sabayon recipe. See, that's where it starts, that light, airy liquid. Now watch how it changes." He pointed to the mixture. We both leaned over the bowl as he whisked faster, moving the setup on and off the heat, pulling air into the mixture with each turn. He stopped momentarily to point out a colander full of tapioca pearls—a plant-derived starch—that had been soaking in milk overnight and were now sitting under a stream of water in a nearby sink. Leaving the whisk idle for a moment, he pulled the milk-and-trimming mixture off the heat and strained it through a sieve. To the liquid, he added the drained tapioca pearls and placed it back on the heat.

"Just needs twenty minutes. This is the tricky part where I need to be doing two things at once," Kenny said, pointing at the pot. He had, without my noticing, started whisking the yolks again.

"Here," he instructed, handing me a wooden spoon. "Stir it quick, on the heat."

I held the handle awkwardly, uncertain of what to do until my cook's instincts kicked in. I switched hands, pulling the pot gently off the heat, and started stirring consistently in a figure-eight pattern.

"Good, good. Now really push it on that heat," he told

me. I slid the pot back over the heat, focusing only on my spoon and the consistency of the tapioca. Feeling it thicken quickly, I pulled it back slightly, nervous that it would scald. Kenny's arm whirred like a machine now.

"The trick is to get this done all at the same time. When it works, it's magic!" he exclaimed, delighted at the thought.

"There are so many variables, though. Sometimes I get the tapioca and it's too big, I don't know why! It's from Thailand, it comes in a box, but some boxes are different, inconsistent," he said, his eyes widening with every statement.

"It's farming," I said, jumping in at a quiet pause. He glanced up at me as though I just now existed.

"You're right—it's farming! It always changes." He laughed. He whisked and whisked and I stirred and stirred, all the while watching each other's bowls. Suddenly, with a flourish, he slid his bowl off the heat.

"We're ready," he exclaimed. His yolks were perfectly stiff and consistent and my tapioca had thickened just so. He put a dollop of the yolks into the tapioca mixture to temper the two, then spooned the rest of the fluffy yolks into the denser tapioca, gently folding the two elements into a lightened, puddinglike consistency.

"One hundred cracks of black pepper please, chef," Kenny announced, handing me a pepper grinder. Counting to one hundred—that I could do. I held the pepper mill over the mixture and cracked diligently as he continued to fold.

With everything fully incorporated, he brought our bowl of tapioca sabayon along with a deli container full of freshly whipped cream over to the station that held our stacks of Raynaud dishes.

"The perfect spoon," he declared, holding up a large soup spoon. He organized the trays so that they were stacked to one side and laid a towel flat on the counter in front of him. Every motion and action was measured and precise, as if he knew exactly how much time the setup and execution would take. He pulled the first dish off the tray, set it on the towel, and dipped his spoon into the pudding, pulling up two rounded tablespoons of the mixture, which he dropped with a flick into the rounded saucer. He picked up the dish with both hands and tapped it squarely against the towel. Three taps. The pudding flattened out and settled.

"Removes any air bubbles and sets it just so," Kenny said before placing the dish on a fresh tray. There were ninety guests on the reservation books that night, which meant ninety Oysters and Pearls would be served. He had eighty-nine more to go.

"The dish changes every day. Some days it might only yield eighty-six portions, or today, eighty-nine," he said, leaning over the dishes with a concentrated stare. Doing this one dish, every single day, I realized, had made Kenny a master. "So many things can change it. The tapioca won't set, the sabayon takes too long. The pudding needs to be just right so the oysters, sauce, and caviar rest right on top. It's a lot of variables," he chattered on. He stopped momentarily to lean toward me with a conspiratorial whisper.

"Chef Thomas has been doing the same dish for fifteen years at both restaurants. It's the one dish he puts his signature on every single day. It has to be perfect," he said, sounding mystified. I nodded out of respect. Chef Thomas may not have been in the room but I felt his presence was everywhere.

Chef David appeared behind us, presumably to check on Kenny's progress. "Fly like the wind, Kenny!" he teased in a booming voice.

"Yes, *chef*!" Kenny called out. Every command from Chef David was answered this way.

Chef David walked me over to the butchery station and introduced me to Santiago, the seafood butcher. A towering man from the Dominican Republic, he'd been on the job since Per Se opened in 2004. He was stationed at the back of the private-dining kitchen in between a sink and a refrigerated reach-in, which he opened to reveal his projects for the day: glistening clear-eyed whole fish, bins of oysters, fish tubs full of squid, urchin, and mussels. A pile of oysters was laid out in front of him along with deli containers to capture the bellies and the liquor. I looked closely and smiled. Those were most definitely our oysters. I recognized the teardrop shape and even the coloring of the shells, a faint greenish hue. I'd probably helped cull or wash that very bag, in fact, and realized that they'd likely come out of the water just two days before. I examined them again: They looked good.

Santiago was disappointed. He'd just broken his shucking knife of seven years, a travesty to someone who shucks 1,200 oysters a week (his calculation).

"It curved a little," he explained, "and it never, *ever* punctured the oyster belly."

He held a new knife, one he didn't seem all that excited

about, and pointed to a container full of oysters he'd already shucked. Each belly needed to be pristine, he told me. No cuts, no tears. The ones I saw looked perfect. I hoped he didn't need me to help shuck. (Stirring pudding was one thing but the idea of ruining even one of his perfect specimens was too daunting to face.)

I watched him speed-shuck the oysters with incredible precision. He held the oyster down on a toweled surface and just barely slipped the knife into the hinge before sliding it around the top shell with one quick flick. He pulled the top off carefully, then scooped the flesh from underneath. Next he picked up a tiny pair of red-handled scissors and laid a raw, intact oyster belly flat on his palm. With the scissor's needle-thin shears, he trimmed away the gills and lip of the muscle, which gave way easily, leaving just an almond-sized belly. The trimmings went into one container, the belly into another. He demonstrated on one more carefully so I could see where to make the snips, then handed me the scissors and a pair of rubber gloves.

"You trim. I'll shuck," he said, grinning. Relieved, I slipped on the gloves and picked up an oyster. The scissor eyes were just small enough to keep my fingers from going all the way through. How had he fit his big fingers through these?

Careful not to go too far into the meat, I snipped once, then twice, trying to cut the fringe off with just two moves. But the meat came out shaped like a triangle, not the beautiful rounded almond Santiago had crafted. I snipped again and showed him the results. He examined it, prodding the belly with a finger.

"It's okay." He nodded, unsmiling. "A little less, okay?"

I bit my lip. Okay, a little less. I picked up another piece of meat and cut this more gingerly, trimming a little here, then a little there before showing it off. Santiago gave a short nod. "Okay. Now count them. We need two hundred, total."

I did a few more, each with a painful slowness, trying to get the shape just right without puncturing the belly or cutting them down too small. These were the bellies that would be showcased on top of Oysters and Pearls. I thought of Kenny's mantra: "It has to be perfect every day."

Santiago watched me out of the corner of his eye but talked casually, trying to put me at ease. He told me about living in the Dominican and how they would eat oysters when he was a kid. The Caribbean kind, he said, big ones. He talked about cutting fish every day for nine years and pointed to a set of knives set to one side. The boning knife looked like it had been whittled down over many years, making it little more than a thin, sharp nub of a blade.

I asked him what he thought of our oysters, whether they were okay for him.

"These are almost *per*-fect, every time. Sometimes we get a bad one, or a couple, but not often," he said. "But, they're getting smaller, no? I like when they're a little bigger, like this. More meat to work with, more belly," he said, picking up one of the fatter oysters in his pile. A mental note for my crew: go bigger on the Per Se's.

He finished his pile and turned to check my progress. I was at thirty-two bellies. He sighed and walked off in search of another pair of scissors. I was crushed—not the impression I wanted to make. I tried to speed up as he trimmed bellies next to me but I was no match. He cut four in the time it took me to do one.

We counted off each as we finished (he continued to outpace me three to one, even after I scaled back my trims to two per oyster) and when we finally reached two hundred, he put his scissors down and gave me a gratuitous smile as if to say "you're done."

"Okay! All set," he said. I handed him my scissors and went back toward the main kitchen, where I found Kenny at the stove. He'd finished plating and showed me where the dishes were chilling in a refrigerator under his station. He was busy concocting another canapé, one he wouldn't divulge. Chef David saw me standing idle and quickly swooped by to place me at another station, next to a chef named Greg.

"Do you have work for our stage?" he inquired.

"Yes, chef!" Greg responded. He pulled out a cutting board and placed a large can of black olives in front of me along with a metal tube and a small paring knife.

"Pit the olives, then slice them like this." He demonstrated.

I got to work on the project, wondering what the olives were for and whether my slices should be as precise as his. He watched as I lined up several and cut them into slivers the same size as his. He gave me a short nod of approval. Beside me, he was lining up and trimming hundreds of minuscule baby leeks and bundling them into groups of five. To my other side, a young kid named Ethan was carefully chopping and rechopping a pile of sweet-smelling agro dulce peppers. They were doing the most tedious of the kitchen's work but seemed to take each job as seriously as though they were plating a final dish. I sliced in reverent concentration.

The mood in the kitchen had changed since my time with Kenny. Things were speeding up and commands were coming more quickly. I turned at one point to see the quiet, imposing presence of Chef Jonathan Benno, a man I recognized from photographs. He saw me glance at him and walked over to introduce himself.

"All going well?" he asked succinctly.

"Yes, chef," I replied. "Thank you."

He nodded curtly, then peered over the shoulder of both Greg and Ethan to see their work.

"Kenny, what are you thinking for canapé tonight?" he asked, stopping the chef de partie mid-stride.

"Chef, I've got a few ideas," Kenny confided and the two leaned together for a hushed conversation. Benno's stance was relaxed, his hands folded together behind his back. Kenny gestured excitedly as he described what he was thinking. Benno nodded benevolently.

"Good work, chef," I heard Benno declare before sending Kenny back to work. I was mesmerized by the room's energy. It was calm and peaceful but with an unmistakable hum. Benno's presence seemed to both elevate and control it, as if he were the queen bee of a hive.

I looked down and realized my station was a mess. It looked as bad as my culling table—covered in bits of olive gunk. Surely I wasn't the neatest or most talented stage they'd ever had. I searched around for a kitchen towel to clean things up, wiping my trimmings and mess into a small hole meant for garbage. Even the prep stations were built for speed.

All around me, there was movement. Hands reached into drawers and compartments, pulling equipment or ingredients out with simple, undetectable motion. The kitchen's overall vibe was fluid, precise, and effortless. There seemed to be a stream of unspoken mischief emanating from the group around me, as though a communal joke were flying right over my head. I wouldn't catch the punch line until much later but standing at my station, I felt I was missing a very large part of the kitchen's camaraderie.

Suddenly, Kenny leaned in from out of nowhere as I finished my last pile of olives.

"Look at you, chef," he whispered. "You're *cooking* at Per Se!"

"I'm *chopping* at Per Se," I replied, smiling. Kenny's enthusiasm was infectious. I finished my olives and proudly showed my results to Greg.

"Nice work," he offered. "Now, tell me what you do again? Where are you from?"

I explained that I worked with Island Creek, that I was a farmhand there. "I'm a writer, too," I threw in casually.

"A writer, eh? Well, we wouldn't want to ruin those hands of yours," he said dryly before taking away the paring knife I held. "How about shredding some mushrooms?"

He pulled out a bin of whole black trumpet mushrooms and showed me how to shred them into thin strips. They would go along with a mushroom tortellini. I sidled up to the bin and got to work pulling individual strands off each fluted specimen. Around me, cooks leaned in close to their cutting boards, putting their eyes and noses right next to the food as they worked. I took note and bent over slightly, getting a good look at the mushrooms as I tore. Feeling and smelling each delicate strand made the experience even more surreal. I tried to imagine standing at my culling station with my crew looking on as I bent my head down like this. Just thinking about it made me laugh. I stood that way in focused concentration until, after ten minutes, my lower back started to scream. Perhaps I could just hold the mushrooms up closer to my face.

I finished the mushrooms and looked up to find a clock on the wall. Underneath it, a sign read: SENSE OF URGENCY. It had taken me an hour to shred the mushrooms. I wondered if I was the slowest stage they'd ever seen. I looked over to see that Ethan was still pulverizing the same pile of peppers next to me. They were almost down to a fine pulp when he stopped to stretch his wrist. Apparently not, I decided.

Greg checked my mushrooms, gave me a nod, and asked if I could help him with the leeks. His tedious job was only halfway done, so he handed me a small pile, along with the paring knife (apparently he didn't care about my hands when time was running short). They were the tiniest leeks I'd ever seen, thin and membranous, like they were made for a one-foot-tall pixie. How did one even harvest leeks this small? I stacked them into groups of five and carefully trimmed off the fragile rooted tips. For whatever reason, I loved this job. I loved the feel of the itty-bitty vegetables in my fingers, loved the satisfaction of getting five perfectly even lengths out of each stack, and bundling them up like Barbie-size bushels of hay. After callousing my hands on the silos and pummeling dried seaweed from our mesh bags, this delicate task felt so refined and civilized.

I felt a set of eyes on the back of my head and turned to see Skip and Shore standing on the other side of the kitchen. It was just after four P.M., almost time for staff meal. Greg slid my cutting board away from me and put all of the leeks into one container. I tried to help but turned and found, instead, one of the back servers, dressed in a vest, a white shirt, and black pants, standing in front of me with a huge plate of food. She set it down on my station, which had been magically wiped clear. Staff meal was served. Kitchen work came to a halt as chefs stood at their stations scarfing down slabs of pork smothered in barbecue sauce.

I ate half of the plate as quickly as I could and, following everyone else's lead, took the remainder to the dishwashing room to be dumped. Getting the nod from Benno, I walked over toward Skip and Shore, relieved to be among familiar faces again. Premeal would start any minute, so we scurried out toward Per Se's immaculate dining room.

The space itself was smaller than I had expected, with three tiered floors and only about two dozen tables. It sparkled with glass and copper accents but it was completely uncluttered with little more than the floor-to-ceiling view of Central Park and a sleek, glass-enclosed fireplace to draw one's attention away from the plate.

The room was full of servers, captains, the sommelier, and managers. I found a seat as the room fell silent; Benno now stood on the top tier to address his audience. He spoke softly but commanded the room as he introduced Skip and Shore, who sat beside him. He started with the backstory of how Island Creek came to be part of the menu, before dropping a few jokes about the Red Sox and handing them both "I ♥ NY" T-shirts. The audience let off a round of yips and catcalls at the sight of the shirts.

Benno then handed the floor to Skip, who looked as if he were about to give an address at Harvard. He stammered through a few points about his own career before Shore jumped in to help him fill in details about the farm, our growing cycle, and the wholesale company. The farm was supplying Per Se with other treats like razor clams and Nantucket Bay scallops, which Skip was able to describe more comfortably—he was much more at ease talking about what came out of the water.

They opened the floor to questions from the staff, who wanted to know how razor clams grow, the name of the guy who caught the scallops, and Skip's favorite way to eat oysters (with green Tabasco and a splash of vodka, he replied). They were insatiable, wanting details about how we harvested, when scallop season began and ended, and why certain seafood labels were so vague. Skip answered each question with as much detail as he could but I could tell that he thought the staff knew more about food than he did. The rest of the meeting was dedicated to going over that day's menu and the reservation list. Questions rang out as Chef David listed off each dish: Is there lobster stock in the mousseline? Where is the sea bream from? Is there bacon in the lentils? How long is the beef braised?

Each answer would prepare them for what would surely be an onslaught of questions from the customers themselves.

The reservation list revealed an equally fascinating discussion. The maître d', Chloe, read off every name on the night's reservation list, complete with personal information. A baroness from Monaco would be dining tonight with a friend who was a doctor. Her birthday was coming up and she'd been to the restaurant twice before.

"The doctor has an allergy to shellfish," one server called out. They had photographic memories of each guest's personal background, it seemed. I wondered how many meals I'd sat through where the staff knew this much about me. This was above and beyond good customer service. It was personal.

The meeting ended promptly at five P.M. and Benno motioned for me to head back into the kitchen. The guys were going back to the hotel, where I'd meet them before dinner. In the meantime, service was about to begin.

The kitchen had been transformed in those thirty minutes. The room was immaculate and calm. A counter at the center of the room had been transformed into the expediting line, now covered in white paper and lined with lime green tape. Every menu (prix fixe, vegetarian, VIPs) was lined up side by side; at the very end I saw a menu for the French Laundry. I noticed that the TV screen overhead was turned on, showing our counterpart kitchen now bustling.

Kenny waved for me to join him at his station, where I was able to stand stiffly against the wall and out of the way. Kenny moved quickly, arranging his *mise en place*, stacking pots next to his portion of the stove. It was like a surgeon readying his operating table with every necessary tool set within arm's length.

"Don't look at my line," he said slyly, covering a few of the deli containers with his arm protectively. "I've got surprises here waiting for you."

Benno stood behind the line, wearing his white jacket and apron, with an eye on both the clock and what was going on around him. Chef David hovered there too, watching the cooks and checking their readiness with quick, barked-out commands. Each chef responded with military precision: Yes, chef!

Suddenly, a server appeared.

"Chef, ordering for table twenty-six," she said.

"Twenty-six," Benno stated.

"Twenty-six!" the kitchen replied in unison.

"Ordering one gougere, one salmon, one O and P, two halibut, two sturgeon," the server sang. Benno repeated the order, directing each dish to different stations. Kenny was already whirling through the order, pulling out a chilled pudding, and heating a pot on the stove. Firing: Oysters and Pearls.

He quickly heated up the poaching mixture: butter, more oyster liquor, champagne vinegar, and vermouth. He swirled the sauce to test its heat, then dropped two almond-sized oyster bellies into the pot. I leaned in nervously, hoping the bellies looked right. He slid aside quickly to give me a view, then turned back to his work. He laid the oysters on top of a dish of chilled pudding, poured the sauce over top, and finished the dish with a delicate dollop of shimmering caviar.

He scurried the dish over toward Benno, head bent over in final examination. He set it in front of the chef, who stood tall, his hands resting casually on the counter. Benno took a close look, nudging the dollop of caviar very subtly to one side with his knuckle, then called a server who swooped in to take it away.

I looked at Kenny, who was trying to hide a smile.

"There's your dish, chef. O and P," he whispered, already en route to his next dish. Two more orders for Oysters and Pearls had been called out. Kenny was on fire.

I tried to stay out of the way. Kenny's station was a blur of spoons, deli containers, hands, and dishes. At one point, David, who'd been watching Kenny closely, was in his face.

"We're watching, Kenny. Get moving," he said with a grin. Someone called out six orders for canapés and just like that, Kenny's station was a beehive. Benno and Chef David flanked him, pulling out containers, pouring the contents into saucepans, laying ingredients on a plate. Three sets of hands worked in one small space for several seconds, smoothly jumping around each other. There was no bumping or jostling, no raised voices or looks of concern. Just motion and energy, all reeling into one elegant and noiseless tornado.

I felt a tap on my shoulder and turned to see a fresh-faced cook holding a white plastic container in front of me.

"Smell," he said, and lifted the lid of the box. I inhaled deeply, letting the intoxicating complexity of truffles fill my head. I leaned in, falling dangerously close to putting my nose directly against the grapefruit-size specimen before the cook snapped the box shut. He smiled and walked away, leaving a potent waft in his wake. Benno was suddenly on the other side of me and motioning me toward the other side of the room.

"You might be more comfortable over there," he said quietly. I took my cue and made my escape from the eye of the storm.

I watched for almost an hour as the kitchen moved through its first round of orders. For all of the commands, aromas, and motion that seemed to shoot through the air, I saw very little actual food. Chefs were pulling tiny stashes out of counter-height coolers, the reach-ins, and other compartments hidden behind the stainless steel surfaces. It was like a laboratory. And each of the chefs looked as serious as a nuclear scientist.

Then, about ten minutes before my stage was to end, I heard a phone ring. The entire kitchen stopped dead in its tracks. Every face turned toward the TV screen, holding a collective breath. Benno walked calmly toward the black kitchen phone that hung in a nook near the hallway and picked it up without saying a word. He could see the TV screen from his stance and kept an eye on it while he listened. The rest of the kitchen started moving again but watched Benno carefully. After a few quiet words, he hung up and walked back to the line.

I saw him whisper something to Chef David and the two shared a private laugh. The room let out a sigh and work resumed just as quickly as it had stopped.

A minute later, Benno looked at the clock and then looked directly at me. He left the line again, this time to lead me out of the kitchen. I waved to Kenny, then followed Chef Benno back to the office to collect my things.

"Was that Chef Thomas on the phone?" I asked, pulling on my jacket.

"No." He smiled. "But close. When that phone rings it's one of two people. The chef de cuisine at the French Laundry, or"—he paused, dropping his voice down a note—"Chef."

I knew he wouldn't give me any more details so I thanked him for the day and told him I could find my way from there. He was anxious to get back to the line.

The second time I walked through the entrance of Per Se, I felt right at home. I'd scurried back to the hotel, gotten cleaned up, met Shore and Skip, and the three of us had raced back to Per Se for our eight P.M. reservation. A small army of greeters welcomed us to dinner, including the maître d' Chloe and some of the familiar faces from the pre-meal meeting. They were warm and inviting this time, looking somewhat awestruck by the men at my side. Skip was a celebrity for them, a food hero whom they'd studied and had now heard speak. And here he was in their charge. Even in his suit and tie and combed-down hair, he looked like he belonged outdoors. The three of us shared a quiet thrill over being guests of honor for the night.

We were whisked through a dimly lit lounge and on toward the dining room to our table directly beside the fireplace. I sat between Skip and Shore to face the stunning room. It had been transformed from the high-energy meeting room I saw at pre-meal to a candlelit stage. The white tablecloth and weighted silver were symbols of occasion. Just sitting before them with a host of suited servers fussing around us made me feel glamorous. The other folks in the room, including that baroness from Monaco and any other of the social elite Chloe had listed off earlier that day, faded out of my view as soon as our captain, named Antonio, filled my delicate crystal flute with an ever-bubbling slug of Premier cru Champagne.

It was clear from the start that our entire meal would be a well-choreographed set of surprises, starting with the menus. Inside Skip's, Benno had put a copy of the front page of a recent *New York Times* with the headline YANKEES WIN THE WORLD SERIES. He couldn't get enough of the joke.

Our culinary journey started with morsels of gougere and salmon "coronets," another Keller signature of salmon tartare served in a bite-size cone. That was followed by a twenty-three-course culinary feast that lasted for five full hours, taking the three of us from mere diners to gustatory disciples. Kenny was right: There were plenty of surprises. The first was what Benno called the Patriot Oyster. It was a version of Skip's favorite way to eat oysters.

"We were out of green Tabasco," our food runner explained with a wink. Instead, Benno had placed a sliver of jalapeño on top of a single naked oyster and splashed it with an almost undetectable hit of vodka.

Oyster dishes were marched out in succession from there: in a chowder, tempura-battered with horseradish, and of course, as the famed Oysters and Pearls. The tiny domed dish was set before me on a stack of four plates—four!—revealing that we were, indeed, some of the top dogs in the dining room.

I dipped my spoon into Kenny's ethereally light pudding and ate. One after another, orbs of flavor exploded on my tongue. First the oyster, which sang with its champagne vinegar-vermouth baste; then the tapioca, which broke easily between my teeth. Finally, the rounded balls of caviar burst into tiny, salted fireworks to ignite and round out each insanely pleasing flavor. I closed my eyes and savored perfection. All of those early March days, those long stretches of aching muscles and those seemingly endless picking tides when I was covered in mud and exhausted were, all of sudden, completely worth it.

Each dish brought with it a description or story from our servers, which Skip lapped up with heartfelt enthusiasm. He was impressed that they could rattle off fun facts about all six salts that accompanied our terrine of foie gras or about the person who collected our abalone off the West Coast. We also tasted a few more signatures, like Keller's white-truffle-oil-infused custard, which was served inside a delicate, uncapped eggshell along with an unctuous veal ragout. I tried to visualize one of the chefs standing at their station, laboriously severing each precious egg. It had likely been a monumental effort to build such an elegantly simple dish.

The complexity marched on in dishes like Nantucket Bay scallops served with a dollop of sea urchin and pickled ginger. Skip's eyes lit up as he chewed, working his way through each layer, trying to decipher, as I did, where the crunch, tang, meatiness, and ocean flavors met. We both finished and stared at each other, mystified.

"I can't get over that dish," he said to me hours later, when we were well on our way through the entrees. And there were multiple entrees. Or tastings, more accurately. Around course ten, Antonio paused to ask, "Are you ready to begin now?" Everything up to that point had been a starter.

We were moved on to more complex dishes, like the butter-poached lobster "mitt," a chunk of flawless lobster meat settled over a bed of tiny tortellini. I practically beamed when I saw the slivers of trumpet mushroom laid tenderly across the dish. The same went for the cod shank, which was touched with not only my somewhat bulky olive slices but with Ethan's pulverized pepper agro dulce.

Next up, we got walloped by actual white truffles. The presentation arrived as a simple white plate of colorless risotto. Chloe appeared beside us with an ornate wooden box from which she produced a massive hunk of white truffle from Alba, Italy. With a seductive lean toward me, she held the intoxicating mass directly beneath my nose before delicately grating the hulking mushroom, covering my risotto in creamy brown snowflakes. Next, she poured a drizzle of steaming brown butter over the pile, melting the edges of the flakes and sending another wave of woodsy aroma up toward my face. I was rendered motionless, stunned into a state of disbelief and arousal, wanting the moment to go on and on and on. Chloe turned to perform the same act with

Shore, whose eyes widened to the size of oysters as he inhaled the display before him. Skip was near tears giggling at our reaction until he received the same treatment, causing him to draw his breath in sharply and then light up with his Cheshire grin.

For a moment, after she silently padded away, we didn't speak. We just sat and breathed deeply over our plates. When Shore took his first bite, he moaned with ecstasy.

"That might have been the most erotic moment of my life," he declared with a straight face. Skip and I burst out laughing.

A few courses later, Antonio asked if we'd like to take a look at the kitchen. It was the first time I'd noticed the other people in the room, who had just sort of swirled around us as a silent backdrop. The room was starting to empty, actually, leaving our table with just a few others to close out the night.

We walked past the wine cellar, a massive, temperature-controlled glass box that sat toward the front of the restaurant, and back toward the kitchen, where we were greeted with a few cheers and loud hellos. Benno came over to shake our hands and ask how we were enjoying the meal even though he already knew the answer: He'd blown our minds. Kenny waved hello and I thanked him profusely for letting me trail him for the day.

"You're my new hero," I admitted, eliciting an "aw shucks" from the talented chef.

We returned to the table for what would be a short parade of desserts, including an entertaining twist called "coffee and doughnuts" featuring feather-light cinnamon-sugar-dusted doughnuts and a cappuccino-flavored semi-freddo.

As we pulled back from the table in a sort of awed digestive stupor, Antonio approached us one last time.

"We hope you enjoyed your meal," he offered generously before adding, "Chef Thomas would like to take care of your dinner tonight."

We all stared at one another, uncertain of how to handle the rare gift. As Antonio slid away, we tried to stammer out a heartfelt "thank you" while masking our disbelief. I did the math quickly in my head—the tally was well over a thousand dollars, probably more. Perhaps, I thought, I could look at this as payment for the little bit of work I'd done in the kitchen that day or, more fittingly, for all of the work that my crew and I had exerted in order to pull hundreds of thousands of oysters out of the water so far that year. It was a spellbinding finish—but almost too good to be true.

The now empty dining room felt as welcoming and familiar as an old friend's home, a place we didn't want to leave. But it was nearing one A.M. and time to say good-bye. Another contingent of captains and servers stood at the exit, complete with goodie bags filled with chocolate truffles and copies of our menus for us to take with us. They waved us off, stumbling into the night, offering us a warm welcome whenever we wanted to return.

Piling ourselves into a cab, we laughed uncontrollably at our incredible fortune. The day had been epic, a culinary experience of a lifetime. All I wanted was to wake up and do it all over again.

Patriot Oysters

C hef Thomas Keller's dish, Oysters and Pearls, undoubtedly stole the show at our meal, but it was the Patriot Oyster that got the biggest chuckle out of Skip. As he mentioned to the staff, his favorite way to eat oysters is with a splash of green Tabasco sauce and, occasionally, a splash of vodka. Chef Jonathan Benno, who didn't have green Tabasco on hand, used a sliced jalepeño instead. Either one works.

> *1 dozen Island Creek Oysters, shucked*
> *1 jalepeño, very thinly sliced in rounds*
> *(or a bottle of green Tabasco)*
> *4 tablespoons vodka*

Top each oyster with a jalepeño slice (or a few drops of Tabasco if using), then 1 teaspoon of vodka. Serve ice-cold.

SERVES 4

CHAPTER TEN

PRO-PAIN

Nothing could shatter my elation after our night at Per Se. In an attempt to make the moment last, I reported my findings (our Per Se cull was too small; A2's quality-control checks were nearly perfect) and then retold the story of the meal to anyone who would listen, including my crew, who rolled their eyes the third time I told them about my clumsy entrance through the main door.

As Berg promised, the pile of dirty oyster bags was still there when I got back, leaving me with nothing but power washing in my very near future. But even that task took on a new glow as I broke up the monotony of the work by mentally reliving my four-star day, from every technique I'd learned from Kenny to our final dessert.

I was still floating a few days later when Berg announced that it was time for the Oyster Plex to be brought back to land. Every other Island Creek float (along with just about every boat in the harbor) had already been put away for the season, leaving Our Girl bobbing lonely in the middle of the bay. It was time to get her back to land, putting us close to a power source and, to my utter joy, a bathroom.

Moving the float seemed to lift everyone's spirits, especially Berg's. While Matthew and I were in Chicago in October, Berg, Skip, and Shore had traveled to Africa for the foundation's first exploratory trip to Zanzibar. They'd spent five days in Stone Town, Zanzibar's most populated city, where the shellfish hatchery would be built, as well as a few of the outlying villages where the shellfish would finish growing. Berg had come back with renewed energy.

"There's a lot of work to do over there," he told me as we readied the float for her big move. "We have a solid plan but we need to put benchmarks in place, to really understand where the foundation's money is being spent," he said. They foresaw it taking up to four or five years to get a successful hatchery in place—a lifetime for a twenty-three-year-old. In February, he would return to the beautiful but impoverished country where, for ten weeks, he and a few other members from the Woods Hole team would start the process of building a hatchery.

In the meantime, he was anxious to get the farm ready for his absence. Ten weeks without him meant someone else would need to harvest and run the show—until then, we still had equipment in the water and seed to plant.

Since the perch that we'd occupied in the spring was now flattened into a neatly manicured parking lot, our plan this year was to leave the Plex in the water. It would be tied up to the farm's "winter dock," where the growers kept their boats during colder months. The float fit perfectly into its new parking spot.

Being back on land was an adjustment after so many months on the water. We went back to using a regular hose hooked up to the dock's water supply to wash our oysters, and Berg and Will tinkered with some electrical lines that allowed us to add power outlets to the float. Berg appeared one morning with a new electric space heater.

"It's for the oysters, Pain," he teased when he saw my face light up. "Yours is over there," he said, motioning to my long-lost friend, our propane-powered space heater. I pulled it out of its hiding place in the corner, turned on the propane, and fired it up, standing directly beside it as it glowed amber orange. A2 laughed when he saw me. "Ah, Pro-Pain," he sighed.

Greg had gone back to college, leaving Will, A2, Berg, and me to return to a tight-knit but occasionally dysfunctional team. The four of us worked well together, but like a clan of siblings, we knew exactly how to get under each other's skin. It wouldn't be for long, though. I'd made the decision to start working in the office after January 1. In just a few short weeks, my time on the crew would come to an end.

We took a brief break for Thanksgiving, which gave Dave and me time to visit my parents down in Houston. I had oysters shipped to them for the occasion, giving my family a new holiday tradition. We opened most of them to eat raw before our feast but saved some to fold into a buttery, herb-filled oyster stuffing.

It had been almost a year since my sister, Shannon, and

her husband, Brian, had announced their plans to adopt; this year as we sat around my parents' dining room table, my sister filled us in on their progress. They'd applied to several adoption agencies and had even been interviewed by a few expectant mothers. They were searching for a baby from the United States and though they'd heard a million different stories about how long the process might take, they were hopeful that something would happen soon.

That night, as Dave and I shared a hoppy bottle of beer to finish off the meal, he asked how I felt about my sister's news.

"I'm thrilled for them," I admitted, realizing that something else had surfaced inside me. As I watched my sister glow with the hope of a new baby, I noticed I was yearning for that same happiness. I nestled in closely to Dave and asked if he was ready to start talking about kids again.

"I'm ready whenever you are," he said, giving me a kiss on the forehead.

We flew back to Boston loaded up with early Christmas presents (we wouldn't see my parents again until after the holidays) and a tiny old coffeepot that my mom had given me to use on the float.

I arrived to the farm after the holiday to find a new face on our crew. Chris was a fresh-faced twenty-something who'd grown up in Duxbury and gone to Williams College. He'd spent the last few years working on sailboats, crewing private charters, and traipsing the seas from Maine to the Caribbean. He would eventually land in the office as the farm's new marketing person, but Shore had instructed him to work on Skip's crew to see how things on the farm ran.

Since he was familiar with boats, he would be a natural substitute for Berg and it would give him the opportunity to learn the oyster farming cycle.

Chris was goofy but razor sharp. Despite having never worked around oysters, he picked up the basics quickly, allowing A2 to cruise through the training process in just a few hours. Chris was enamored with oysters and took every opportunity to open one up and taste. I found it funny to see such a well-pedigreed upstart dressed in lumberjack clothes and a pair of work boots, his floppy brown hair piled under a trucker's cap. He had a silly sense of humor yet managed to speak seriously about everything from his favorite artist of the moment (an instrumental Afro-jazz musician) to all the places he'd lived (Paris, New Zealand, a cabin in the middle of nowhere, Maine). Chris and I became fast friends, teasing each other as easily as A2 and I had. At the time, he was living in the city, so we started carpooling and would spend our daily treks to and from Duxbury swapping stories about our most memorable travels, unforgettable meals, or dissecting our favorite topic: oysters.

We celebrated Chris's first few days on the farm with a beer at the Winsor House. The Winny had become a weekly routine that fall, giving us a carrot to work toward during those grueling days of power washing or dumping seed. Even if it was just for one pint or, when I desperately needed to warm up, a glass of red wine, the ritual of bellying up in the low-ceilinged bar and chatting with our favorite bartender, a shaggy-haired artist named Susan, became a marker of the early winter and the slowing season. We usually ran into growers like Don Merry or John Brawley, who had a Ph.D. in marine systems ecology and was also a charter boat captain. They'd gather there as soon as the fading sun pushed them off the water, which now happened earlier and earlier each day. We'd pull our bar stools up in front of the fireplace as Brawley told us a good fishing story or Don reported on his successes or failures as a deer hunter (one of his favorite pastimes off the water). In my work clothes—mud-splattered jeans, a ripped and faded hoodie—I felt at home there, like it was right where I belonged.

That night, Skip, A2, and I regaled Chris with stories about the summer. He tried to follow along as we described Maggie's quest for the perfect cull and our brutal experience with the upwellers. It sounded odd, so many months later, telling these stories to another FNG. I'd come a long way in six months.

"We didn't even get to the good stuff," Skip said, goading me. I asked what he meant, seeing as how the whole summer had been full of good stuff.

"I dunno, I mean we never went over to the Deck by boat, we never did any bridge jumping," he said, sounding a little dejected. The Deck, part of the 14 Union Dockside Bar & Grill, was a waterside bar in Plymouth, which I'd been to, but never by boat. And bridge jumping sounded like one of those suburban legends about things that high school kids do when they're bored.

"I thought we had it pretty good," I replied, trying to cheer him up. Skip raised his eyebrows and smiled.

"I think we did, too. But . . ." He hesitated. "I still think you should come back next summer and do it again."

"Ahhhh, I get it," I replied. "You don't think I got the full experience?" I asked.

"Nope," Skip replied with a lopsided grin. "One more summer might do it. Plus, who's gonna take care of the seed next year?" he asked earnestly.

"We'll see," I said firmly. Part of me did want one more summer on the farm. One more summer with the crew, one summer with the seed. My one-year anniversary with Island Creek was coming up in just three short months. It was time for me to make a decision.

That night, as I made my way home from Duxbury, my sister called. She had exciting news to report: "We're being interviewed by an expecting mother this week," she said. They were one of two couples that the mother, who was due in less than two months, was interviewing, meaning their chance of having a child was now fifty/fifty. I could hear it in her voice: This might just be the one.

I sat by my phone all weekend hoping for good news. The call finally came on Saturday evening, just as I was sitting down at the bar where Dave worked to watch the beginnings of our first winter snowstorm roll in. It was my sister shouting into the line, *"You're going to be an aunt!"*

Their phone interview had gone perfectly, and just an hour after it ended, Shannon got a call from the agency stating that they had been chosen as the adoptive parents. I listened with tears in my eyes as she told me that their daughter, who they'd already decided to name Gracyn, would arrive in late January.

On the farm the snowstorm ended up dumping a few

inches of powdery whiteness onto our now-docked Plex, bringing winter front and center for my crew. Suddenly, there seemed to be more work than time to do it. First and foremost, we needed to finish planting the seed despite the bitter cold we were about to face. I finally caved and pulled out all of my long underwear and winter gear. But I felt more prepared this time around, as though months of working outdoors had toughened my threshold for the elements. Whether in response to the cold or simply from the number of good meals I'd eaten in the last few weeks, I was already gaining some winter weight. All of my meals, not just the ones I'd eaten at four-star restaurants, were now packed with extra calories, whether that meant entire foot-long meatball subs from the town's local grocer, Foodie's, or platters of pork fried rice and sweet-and-sour chicken at Tsang's. I craved fattening, heavy food and didn't even mind the extra padding.

Later that week, Berg had us out on the tide. It was my first time out there since the last new moon—a measurement that I'd grown fond of referencing since it was more accurate as a tide calculator than a calendar month was. We were still days away from the actual new moon, giving us several days of very long, very low tides, which we could use to pull the final seed bags from their cages. Once we reached the cages, I pulled on my bulky spaceman gloves and jumped out of the boat, feeling that cold, familiar rush of the water against my waders. Inside the bags, the seed had grown monstrous, making them bulge around the middle. And even though I wore long johns, heavy jeans, rubber waders, and about eight layers of shirts, the frozen air ripped through me like paper. The only thing I could do to keep warm was continue moving.

Skip was out on the lease with us—a sight that had grown rarer now that it was colder. (Being the boss meant less time on the water, especially when paperwork called.) As we pulled the last of the bags onto the boat, he called us over to show us a system he'd devised. Over the course of the fall, we'd taken to dumping our returns (the too-small, chipped, or misshapen oysters that needed more time on the lease to regrow) directly into black mesh bags, which Berg had dropped onto the bay floor in a messy pile. Because the oysters couldn't stay in the cages over the winter (they would ice over if they were exposed to the cold air) we would leave them in bags directly on the bay floor where, like the newly planted seed, they'd get covered in a fine layer of mud, which could actually protect them from the cold. Skip's plan was to lay the bags out in packs of one hundred where they'd sit in a grid, twenty-five long by four across, all tied together with plastic zip ties. Over the next few sets of tides, he wanted us to lay the bags out into grids and secure them together. Eventually, in the dead of winter, whoever was harvesting could simply pull up one bag from the grid with the hauler, bringing with it the entire grid in one harvest. This would be a time-saver for Chris or whoever else was harvesting in the frigid cold that year.

We got busy lining up what amounted to seven hundred bags into seven different grids, careful to count out exactly one hundred with each grid. It was an ingenious system of preparedness that stemmed from fifteen years of experience. Skip was preparing for the worst because he'd lived through it before. In the winter of 2005, New England saw a six-week stretch of sub-twenties temperatures. Ice blanketed the bay, becoming twelve inches thick in some spots. The farmers had to take their boats out of the water and were forced to stop harvesting. But a few weeks into it, Skip started getting antsy. Per Se was a brand-new customer at the time and he had committed to supplying them on a weekly basis. He was determined to get out there and get them some oysters. On top of which, he was bored. He hated standing idly by just because of a bit of ice. So he, Don Merry, and his dad, Billy, took a pickup truck down to the water's edge and carefully drove it out onto the ice. It was so thick, it didn't even crack under the truck's weight. So they grabbed a chain saw, tied a boat up to the back (just in case something went wrong), and drove over the ice out to Don Merry's lease. Once they got out there, they cut through the ice with the chain saw, taking out small chunks until they'd made a hole large enough for one of them to stand in. It was low tide at the time, so Skip jumped in with his waders on and, together, the brazen team fished up a couple bags of oysters, which Don had laid down on his lease for this exact occasion. They bagged the oysters up and got them to Per Se the next day.

Skip recounted the story while we finished laying out the grids, leaving us all looking at one another in disbelief and wondering just how bad this winter might get.

· · ·

By the time we finished laying out the grids the tide was just starting to creep back in—we still had a ways to go before we could get the boats off the ground.

We quickly caught our breath before moving onto our next task. Time on the tide was now precious and all three hundred cages still needed to come out of the water. During their time out there, they'd physically grown into the landscape, nestling so deep into the silt we couldn't see the bottoms. It would take at least two of us to wrestle them out and stand them upright. This was the moment I had not anticipated way back in June.

A2 and I partnered up and tackled our first cage. With bent knees and flexed back muscles, we pulled at the metal bars, waiting for the sucking sound of air to let us know we'd released it from the ground's death grip. A2 grunted as he pulled, which made me laugh, more out of sympathy than actual humor. We moved on to the next cage, bending low once again to grasp the cage and yank it upward. No matter how much I concentrated on using my legs, my back took the brunt of the work. I wondered what torture lay ahead of me the next time I tried to lie flat on my back and realized I was now the one grunting. We kept at it, cage after cage, as the water pooled in around us. Some of the cages were buried a foot deep in the mud, leaving A2 and me wincing to free them.

Finally, Berg announced it was time to go in. We needed to drop the seed bags onto our barge float (we'd left that one attached to our mooring in the bay for projects like this), then return to the lease to load up the cages and get them out of the water.

With two boats, we were able to haul about one hundred cages off the lease and back up to our storage space by lunchtime. Our day was only halfway done. We reconvened at Foodie's where, over a meatball sub and two candy bars, I asked Chris how he was handling the work. He looked ragged, like he was already zapped of energy, but said the work didn't seem so bad.

I felt his pain but realized that I was actually in decent shape. I was no longer exhausted by days like this. I could keep up with the boys even on the most frigid days.

After lunch, Berg and I ran out to the Back River to gather up the last of the buoys, braving the gusty winds at top speed to make the trip go by faster. We slowed to a crawl as we approached the SHELLFISH LEASE signs when Berg nudged me without a word. I looked up to see a white-and-gray spotted seal lounging on one of the buoys. It perked up when it heard us coming and sat watching as we unhooked our buoys and pulled them into the boat. A few minutes later it slipped away, back underneath the water.

We ended the day dumping seed, which Skip returned to help us with, then corralled our now empty bags for one last run up to the shop. The bags would go back to the pile to be power washed, and the last of the seed would be planted. We were finally nearing the finish line.

That night, I stood under a scalding-hot shower for almost an hour. It felt good to know we were making progress and that the farm would soon be in winter mode. Memories of my first exhausting week on the farm came flooding back. I looked down at my hands, now swollen and calloused, and thought proudly of all the work I'd done. I was coming to the end of the cycle. I wondered what would happen to those hands once I was back sitting at a desk. I was reaching my own finish line, where indoor heat and an endless supply of hot coffee beckoned from the other side. But I worried that my body would forget all of this work and all too quickly reacquaint itself with a more submissive posture. More important, I worried that I would miss my crew.

The next morning started with snow, which we worked through to get out on the tide. The scene was breathtaking as snowflakes melted on the mud around us and up on shore; the coastline's beautiful, old 1800-era houses glistened in the early-morning dusting. The sun poked out briefly from behind a thick layer of clouds, streaming laserlike rays down over the horizon. I took the moment in silently, not wanting my memories of this scene to fade.

We were out there to finish securing all of our bag grids, but my bulky gloves refused to grasp the tiny ties. I finally tossed them off, feeling the twenty-five-degree air pierce through my skin like razor blades. As quickly as I could, I pulled zip ties through the black mesh before my fingers stopped working. Skip looked over and nodded toward my gloves on the ground.

"You going bare-handed, office girl?" he asked. I smiled and got back to work. After the tide we spent the afternoon counting oysters, a marathon session, which ended with us putting one hundred bags into the cooler. As we counted, I watched Chris carefully. He looked like he was about to hit a breaking point.

"I keep losing track," he whined. But I knew where he was coming from. With nothing to look at but piles of oysters, this felt like the most monotonous job in the world. I told him to slow down and count by twos to fifty, just like Berg taught me. He sighed before picking up a yellow bag to start again.

"One . . . two . . . three. . . ." I heard him count to himself, tapping his oysters together rhythmically. I smiled to myself.

That week, we started getting reports that the coldest temperatures of the year followed by a classic Nor'easter were about to barrel in on us. Duxbury was forecasted to get the brunt of the storm, up to eighteen inches of snow. Berg tried to prepare us with a pep talk explaining that our biggest threat was frozen oysters. Once harvested, if fully frozen (as opposed to being chilled on a bed of ice), oysters open up and quickly die, meaning their time out of the water was beyond precious. It was lethal.

As the week wore on, temperatures slid down to the teens. Friday morning, my car struggled to start up in the cold and when it did, my digital thermometer blinked at me: nine degrees.

I got to the float to find that our hose, which had been left outdoors overnight, was frozen solid. I picked it up to take it inside the float, where I found Chris cursing at the space heater. We were out of propane.

"On the coldest day of the year?" I cried. The temperature

wasn't expected to get above nineteen degrees that day. Berg, who had just come in with a haul of newly harvested oysters, rolled his eyes at me and grabbed the tank to refill it, leaving us to figure out how to defrost the hose. Quick on his feet, Chris ran it up to the Maritime School locker rooms and threw it under a hot shower.

Washing the oysters took hours—as soon as the water hit them, they iced over, meaning we needed to get them warmed up as soon as they were washed. Berg came back with a now-full tank and got the propane fired up, which brought the Oyster Plex to a balmy fifty degrees, though we had to keep the garage door open a crack in order to slide crates in and out.

Will took one for the team as our washer, hosing each crate down quickly to keep the oysters from freezing. It was a hellish job—standing outside, being spritzed with ice-cold water, no protection but gloves and a couple of layers—but he handled it gracefully. After sliding around on the icy surface for a few hours, he came inside to warm up his hands and proudly showed off a four-inch-long icicle growing out of one of his elbows.

The oysters themselves seemed to be okay, too. Berg opened one every hour or so just to see how the meat was faring.

"This temperature swing really stresses them out," he said, carefully prying one of the little guys open. The liquor surrounding the meat crystallized briefly as it met the frigid air. He handed me one to taste. The icy juice gave the meat a delightfully pleasant crunch. I chewed for a bit to release the belly's sweetness. The oysters were at their absolute peak.

"I don't care what anyone says, this is the absolute best time to eat oysters," Berg said before slurping one back.

"You mean standing outside in fifteen-degree weather?" Chris joked as he opened one for himself.

"No," Berg laughed. "December. Right now. They're so full of sugar they're like candy." Because oysters go dormant in the winter, they spend the fall bulking up on food, creating a surplus of glucose in their meaty bodies, which they live on for months until the water gets warm enough for them to start feeding again. That glucose translates to sweetness, and that day the oysters were packed with sugary goodness. We slurped back a few more for quality control before Berg sent us all back to work.

Eventually, with all of the oysters washed and bagged, we rewarded ourselves with another inhumanly large lunch at Foodie's, where I devoured a pint of macaroni and cheese. We returned from lunch to find the windowpanes of the Oyster Plex frozen over like chiseled glass. Berg announced that once we got the bags up to the shop, we could call it a day. The blizzard was expected to hit sometime on Saturday, so he was anxious to get things wrapped up before burying himself indoors for the weekend. I was up in the bed of the farm truck stacking bags when my phone rang. It was Skip.

"Hey, E-Rock, I've got a question for you. Just wondering if you're coming back next summer?" Parts of his statement were muffled as I tried to keep stacking bags while holding the phone with my shoulder. "I want to sit down and talk to you about seed. I'm thinking I might build another upweller and get us up to four next year." I stopped what I was doing and got off the truck.

"I just put in a huge order with Dick at ARC. I'm doing it much bigger this time around. I'm thinking we get a whole crew dedicated to seed and you could run it. It would be a huge operation that stands on its own. I wondered if we could sit down . . ." He paused, waiting for me to answer.

"Wow, Skip. Really? A huge operation?" I stammered into the phone. "I'd love to sit down, but . . . well, when do you want to know?"

"How about sometime in the next month?" he said.

I put my phone down and stood thinking for a minute. It was decision time. While I couldn't grasp how we would manage four upwellers or having a whole crew on seed, I realized I wasn't ready to leave.

I could feel Chris and A2 watching me.

"Skip wants to talk about next summer," I said. A2 laughed and shook his head. He secretly believed that I would never leave. Chris cocked his head to the side with a smile.

"So does this mean you're staying?" he asked.

"Yeah, I think it does," I replied.

The blizzard ended up dropping almost two feet of heavy, wet snow across Massachusetts a few days before Christmas. Dave and I were scheduled to take a road trip down to

Tennessee to spend Christmas with his family. We'd still make our trip—and we'd also make it to the farm's Christmas party, which was scheduled to go on in spite of the snow.

The day before Dave and I were to leave, the crew and I spent all morning digging out trucks and boats and all afternoon setting up for the party. It was mostly for the growers, their families, and some friends of the farm: a pretty modest affair with our raw bar boat set up in the garage, a keg of cheap beer, and snacks we pulled together in the office kitchen. Dave made it down after work and found us all huddled in the shop in our heavy winter coats and hats. Skip decided to pull out his *perron,* a Spanish pitcher that had a long, funnel-necked spout. He used it to feed everyone shots of bubbly cava; we passed it around the garage like a bunch of frat kids, collectively downing two bottles of sparkling wine in just under ten minutes.

The party devolved from there, eventually turning into a massive snowball fight. Dave and I left just as folks were headed over to Don Merry's house to warm up. Our car was already packed for our road trip, so after a couple hours of sleep at our friends Matt and Meghan's house, we were on the road the next morning headed for Knoxville, Tennessee.

The trip turned out to be exactly what Dave and I needed. It was a quiet holiday and I spent most of the week sleeping, recuperating, and reflecting on the last nine months. I thought back to the anxiety and excitement that had consumed me before my big leap to join the farm and then of the uncertainty that followed during those first rocky few weeks of work. I thought about the farmers and my crew, who had all become more like family than friends. In between all of the difficult, exhausting, and ultimately thrilling parts, I realized how much the farm had taught me about my threshold for work, my ability to push through pain, and my own strength.

Dave and I spent that week talking about what was next. I was staying on the farm through the summer, I decided. That would give me the opportunity to see this year's seed crop come to size and allow me to go through the seed process one more time.

"One more summer," Dave agreed. "And then we can have our life back," he concluded. I resolved to make the upcoming year about balancing my life with Dave and my life on the farm.

The time away also had me reevaluating what I wanted to take away from this experience. I never set out on this journey to *become* an oyster farmer. I'd done it to learn about food in an unfiltered way, to see what it meant to grow something from beginning to end. Along the way, I'd unearthed a fascination with growing food with my own hands. But being an oyster farmer wasn't my calling in life, not like it had been for Skip. I couldn't see myself applying for my own oyster lease, running my own upweller, or launching my own oyster business.

But one more summer would buy me some time. Now that I'd gotten my hands dirty, it was time to figure out where my life was headed next.

. . .

My last four days on the Oyster Plex were blustery, snowy, and cold. The weather and wind prevented us from going out on the tide until the afternoon of my second-to-last day. It wasn't a long tide but we'd be able to get the last of our bag grids tied together and maybe, just maybe, pull in the last of those cages. As I walked along the edge of a row of bags, hunched over to attach zip ties to each one, I stepped gingerly around a rock that I knew was underfoot. I'd become so familiar with the terrain, it didn't occur to me to look anymore. Around me, I could sense that the water was icing up. I stepped into a nearby puddle to break the ice with my boot.

"You know what that's called?" I heard Berg's voice to my left. My jacket hood and hat shielded him from my view but I could feel him standing, hunched like me, just a few feet away. He'd been working beside me all day, occasionally tossing out little reminders that this was my final tide.

"What's that?" I asked, standing to face him.

"Skim," he answered, pointing to the thin edging of ice that had formed between the water and the mud behind me. I remembered seeing the water and ice do the same thing on my very first tide. "As the water drains out and comes into contact with the mud, the air cools it instantly, causing the ice to skim over the surface. It's called skim ice."

I would miss Berg's lessons. He knew so much about the bay and without realizing it had passed a million of those details on to me, from hidden obstacles that lay right beneath the mud to what the tide would do on any given day. I'd gotten to know this landscape like the back of my own hand. The channel marker that outlined Skip's lease.

The invisible boundaries of the cages when they weren't there. The herons, green crabs, horseshoe crabs, baby lobsters, and squid that inhabited our lease when we weren't out there to disturb them. I even had favorite sections, like the stretch of land that sat just north of our first row of cages. We'd picked it dry during dozens of tides, but every time I walked the length of it, I would always find an oyster. I picked up an oyster out of the mud near my feet and felt its weight in my palm. I'd finally come to understand that it wasn't just the fact that these little guys grew; it was the people who grew them. It was us, our hands and our efforts to raise them up from seed, to nurture and care for them, then leave them alone to grow before picking them at just the right size and shape. Our day-to-day work gave life to those oysters. Nothing more and nothing less.

Skip walked over a few minutes later as we finished up the last of our work. A full moon had risen up over the beach as the afternoon sun faded behind an ominous row of clouds. We were expecting snow.

It arrived the next morning, my final day on the farm and the last of the year. As it blanketed the deck of the float and our docks, Chris, Berg, and Will made a few final runs to the lease to get the last of our cages. December 31 and we were finally putting our equipment to bed. As A2 and I packed the last of our bags, he gave me a pre-office pep talk.

"Just don't go forgettin' where you came from, okay, Pain?" His time was coming to an end, too, making us both a little nostalgic for what we'd been through together. We celebrated my final day—and the fact that our cages were out of the water—with lunch at Tsang's, where over a huge platter of crab rangoon and pots of steaming hot tea we watched the snow fall on the world outside. I felt warm and satisfied, like being at home around my family's table. We belly-laughed our way through lunch, reminiscing about our crazy run together. We were a family now. But somehow, I knew it would never be like this again.

Oyster-Mussel Chowder with Pancetta, Sunchokes, and Almonds

Oysters are now a tradition at most holiday meals with my family. We usually order a bag of one hundred from Island Creek to be delivered wherever we're celebrating, whether that be Texas or North Carolina, and start the holiday meal with several dozen shucked on the half shell. We'll use another dozen or so for a cooked dish, then shuck more oysters for cocktail hour throughout the weekend. Everyone gets in on the shucking action and my mom and I continually search for ways to incorporate oysters into the meal. This year, we'll try this recipe, which was very generously provided by Chef Jody Adams of Rialto Restaurant in Cambridge.

> *2 tablespoons unsalted butter, divided*
> *1/2 cup peeled and thinly sliced sunchokes*
>   *(Jerusalem artichokes)*
> *Kosher salt and pepper*

½ tablespoon unbleached all-purpose
   flour
1½ cups almond milk
20 mussels
1 ounce pancetta, cut into ⅛-inch dice
1 cup thinly sliced leek rounds, rinsed
½ cup fennel, cut into ¼-inch dice
1 teaspoon minced garlic
1 cup white wine
¼ cup heavy cream
16 shucked oysters
4 Marcona almonds, toasted and chopped
4 teaspoons roughly chopped chervil

Melt 1 tablespoon butter in a small saucepan over medium-low heat. Add the sunchokes, season with salt and pepper, cover with parchment paper, and cook for 10 minutes or until tender. Add the flour, and cook 1 minute. Add the almond milk and cook until thickened, about 4 minutes. Puree the mixture in a blender until very smooth. Adjust seasonings, if necessary.

Next, wash the mussels and de-beard. Melt the remaining 1 tablespoon butter in a large sauté pan over medium heat. When the foam subsides, add pancetta and cook 3 minutes, or until rendered. Add the leeks, fennel, and garlic, season with pepper, cover with parchment, and cook 7 minutes or until tender. Add the mussels and white wine. Cover and steam open the mussels, about 5 minutes.

Remove the pan from the heat. Remove the mussels from the shells and discard the shells. Set the mussels aside in a bowl, discarding any that haven't opened.

To serve, put the pan with the mussel liquid back on a medium heat. Swirl the sunchoke puree into the mussel juices. Add the cream, oysters, and mussels and stir until the oyster edges have just started to curl and everything is hot. Ladle into 4 warm bowls. Garnish with almonds and chervil.

SERVES 4 AS AN APPETIZER

IV

Half Shell

*The outcome is a little luxury item, of
rather large economic consequence but no
great importance to the world's nourishment.
It should be.*

—Eleanor Clark, *Oysters of Locmariaquer*

CHAPTER ELEVEN

O.P.

Office life bore absolutely zero resemblance to life on the farm. Where three-inch rings and bulky gear dominated my former landscape, here sat fax machines, desks, and order. Familiar territory, yes. I'd worked in offices before. But my insides now bristled at the confined space. My first morning behind a desk had me craving the openness of the water. Cold or no cold.

To get to know my new surroundings, I poured myself some coffee and tried to settle in and observe. It was hectic and sometimes loud, which surprised me since very little seemed to actually be *happening*. The phone rang—which it did constantly—and Lisa, the farm's accounting pro and office manager, answered in a deep, singsongy voice:

"Island Creek, this is Lisa . . ." (short, throaty laugh)

"Hi, Vinny. What do you need today?" (pause)

"Two hundred to Great Eastern? Yup, we can do it." (pause, short laugh)

"Thanks, Vinny. Talk to you tomorrow." (click)

Then . . . "*CORYYYY!!!!* . . . Cory! I need two bags for Great Eastern," she shouted through a phone-based intercom connected to the shop, which sat fifty yards away. I could hear the blare of a whiny jam-band guitar careening through speakers that sat, evidently, directly next to the phone. Cory picked up and yelled something incoherent back at Lisa, who hung up and sighed heavily, muttering to herself.

The phone rang again and this time, Lisa was tied up on the other line. I picked it up after a few rings.

"Good morning, Island Creek . . ." I said uncertainly.

"Yeah, it's Sally at Shellfish Supply. Lisa there?"

"She's on the other line, can I—"

"Tell her we need five regulars over at Araho for tomorrow delivery. I also need twenty pounds of razors and does she have any Wellfleets?"

"Uh, Wellfleets? I, um . . ."

"Look, just the regular and razors. Thanks." Click.

I was scribbling down the order, still holding the receiver, when Lisa hung up her line and looked over at me.

"Who was it, Sally?"

"Yeah, she said something about regulars? Five, I think? And razors. Does she mean razor clams?"

Lisa looked at me, dumbfounded, then picked up the phone and made a call.

"Hi, Sally, it's Lisa. . . . Yeah. She's new. What do you need?"

I avoided the phones after that. I looked over at Matthew, the company's sales rep, who stared at his computer screen, oblivious to the phones, the other people in the room, and miraculously, the noise. Shore, who had temporarily moved his office into the conference room to make room for me, was nowhere to be found. Lisa appeared to be the only one in the room doing anything.

My office role was loosely defined. Shore had asked me to help out on the phones (which would take practice), help him with some marketing strategy ideas, and produce some content for the farm's ever-evolving Web site. Together, we outlined some specific duties, but for the most part, he said, I should see where I was needed and jump in when I felt comfortable.

Apparently that would take some time. Which I had plenty of, I realized, feeling the day draw on interminably. With little to no understanding of the order process or what I could do to help, I felt myself watching the clock, wondering what time everyone would break for lunch or when I could sneak out to visit the guys on the Oyster Plex. I broke up the hours reading through the company's customer list, then checking in with my sister, who was on her way to Indianapolis to pick up her newly born adopted daughter, my niece Gracyn.

Day Two went much the same way, with me avoiding the ever-ringing phones, scrolling through the company's Web site to see if there were updates I could make, and keeping track of my sister. That night, I went home and cried. This wasn't what I expected nor did it seem to give me any actual insight into the business of running an oyster farm. I couldn't tell from Lisa's clipped conversations or Cory's buzzing in and out where our oysters ended up or even how the office functioned. When I asked, I was given a few basic answers but not enough to give me a full picture. I felt useless.

Then, on day three, a bomb went off.

Shore texted me that morning to tell me to come in later in the afternoon. Skip needed my help with something that night so I should be prepared to stay down in Duxbury until late. He suggested I arrive around noon to balance out the hours. When I did saunter into the office, I found both Lisa and Cory sitting stone-faced at their computers. Matthew was nowhere to be seen.

"Is Matthew coming in today?" I asked.

"No," they stated firmly in unison. There were only a handful of desks in the room, so instead of setting up my laptop at Shore's, I sat down at Matthew's. A few minutes later, Skip walked through the front door and gave me a funny look.

"Moving right in, eh?" he asked. Lisa shot him a look.

"Shore hasn't told her yet," she said to Skip, who shrugged and walked back toward the conference room.

A minute later, Shore came out of the conference room.

"We had to let Matthew go this morning," he told me abruptly. "Things weren't working out between him and the company."

As stunned as I was by the news, I could see that Shore was a wreck. I found out later that it was the first time he or Skip had fired anyone. And with the wholesale team consisting of just five people, it was a fairly personal loss.

News traveled fast that morning as Shore, Skip, and Lisa made announcements to the growers and our customers, leaving me to play defense with anyone who called or came to the office looking for our former employee.

By now I was fully convinced that I'd made a horrible decision leaving my crew. Sure it was frigid out there and the work was backbreaking, but at least I didn't have to deal with office politics. The biggest drama of my crew's day had been what to eat for lunch and now here I was listening to speculation about the company's future, about other people's jobs, and about what Matthew had done wrong.

Trying to shake off the awkward vibe, I drove down to the water to check in on my crew. They'd already heard about Matthew, and I arrived to find Will and Chris gossiping about what could have gone wrong. They looked up from the cull and for a split second neither of them recognized me. My hair was down and instead of the bulky hooded coat I'd worn all fall, I was in a long black jacket and somewhat stylish winter boots. I'd also put on makeup.

"Office *Paaaain!*" Chris hooted, like I'd walked in wearing a bikini. "Can we call you O.P. for Office Pain?" he jabbed.

"Three days and you're already one of them," Will chimed in. I immediately pulled my hair back into a ponytail. Will handed me a pair of gloves, which I happily sunk my hands into, and I got busy sorting through oysters. I'd missed all kinds of great things, they informed me, like going out on the tide earlier in the week and A2's announcement that he'd be leaving the farm in February to move back to New Hampshire. They teased me about my new office persona

("Do you guys just sit around and drink coffee all day or what?") to which I tried to describe my boredom without revealing just how conflicted I felt about being there. Instead, I gave Will a hard time about his crazy hairdo (he hadn't cut it in months and without a hat on, he resembled a well-coiffed superhero) and got a report from Chris on how the oysters were coming up. Twenty minutes went by before I realized I needed to get back. The guys waved good-bye, howling at me to take off the makeup and come back to the crew.

I walked away with the feeling that I didn't really belong there, either. At least not dressed like this. And I dreaded going back to the office. But when I got there, I found that the mood had shifted. Skip was getting ready to entertain a houseguest that night and needed some help prepping for a big feast. His guest of honor? Chef Jonathan Benno from Per Se.

Per Se had been closed for a rare but lengthy renovation, giving Benno and his wife and daughter time to visit family up in Maine. Earlier that fall, Benno had announced to the public that he was leaving Per Se to open his own restaurant, which would live just a few blocks from his former employer's (it would eventually be called Lincoln). This trip would be one of the last he and his family would get before the madness of opening a new restaurant would take over his life; on their way back to New York, Benno decided to stop by Duxbury for his first visit to the farm. Skip, thrilled to have a top-notch chef in town to visit, suggested Benno stay with his parents, Nancy and Billy, and have dinner at his house.

Skip invited Shore, me, his close friends and neighbors Peter and Ligaya, our delivery driver CJ and his new girlfriend, Asia, and Nancy and Billy. When I returned to the office that afternoon, I found Skip standing in the kitchen with a piece of paper in hand, fretting about the menu. He wanted to keep it simple, he explained. A Caesar salad, spaghetti with clams, steamed lobsters, warm bread, and an easy dessert. All family style.

Looking for another excuse to get out of the office, I offered to grocery shop and then met him back at his house to coordinate the meal. He lived in a tiny, two-bedroom cottage that faced the water from a hillside. There was a gas-lit fireplace, a TV he never turned on, a small but cozy dining room, and signs of his two daughters, Samantha and Maya, everywhere. A wall inside the kitchen was marked from top to bottom with pencil tics and names, recording the height of his girls and every friend and family member who had ever visited (later that night Skip marked my five-foot-three height with a simple "ERock"). I set up shop inside his miniature kitchen, which was cluttered with mismatched glassware, cabinets bulging with pots and pans, and bottles of wine stashed in hidden corners, and got busy prepping the salad and a cheese plate.

Don Merry called just as Skip was setting the table (a mix of old forks, knives, and mismatched cloth napkins, which Skip called "farmer chic") to announce he'd just shot a duck. Could he swing by before dinner with some roasted duck? CJ called a few minutes later: He was going to stop by Coppa, a new restaurant opened by our friend Jamie Bissonnette and his partner, Chef Ken Oringer. Would Skip like some charcuterie to kick things off? If Skip had been worried about trying to impress a four-star chef, he didn't show it. And Benno was in for a treat.

When Benno, his family, and the other guests arrived, we gathered on the overstuffed couch and chairs in Skip's living room and dove into plates of charcuterie and cheeses, slivers of Don's freshly shot duck dipped in a raspberry jam, and a plate of freshly shucked clams and oysters. Chef Benno ate everything with gusto, plucking up bits of duck, then licking his fingers clean. Skip looked on, utterly pleased.

We sat down at Skip's crowded wooden table to platters of pasta that overflowed with tiny littleneck clams still salty from the bay, a gorgeous anchovy-dressed salad of torn romaine lettuce, and freshly steamed lobsters that glowed like embers in the middle of the spread. Benno gaped at the feast, taking in everything before him. He humbly thanked Skip for all of this hard work and immediately started passing the family-style platters. Halfway through the meal, he admitted that he rarely sat down to enjoy a meal, let alone one someone else offered to cook for him. This clearly meant the world to him.

Skip was in a celebratory mood all night. He opened a couple bottles of wine from his cellar—he'd been collecting wine for a decade—while his neighbor Peter presented the group with a 1988 Australian Cabernet. The cork crumbled a little when he opened it but we all savored a glass as he and his wife, Ligaya, regaled us with stories about smuggling the bottle home in a suitcase years earlier. Over dessert, Skip's mom, Nancy, who had a jovial personality, entertained us with stories about how she and Skip used to catch eels together when he was a kid.

At one point, I snuck into the kitchen to refill the salad bowl and found Skip opening another bottle of wine.

"How do you think it's going?" he whispered excitedly.

"Are you kidding? I think Benno's in awe," I replied.

"That's so great." He smiled. "I love this. I love having the house full, cooking for my friends. I don't do it enough anymore."

I looked out at the room and smiled. "Good thing you're opening a restaurant, too," I laughed.

Our dinner with Benno seemed to break any lingering negativity that hung over the office. The Island Creek Oysters Bar, which was now closer to becoming a reality, suddenly loomed on the horizon. The guys were now eager to get started.

I eventually fell into the rhythm of office life, learning to get used to the incessant phone, the zany back-and-forth between Lisa and Cory, and the open-door policy that had us welcoming visitors several times an hour. Working inside an old house came with perks like a fully working kitchen, where Skip would often cook up eggs and toast for breakfast and the fridge was always stocked with beers. The growers, especially, took advantage of the space, treating it like a clubhouse whenever they came in to pick up their weekly income checks or catch up on farm gossip. While I'd been introduced to them all out on the water, being in the office gave me a chance to see another, more relaxed side to them.

There was Christian, short and stocky with salt-and-pepper hair and a wry smile, who always came in with a story about his crew, a group of cut-ups and stooges. Gregg Morris would wander in holding a massive sixty-four-ounce mug of coffee ("I'm down to one cup a day," he'd quip) and shout out a ringing "How's it going, gang!" to anyone in the room. Scott Doyle, who ran a lease with his brother Brad, would lean against the doorway, one hand on his hip, and talk to Shore about golf or fill us in on the shenanigans of his two little boys, Scooter and Petey. Mike George liked to sit on the edge of a desk and talk about what he had planned for the landscaping around his house. Having worked in sales as a software implementation expert, he often asked how the business was running (but always reminded us how happy he was being on the water full-time). Mark Bouthillier, whose two kids, Van and Emmaline, shared his freckled face and reddish hair, would grab the nearest golf club (there were several lying around the office) and putt golf balls around the office's carpeted floor. Steve Gilbert, who the guys called Pogie, would offer a report on the bay or his two cents on the weather. Billy, who still sold lobster, oysters, and shrimp from his neighboring seafood shack, Bennett Lobster and Seafood, would drop in with hand-written messages for Lisa or to give us an update on the farm's six chickens, who lived in a coop on the side of the office. Sometimes he brought their fresh eggs in, still warm from the nest.

All of the growers had worked for the wholesale arm at some point, whether it was driving the truck into Boston every day like Mike George had or shucking oysters at a charity event to promote the brand. Before the company was incorporated and Lisa was hired, the growers often took turns working the phones to fill orders and load the truck for its daily deliveries. At that time, there was no office, just a phone set on top of some bookshelves inside a bathroom in Billy's seafood shack.

With the incorporation of the wholesale arm of Island Creek Oysters in 2007, Skip hired Shore and Lisa to handle all of the ordering and marketing, which freed the growers up to do what they did best: grow oysters. The two worlds were divided, with suits handling the money and boots doing the dirty work. It was a palpable divide by the time I got there, one that had actually grown somewhat tense that winter.

It was an especially tough season for the farmers, with frigid temperatures in January and February, which brought large swaths of ice to the bay (though it was nothing like that winter in 2005). Growers whose leases sat at the north end of the bay, closest to the Powder Point Bridge, were seeing a lot of oysters die off in their planting fields, most likely from the ice that was forming around the base of the bridge, then breaking off and drifting over the leases. Then came March, when we were hit with three weeks of horrendous rain, forcing two rain closures from the state within one single month—Billy and Pogie both called it "unheard of."

On top of the nasty weather, there were rumblings that the seed crop from the previous year, planted just before I got there, wasn't performing very well. Yields were down overall, meaning growers weren't getting nearly as many perfect oysters out of each cull as usual. The result was an oyster shortage, the consequences of which eventually trickled into the office and specifically down to Lisa. After years of having a surplus of oysters to move, she and Shore were suddenly forced to turn down orders. The farm had several tiers of customers, including wholesale customers (larger seafood houses that bought our oysters at wholesale prices, then sold them to restaurants or retailers at a marked-up rate), restaurants (the farm sold directly to chefs, as it had been doing since Skip took his first bag of oysters to the back door of Chris Schlesinger's East Coast Grill back in 2001), and household or retail customers (online business that shipped fresh oysters by the dozen overnight anywhere in the country). During the shortage, it became Lisa's job to determine whose order to fill and whose to deny.

In the midst of all of this, we got word of a catastrophe taking place in the Gulf of Mexico. The *Deepwater Horizon* oil rig exploded off the coast of Louisiana on April 20, two days before Earth Day. The explosion killed eleven men on the rig and then proceeded to dump millions of gallons of oil into the waters of one of the country's most productive seafood resources. The oyster industry, especially, was hit hard by the spill (oysters, unable to move, were one of the most vulnerable victims). Within weeks of the rig exploding, we started to get phone calls. Folks around the country were looking for oysters. And Island Creek couldn't provide them.

The stress felt by the growers probably went double for Lisa. As the first line of defense on the phone and with the company's customers, she was the one forced to explain the circumstances and to apologize on behalf of the company. She handled it gracefully, though, and vented her frustrations only momentarily.

Lisa's second in command, Cory, was forced to play bad cop. He fulfilled orders every day by tagging the bagged oysters with state-mandated shellfish tags and loading them onto the delivery trucks. But he was more than just a freight loader; Cory was certified by HACCP, an FDA-mandated food-safety system, and was responsible for keeping the entire operation up to the state's rigorous seafood wholesaling codes. Cory was the perfect person to do the job—he took it seriously, running quality-control checks on every bag of oysters that came to the shop. He also reprimanded growers or crews when they brought in oysters that weren't up to the company's standards. He and Lisa operated as a unit, shifting their attitudes daily based on what the growers were bringing in and how many orders they needed to fill.

For several weeks, interactions between Cory and the growers became tense as he cracked down on their cull (because there were fewer oysters, guys were getting looser about what they put into bags) yet demanded higher numbers from them. Shore stepped in frequently to moderate, reassuring the growers and the wholesale team that this was only a temporary blip. By summertime, when the next crop of oysters came online, the company would be back to operating at full speed.

Shore, meanwhile, was trying to keep the company's marketing strategy on track. He often used the winter months to seek out new and unique opportunities for the company's brand, and this year, he and Skip had decided to work with Harpoon Brewery to launch the brewery's first oyster stout. The idea sprang, naturally, over beers and oysters. Shore, Skip, and a few of the guys from Harpoon were out for drinks one night and Shore asked if there was a beer that went best with oysters. One of the brewers said that indeed there was. Oyster stout was traditionally an old British style of ale, dry and full-bodied, made to stand up to the briny crispness of oysters on the half shell. Harpoon's brewers did some research and found an article by famed beer guru Michael Jackson that stated that as early as the 1700s, when oysters were as abundant as salty bar snacks are today, porters and stouts were the drink of choice to go with a plate of bivalves. Guinness made entire ad campaigns around the partnership. Much later, around the early 1900s, oysters were added to the brew itself, which Harpoon thought made a lot of sense.

The two small, local companies decided a partnership was in order and Harpoon put an oyster stout on their brew schedule. Brewer Katie Tame (a sweet and serious curly-haired twenty-something who was, at the time, Harpoon's only female brewmaster) started experimenting with recipes in which she could incorporate freshly shucked Island Creeks. The one she settled on put oyster meat directly into the kettle in what was called the mash. The meat would disintegrate under the roaring heat of the boil but it would leave behind a lot of protein and just a hint of briny minerality.

As the brewery process got under way, Shore and I worked on setting up launch parties and industry events so that we could introduce the beer to the restaurants that served our oysters. It was a special release for Harpoon, part of their 100 Barrel Series, meaning it would only be available for a limited run. More important, it was an opportunity for Island Creek to expand its reach from just a small oyster brand to a well-established seafood presence, one that contributed to Boston's food culture. This wasn't just about selling oysters (which they most likely would). It was about giving Island Creek's brand culinary cachet.

On Brew Day, Katie had Skip, Shore, and me down to Harpoon's South Boston facility to help shuck the oysters: 180 for every batch of beer (they were brewing three batches). A few weeks later, we returned to the brewery for bottling day, where, under the clank and roar of the bottling machine, we tried our first taste of Katie's concoction. It was chocolatey at first, then smoky, roasty, and dry. Inhaling the sweet, malty brew, I swore I could smell the ocean on the beer. Skip, who, like the rest of us, wondered just how good a beer brewed with oysters could taste, looked genuinely surprised to discover that it was delicious.

We helped the bottling team secure gold foil caps to each twenty-two-ounce bottle (all of the 100 Barrel Series beers were sold as large-format bottles) before heading out with a few sample bottles to try with some oysters. We smuggled a growler of the stout into Eastern Standard, asked the bartender for some glassware for our contraband, and tasted it with a few dozen Island Creeks. The two turned out to be a perfect match. The oysters themselves actually enhanced the minerality of the beer, rounding out the stout's smoky sweetness. They didn't compete; neither outshone the other. The two flavors just mingled and inter-twined on the palate, leaving a long, pleasant taste of each.

For several weeks in February, we hosted dinners, we threw parties, we shucked oysters, and we drank our fair share of stout. The beer was a huge success. Restaurants couldn't get it fast enough and in just three weeks, the brewery was sending out its very last kegs. It was the fastest-selling 100 Barrel Series they'd ever pulled off.

There wasn't much time for us to recover from it, though. Island Creek was headed to Miami for its first ap-pearance at a major food festival. The farm hired my friend Nicole, of All Heart PR (she'd been essential in promoting the Oyster Fest) as their publicist. Her goal was to give the company exposure on a national level. Up there with the ranks of Aspen's annual Food & Wine Classic and the New York City Wine & Food Festival, the South Beach Wine & Food Festival is one of the country's elite foodie events, featuring a host of chefs (both actual ones and TV ones—Rachael Ray hosts her own Burger Bash annually). Setting up the Island Creek raw bar there would put the farm in front of dozens of renowned chefs (potential customers), some heavy-hitting members of the press (potential public-ity), and a new contingent of oyster lovers (potential prof-its). Not to mention, it would get them on the beaches of Miami in the dead of winter. Graciously, Shore asked me to tag along.

A few days before the trip, we said good-byes to both A2, who was leaving the farm to move to New Hampshire (I made him promise to visit often) and to Berg, who was on his way to Africa with Skip. (Though he was disappointed to miss the Miami trip, Skip was eager to get the foundation's first project off the ground.) Berg had managed to extract himself from all of his farmwork, handing the reins over to Skip's two remaining crew members, Chris and Will, and had packed up his life for a ten-week stay on the other side of the world. Aside from the anxiety of travel and relocating to a remote island, Berg was eager for the trip. Skip and grower John Brawley, who was also headed over to represent the farm, would stay in Africa for only a few weeks, leaving Berg there to work on building the shellfish hatchery. Over the course of the lengthy and sometimes frustrating trip, he sent us reports on his adventures, tracking the hatchery's slow but steady progress for everyone back home.

I, meanwhile, prepared for our adventure in Miami. My companions, Shore, CJ (who brought his girlfriend, Asia), Nicole, and I would be shucking and schmoozing with the culinary masses for four days. We were on a tightly packed schedule, similar to Nantucket, setting up the oyster boat at three events over the course of thirty hours. With each event we had the same agenda: Get Island Creeks into the mouths of any and every big culinary name we came across . . . and then hand them a free T-shirt.

We hit the jackpot our first night there. It was a chef-only afterparty hosted by American Express inside the lobby of the swanky Tides Hotel. We were one of just a few food purveyors on site, and within minutes of the party starting, the ever-attractive raw bar was swarmed with culinary superstars. One of our first guests was prolific restaurateur Drew Nieporent, owner of Nobu and Tribeca Grill, who raved about the oysters before launching into a story about how he had brought oysters home for his wife on Valentine's Day but realized too late he didn't have a shucking knife.

"I had to use a cheese knife to open them. I just about killed myself!" he roared, getting a laugh from everyone in the room. Joe Bastianich, wine guru and partner to another culinary über-personality, Mario Batali, who co-owns big-name spots like Lupa, Del Posto, and Babbo, sidled up beside Nieporent and sucked back a dozen of our oysters, then returned later to take at least a half-dozen more. Around us, the room filled in with a host of other stars: the cast of the Food Network's *Ace of Cakes,* including punky pastry chef Duff Goldman and his cute, hipster redhead cohort, Mary Alice Yeskey (who immediately threw on an Island Creek T-shirt over her party dress); spiky-haired blond chef Anne Burrell from *Secrets of a Restaurant Chef*; Boston chef Ken Oringer with an entourage of friends; chef Ryan Hardy from Aspen's Little Nell resort; and Ming Tsai, host of TV's *Simply Ming* and a close friend of the farm.

What we weren't expecting was a very special appearance from superchef Daniel Boulud, who, during one of his swings through the party, jumped behind the raw bar to shuck oysters with us. I'd seen the petite French chef's picture plastered in magazines and read about his rise from life as a country boy in Lyon through the kitchens of France, and I'd eaten at his respected New York City restaurant, db Bistro Moderne, which features a succulent, outrageously priced truffle-stuffed burger. Once, when I was working at *Boston* magazine, I covered the James Beard Awards—dubbed the culinary Oscars—and during the award ceremony's rowdy afterparty, I found myself close enough to the bar that when Boulud stood on top of it to spray the crowd with a magnum of Champagne, I got hit with the spray. Boulud was a party animal whose presence at fetes like this turned the crowd from vaguely entertained to hog wild.

And here he was, standing behind our raw bar shucking oysters.

Wearing a collared shirt unbuttoned to show a bit of skin, Boulud nudged his way in between Ken Oringer, who was now standing behind the boat (a superstar in his own right, Ken knew how to draw an audience), and me. With a flourish, the French chef grabbed a shucking knife and an oyster and proceeded to demonstrate for the now massive crowd how he opened oysters. The man was fast but not very precise as he flung oyster shells wildly into the audience. On the other side of Boulud, Oringer stood by, egging the superchef on.

"Come on, Chef, I know you can shuck faster than that," he urged. Boulud laughed and in his lilting French accent, replied, "I don't want to hurt anyone!"

It was surreal, like standing next to the president, or a paparazzi-hounded A-lister. He was the brightest presence in the room. And he was a riot.

Shore and I leaned over Boulud's shoulder to watch his method. He put the tip of the knife through the side of the oyster—a slightly more dangerous but super-quick opening—and flicked the meat away from the shell with a flourish.

"Easy to shuck, these oysters," he declared after opening a pile. He slurped one back and closed his eyes, letting out a long hum of approval. A minute later, he was holding up his hand, declaring he'd cut his finger. We, and the audience, applauded the chef as he disappeared into the crowd.

"Holy crap. Daniel *fucking* Boulud just shucked our oysters," Shore said to me as we got busy refilling the raw bar. I grinned and patted him on the back. "Not bad for a little oyster farm from Duxbury," I replied.

The party didn't wrap up until almost two A.M., at which point we had to move the boat over to another hotel for an early brunch the next morning. After gathering up the boat and all of our goods, we walked the boat through the lobby and out onto Collins Avenue, Miami's main drag. Despite the crazy-late hour of night, the sidewalks were mobbed. CJ, who looked like an urban cowboy with his long blond hair breezing around his shoulders, and Shore, ever the clean-cut prepster, each held an end of the boat and marched it through the crowd. They were stopped no less than ten times for people wanting to snap pictures.

It was well past four A.M. when we stumbled back to our own hotel, but after a quick nap and turnaround, we were back in action by ten A.M., setting up for brunch with Chef Michelle Bernstein at the Delano Hotel. One of the founders of Miami's burgeoning culinary scene, Michelle is a sassy, passionate woman who not only adores the Latin cuisine she feeds her city but the city itself. She advocates for Miami whenever she can, appearing on TV, showing up in magazines, and cooking at guest events like this. She also knows Skip from a trip he'd made to Miami years ago—it was clear that she had a special place in her heart for the New England oyster grower. She greeted Shore and CJ warmly and quickly embraced Nicole, Asia, and me just for being part of the crew.

Unfortunately, while the raw bar had been a perfect fit at the chefs' afterparty, it stood out for doing the opposite at the Dolce Brunch. The much smaller, seated luncheon featured a very brief opening reception where guests mingled just outside the dining room as they waited for brunch to start. We shucked enough oysters to fill the raw bar but quickly realized that the guests, who mainly hailed from Miami or other parts of South Florida, were not interested in eating oysters at ten A.M. A few courageous souls approached the raw bar excitedly to drip Michelle's strawberry-and-black-pepper mignonette over the half shells, but for the most part, we were left with a raw bar half full of oysters, which we took back into the kitchen for the staff to enjoy.

From there, we moved on to another late-night event inside the striking Setai Hotel. Ming Tsai, the owner of Wellesley's Blue Ginger restaurant and charismatic star of public television's *Simply Ming,* was hosting the festival's rowdy Dim Sum Disco, where guests grabbed light bites and snacks from a lineup of chefs stationed around the hotel's open kitchen. We were completely in our element there as guests lingered at the raw bar, took photos, and generally adored our oysters. CJ and Shore helmed the raw bar, where Ming had set out a number of Asian-influenced mignonettes while Nicole and I stood off to the side to shuck oysters for the servers who were passing them out to the crowd. As the night carried on, Ming grew more and more animated, getting us to dance for the crowd while the staff brought over an endless supply of cocktails.

We wrapped up the night and the weekend at a tiny bodega near our hotel, drinking cold beers on the patio. Nothing, not even Nantucket, had prepared us for the whirlwind that was Miami. But we'd taken full advantage of every opportunity, getting the oysters and the Island Creek brand in front of hundreds of people. For Shore, that made it completely worth the trip.

We returned to the farm to find snow still on the ground but turned a hopeful eye toward spring. My one-year anniversary came and went uneventfully but I noticed the same weather patterns emerging—cold, damp, and foggy mornings. But besides those weeks of torrential rain in March, we were blessed with a quick and painless end to winter and a promisingly warm month of April. Spirits were lifting as the growers saw signs of their oyster crops perking up and started to place their orders for that year's seed.

We were also, finally, moving forward with opening the restaurant. After several months' delay, the construction team was ready to demolish the existing space (formerly a restaurant called Great Bay) and start constructing the new interior. Skip and Shore had looped me into the plans, offering a peek of what was to come. The restaurant would occupy a huge space with seating for up to 180 people. There would be a massive bar complete with a raw bar set right in the center of the restaurant and a spacious dining room and lounge. All of this was agreed upon by Skip, Jeremy

Sewall, and their third partner, Garrett Harker, proprietor of Eastern Standard and a veteran of restaurant management. G, as he was dubbed, brought an incredible amount of knowledge to the team. In fact, he was the main reason the project had gotten off the ground.

Discussion of Island Creek opening a restaurant had started long before I arrived. Originally, Skip thought about opening a tiny oyster bar somewhere in Boston's Beacon Hill. Something small, informal, and jewel-like that would serve oysters and beers. Some time later, Shore met Garrett at a swanky foodie event and the two hit it off. Shore casually mentioned that the farm had always wanted to open a restaurant and Garrett, apparently, took note.

Around the time I joined the farm, the restaurant Great Bay, which Jeremy had originally opened years before and then left, announced it was closing. It sat within the Hotel Commonwealth, a stately newish building that took up one whole block of Kenmore Square smack in the center of the city. Eastern Standard, Garrett's beautiful and very popular brasserie, was in that same hotel and had, unlike Great Bay, found a loyal and voracious audience. When Great Bay closed, the hotel's owners turned to Garrett to see if he was interested in taking over the space. Garrett immediately thought back to his conversation with Shore.

There were some long discussions between Garrett and the farm as the guys weighed the consideration. Skip ran the idea past his pal Jeremy to get an industry veteran's perspective and quickly realized that one of his closest friends in the chef community would actually be a great fit for the new restaurant's team. Eventually, he, Jeremy, and Garrett formed an agreement: They would partner up to open the Island Creek Oyster Bar inside the old Great Bay space, bringing a taste of the oyster farm life into the city.

A lot of planning had already taken place by the time I came to the table, including the architectural design, specific design elements, and a sense of the menu and concept. I wasn't sure how I could help the team at first, having had no experience opening restaurants, but Shore pulled me into the planning discussions and I quickly found my place. What they needed was to capture the story of this restaurant, to gather everyone's thoughts into a fully formed concept that would help the staff, and later consumers, understand what this restaurant was all about. I could help them write it.

Our first big sit-down took place in March, one of the final days before Great Bay was torn down and gutted. I sat at a long table along with Garrett, Skip, Shore, Jeremy, his business partner Ron Vale, our publicist Nicole as well as Eastern Standard's publicist Marlo Fogelman, the restaurant's bar director Jackson Cannon, and the oyster bar's general manager Tom Schlesinger-Guidelli. From Garrett on down the line, I was looking at some of Boston's most notable restaurant players. Nicole and Marlo each controlled their own powerful corners of Boston's culinary media. Jackson, who was the bar director at Eastern Standard and often credited for helping launch the city's recently surging cocktail culture, sat next to Tom, who was the nephew of one of Boston's most notable culinary godfathers, Chris Schlesinger, and an up-and-coming fixture in his own right. It was a brilliant team, one that crackled with dynamic personalities and had the potential to influence the city. It was the start of something powerful.

We talked about restaurants, our restaurant, in a way I'd never experienced. It was an intense, esoteric discussion about what we wanted the space to feel like, how we wanted the diners to perceive the experience, and about our beliefs in food and how that would translate on the menu. Garrett challenged us to think beyond the restaurants we'd experienced in the past and create something completely unique, something that didn't exist yet. It wasn't just about the design, the menu, or the reservation system. It was about building a concept from scratch.

Telling the story turned out to be the easy part. There was a farmer, a chef, and a restaurateur, all three of whom had honed and perfected their respective crafts. Together, they would create a space where diners could get to know everyone who had a hand in growing their food, from the oyster farmer to the dairy farmer to the winemaker. It was to be a new kind of farm-to-table restaurant where the farm not only existed in the same space as the table but actually stood front and center in the dining room—Shore, Skip, Chris, and a few of the growers were going to be at the restaurant, working the floor or shucking oysters behind the raw bar nightly.

There were struggles, of course. The three-way partnership involved massive contracts and legal documents, which Skip and Shore pored through for almost six months before forging a final deal. There were construction delays both at the beginning and throughout the process as the scope of the project widened and the space transformed from an idea into the hard reality of materials, timing, and permits. The most unexpected challenge came down to the farm itself as Skip struggled to embrace such a sweeping change for the little company he'd founded all those years ago.

Island Creek had matured tremendously since those first hardscrabble days before upwellers, the Oyster Plex, or a brand name existed. It had evolved on the backs of Skip and the other growers who worked tirelessly to bring consistently perfect oysters out of the water twelve months a year. It had been recognized as a locally supported, family-run, small-town operation. It had thrived thanks to a small band of fiercely loyal restaurant chefs who believed in the product and the guys behind it. Opening a restaurant would be the company's first major growth spurt.

Weathering a firestorm of attention, scrutiny, and criticism would challenge any small business. But for Skip, who was now about to compete with his own customers, in the middle of the city that helped build Island Creek into the brand it had become, this was personal. He fretted about the speed with which his humble little oyster farm would be launched into the glare of the city's spotlight. More than anything, he wanted Island Creek to maintain its own identity. To be the oyster farm—and product—it had always been and to celebrate the guys who had gotten it there. It might be a more grown-up version of itself, but he wanted to be certain that the core of the company never changed.

To help transition the company from small-time oyster farm to a restaurant-owning brand, Shore and I worked on creating the company's mission statement, a sentiment that had been floating in the ether since Skip started way back when but had never existed on paper. We came up with this:

> Island Creek Oysters exists as a place where people can look forward to coming to work every day. From there, it is all of our jobs to change the way people think about seafood. We do this by creating a unique user platform (wholesalers, chefs, consumers) that consists of the highest-quality products, an unparalleled commitment to the farmers and fisherman we work with, and education for all. Through this effort we can enrich our own lives, as well as those of the people we work with and who eat our food.

Establishing the company's purpose helped Skip look ahead and define the role of the farm in a larger context. It also opened the door to create a new brand image for the farm, one that was current yet still reflected what the guys considered to be their core values. The simple, rustic old logo needed an update.

The first time we sat down to discuss ideas for a new logo, Skip admitted that the green, somewhat basic font that spelled out "Island Creek" was, in his opinion, ugly. But still, he'd become attached to it.

"We used it because it was all we had. I think someone drew it on a napkin at a bar and the idea just stuck," he explained. "But, then we got our first delivery truck and the first thing we did was put the logo on the side of it. I remember seeing it for the first time and feeling so proud of what we'd created. It was a huge deal to me." He would have a hard time letting it go. But as the three of us talked through his feelings and weighed all of the potential downfalls that might come with this monumental next step, Skip slowly turned from skeptic to believer.

For me, it was thrilling to see this small business, whose purpose and roots were so firmly planted, grapple with the adjustments of change. I found myself playing therapist to Skip's concerns, strategist to Shore's development ideas, and key decision maker within a very small team. My opinion mattered and my ideas were valued. No longer just a farmhand or Skip's seed girl, I was on the very inside track of what was already a close-knit circle.

In the meantime, summer was nearing. Skip was putting his seed program in place—with a bigger order and an additional upweller, as promised. And Shore and I were now entrenched in Oyster Fest plans. After a few persuasive discussions, he'd convinced me to take over as festival director this year, working by his side to officially run the show.

So between managing Skip's 12 million baby oysters, planning a three-thousand-person party, and weighing in on the forthcoming restaurant, I was, like any small business employee, wearing every hat possible—and I found myself enjoying every minute.

Berg returned from Africa with not only some incredible stories but a newfound appreciation for farmwork. He was ready to whip his crew back into shape and gear up for another busy summer. Chris, meanwhile, had started working in the office full-time. I happily handed over the marketing duties I'd very lightly managed and focused solely on getting ready for the seed season and festival planning. I made an agreement with Skip and Shore to budget my time throughout the summer, putting in full weeks on the farm when I was needed but then working in the office as often as necessary to make sure the festival came together. It would be another whirlwind summer—but this time, I knew exactly what I was in for.

Ming Tsai's Grilled Oysters with Garlic Black Pepper Sauce

Chef Ming Tsai is a total character. Charismatic, larger than life, and incredibly friendly, he's also got a mischievous side, which the ICO boys love. But he's a tireless worker and gives his time and energy to a number of worthwhile causes, including the Island Creek Oyster Festival. He served this dish to three thousand fans at the festival in 2010.

Grilled Oysters

2 dozen Island Creek Oysters in the shell, rinsed and cleaned

1 cup black pepper–garlic sauce (see below)

1 cup tomato concassé, (peeled, seeded, and cut into 1/4-dice)

1/2 cup scallions, green parts sliced thin

Preheat grill. Place oysters on grill, deeply curved side down, cover, and grill until they open. Once opened, remove top shell, leaving the oyster meat in the bottom shell for serving. Spoon 1 tablespoon of the black pepper–garlic sauce mixture over each oyster. Garnish with tomatoes and scallions. Serve and enjoy.

Garlic Black Pepper Sauce

MAKES 1½ CUPS

2 tablespoons grapeseed oil or canola oil

10 garlic cloves, thinly sliced

½ cup scallions, white and green parts,
    cut ⅛-inch thick

1½ heaping teaspoons medium-ground
    black pepper

1 cup dry white wine

1 cup homemade chicken broth or
    low-sodium canned chicken broth

1 tablespoon fish sauce (nam pla)

Juice of ½ lemon

4 tablespoons (½ stick) unsalted butter,
    cut into 1-tablespoon pieces

Heat a wok or large sauté pan over high heat. Add the oil and swirl to coat the pan. Add the garlic and stir-fry until soft, about 30 seconds. Add the scallions and black pepper, and stir. Add the wine, broth, fish sauce, and lemon juice and cook until the liquid is reduced by half, about 2 minutes. Transfer the mixture to a blender and blend on high speed to purée. With the machine running, add the butter to form a creamy sauce. Use immediately or store until ready to use.

SERVES 4

CHAPTER TWELVE

PART-TIME PAIN

Like most food systems, oyster farming is cyclical. Spring begets seed, seed begets upwellers, upwellers beget the nursery, and so on. I had that first tingle of déjà vu the moment we arrived on Nantucket for that year's wine festival. It wasn't exactly the same—new faces like Chris, who was learning the ropes as the farm's new marketer; Nicole, who was there to help us shuck and schmooze; and various significant others were sprinkled among the group—but I had the sense that history was primed to repeat itself. Nantucket begets mischief and mischief begets memories.

We were scheduled to shuck at many of the same events as last year, starting with the White Elephant demo where, this time, Skip was entirely at ease thanks to a new set of stage cohorts including Jasper White, the white-haired, bespectacled chef of the Summer Shack, and our friend

Angela Raynor from the Pearl. The three bantered with the audience while the shuckers—myself, Chris, and Shore included—toasted our arrival to the weekend.

The Raynors had opened their ceviche restaurant, Corazón del Mar, so we made our way over after the demo to try out Seth's new menu. By now, I was fully enamored with his style of cooking; by opening a Latin-inspired restaurant he'd completely stolen my gustatory heart.

I've always been smitten with Mexican food. When I was twelve, my father's job transferred us to Mexico City, where for almost four years we lived the grand life of an expat family. The city was loud, massive, and completely foreign but I loved the energy immediately. As soon as my sister and I were old enough to move around the city unsupervised, we'd spend afternoons after school at a divey, hole-in-the-wall taqueria near our house where we indulged in the nation's ritualistic, two P.M. late-lunch *comida*. I'd order a trio of tacos *al pastor,* which the chatty, mustached chefs would shave from a fragrant hunk of spit-grilled pork hanging in the open kitchen, and top with diced onions, cilantro, bits of pineapple, and a squeeze of *limón.*

At Corazón, Seth not only captured those exact flavors from my youth, he brought me back to it. We sat on the second floor around a colorful and authentically decorated bar (punched-tin ornaments and blown glassware lined the shelves) and ordered platters of tacos *al pastor* made from a deliciously classic spit-roasted pork, and tacos *de lengua* filled with the smoky chew of braised beef tongue. Made with fresh corn tortillas, bits of pineapple, and flecks of cilantro, the *al pastor* was precisely what I remembered:

char, sweetness, salt, and juice. I savored each transportive bite and eventually, of course, ordered more.

History did repeat itself in many ways. Late nights followed by early mornings and hours and hours of shucking behind the raw bar. Another family-style feast at the Pearl and a romp through the island's favorite booze hall, the Chicken Box. Will spent yet another night at the Jared Coffin House with a drunken companion. And we added another shucking event to our rotation, setting up the oyster boat inside the Straight Wharf Restaurant, which sat waterside near the town's hub. Owned by a lovely pair of chefs named Gabriel Frasca and Amanda Lydon, the restaurant was known as both Nantucket's hardest fine-dining reservation as well as its wildest pick-up scene. By the time we started shucking, the crowd was a rowdy, drunken mass slurping oysters and free wine like it was the end of time. Skip deemed it the biggest "shitshow" he'd ever witnessed— a high honor indeed.

The festival itself brought the same entertaining set of Nantucket Red–clad tipplers as well as many of the same deliciously oyster-worthy wines. Dave came down to join us this year for our last night on the island and he and I spent Sunday afternoon basking in the sun on the Nantucket Yacht Club lawn. Afterward, the party moved to the Boarding House patio where Dave took part in the Island Creek tradition: Dark and Stormy cocktails, oysters by the boatload, characters, and laughter.

"I think I get why you love this so much," he said as we wandered the cobblestoned streets at the end of the day.

"All you guys do is shuck, party, and hang out with cool people," he mused.

"Yup," I nodded. "Not such a bad life, huh?"

"I doubt you'll ever want to leave," he responded.

Back in Duxbury, the farm crew was trickling back together. I hadn't been out on the water since December and after all those months wading through the rhythms of office life, I was itching to get back outside. My first day back was also Maggie's. She'd finished up her year at school and had already committed to another full-year program, this one at Boston University. Within minutes of settling into the Oyster Plex, we were catching up on all that we'd missed in each other's lives. She had a new boyfriend; I caught her up on the restaurant plans. I was sad to report that Catie wouldn't be back this year, but Pops, Eva, and Quinn would; we'd also gained new faces like Michelle, a young University of New Hampshire student, Matt Titus (just Titus for short), who would eventually transition up to the shop, and Gardner, Shore's best friend growing up who'd recently left his job at a financial firm (our crew was turning into the Neverland for real-world dropouts).

The camaraderie and energy of the crew flowed easily but I struggled to feel fully immersed—because of my arrangement with Skip and Shore, I was now splitting my time between the water and the office. My first week back was spent running back and forth between the two worlds: culling in the morning, then answering e-mails all afternoon.

Having to mentally shift gears every few hours kept tripping me up.

In late May we had a long string of drainer tides, which called for a three A.M. wake-up call one morning. At four-thirty, we were all on the dock, where Berg greeted everyone with a new pair of waders. I pulled mine on, inhaling the fresh wader smell, and wondered how long it would take to get them muddied and leaking. Out on the tide, they bobbed softly against my legs as I traversed the muddy expanse. I caught up with Will while we picked.

"Not sure if it's the weather or water temperatures, but the snail eggs weren't nearly as bad this year," he observed. Being on the tide with Will brought me right back to the winter, and I shuddered to think about frozen fingers and toes. But we were looking at a long stretch of sunny days, a more pleasant beginning than last year.

After the tide, I scooted up to the office to sit in on a meeting with Shore and Chris, who both laughed at my getup. My baseball cap was slick with mud, I had a dark line of dirt caking my arms, and I stank like sweat and seawater.

"Good to be back?" Shore laughed. After our meeting, I ran back down to the water to cull. I stood at the table with Will, Maggie, and Pops, where we dove into a conversation about my new, competing roles. I tried to downplay the impact it was having on my concentration but the truth was, running around made me distracted. My mind wandered off to the festival plans. We were having a committee meeting that night that I was supposed to lead but hadn't prepared for. My list of to-dos was growing by the second and part of me felt like I was wasting time being on the water. I slipped away during a late-afternoon coffee break, telling Berg that I had to get back for some meeting prep.

"No worries, Pain. Anytime you need to cut out, just let me know," he said, to my surprise. I was expecting an eye roll or some muttered comment about being a suit. Instead, he actually looked sympathetic—a trait I could only attribute to his time over in Africa.

"Comin' out on the tide tomorrow? We're headed out at four forty-five A.M.," he said casually as I gathered my things. Crap. The tide. I'd forgotten. I was already stuck in Duxbury that night for a festival meeting, which meant I wouldn't get home until nine P.M. A three A.M. turnaround seemed impossible. Maggie chimed in from behind me.

"You're welcome to stay at my place," she offered. During the summers, she lived at her parents' house, less than a mile from the harbor on Washington Street. I took her up on it and told her I'd be by after my meeting. Berg gave me a fist bump before tossing out, "Good to have you back, Pain."

The festival meeting went smoothly despite my lack of preparation. My job was to refine the event overall, which meant, of course, that every question that came up and decision to be made came down to Shore and me. My head ached by the time it was over. What exactly had I signed up for?

The following morning, I woke up at 4:30 A.M., giving myself just enough time to pull on an old sweatshirt and yesterday's shorts. I'd slept in Maggie's older brother's room, where outside one of the windows a cacophony of birds chirped wildly before my alarm went off. Maggie and I met in the galley kitchen of her parents' beautiful old cottage, smiling sleepily over our commitment to this maddening summer schedule.

"Can you believe we're at it again?" I asked, inhaling the steam off my coffee.

"It's good to be back." She smiled, pulling her wispy hair into a loose ponytail. "And seriously, please consider this your second home this summer," she added. "You're welcome anytime."

It was an offer I couldn't pass up. Dave and I had agreed that in order to make this summer work, I would occasionally need to spend a few nights in Duxbury. The extra sleep would help me cope with the crazy hours and in the long run, would help me keep that work-life balance I so desperately needed. It was just a few short months, I reminded him. A few nights away from each other would probably help us in the long run.

Maggie and I met the rest of the crew on the docks, where Berg was waiting with a boat full of crates and buckets. The sky was still dark enough that we could see a few stars as we pulled out to the tide. Despite the hour, the crew was in good spirits. Berg announced that we would be picking around the edges of the lease in order to clean it up for a new seed crop, just like we'd done on the opposite field the summer before. Being out on the lease brought home just how serious our oyster shortage had been. The field looked almost empty. We got to work picking oysters quickly through the morning as the world woke up around us. By the time the tide was coursing over my shins, we were stacking the crates into neat piles and loading up the boat. I did a quick count in my head. Twenty crates would get us around eighty or ninety bags, enough to finish our number for the week. Berg watched as I did the count in my head.

"Haven't lost your oyster math, have you?" he joked. "Think we've got enough?"

"Yup." I nodded confidently. "Should be around eighty bags."

He nodded back with a quick "Let's hope so."

As we swung the boat around to its perch along the dock, I saw Skip walking through the parking lot, carrying a drill under one arm. He waved to our group and pointed toward the other dock. The upwellers were going in.

I ran over to join him and found him lying facedown on the dock, his head submerged in the upweller's rectangular hole. He was securing a silo into place with wing nuts and asked me to give him a hand. Without thinking, I jumped into the trough, feeling the still-chilly water rush over my knees and skim the bottom of my mud-splattered shorts. I held the box in place as he inserted the bolt and screwed it onto the trough, happy to be back in my element.

Berg walked over to see if he could help. Skip had the two of us put the rest of the boxes in place while he ran up to collect his seed. The packets had arrived that morning. He reappeared a few minutes later carrying a white Styrofoam box filled with tenderloin-size packages of the season's first seed. Once again, a group of onlookers gathered around us to watch the babies go in. Chris had taken a break from the office to videotape the seed's arrival, and Gregg Morris stood to the side, fresh off the tide in a pair of worn-out waders, holding his own box of seed.

Skip did the honors with the first packet, lowering the seed down into the water gingerly. Berg kneeled next to him and watched as the seed sank slowly to the bottom. I'd noticed that Berg had taken a growing interest in the seed and thought back to last summer. Back then, he'd been very hands-off with the seed crew and, to our dismay, rarely offered to help until the boxes bulged with fully grown seed. This year, he seemed genuinely interested, and I guessed it was so that he could take that knowledge and apply it to the project in Africa.

With a grand gesture, Skip turned the upweller switch on and we watched the water churn over the baby oysters. Skip gave me a knowing grin.

"Okay, you know what to do, right?" he asked.

I beamed confidently. It was time to take care of the babies.

A week later, the seed program was in full swing. As promised, Skip had installed a fourth upweller and given me the reins to run a larger seed crew. I recruited Eva, who was newly graduated from Brown and on her way out into the real world, as well as our newest crewmate, Michelle, who had just finished her freshman year at UNH; she was majoring in eco-gastronomy, a program that didn't exist until a few years ago (it made me want to re-enroll as a college freshman). And we pulled Maggie onto the team, giving me an easygoing group to direct. We immediately got into the routine of washing the seed every morning. A few days into the process, Berg stopped me on the dock and asked if I needed a hand.

"I want the crew to be more unified, to really work together this year," he explained. "So whatever you need help with. Lifting silos, grading, whatever. Just tell me and I'll get the guys to pitch in."

Thankful for the offer, I asked if they could help us each morning by pulling the silos which would free Eva and me to start washing right away. He gave me a fist bump and agreed with a kindly "Whatever you need, Pain."

And just like that, we found our rhythm. The guys fumbled through the various upweller call signs at first ("Is this eleven or twelve?" or "Did you pull that one from spot twenty-eight?") and grumbled as they maneuvered around the rowing crews, who were back on the docks for their early-morning class schedule. But the work was over within minutes, leaving the entire morning for my team to get to work.

Because we'd added that fourth upweller and had more seed, I kept diligent track of what went into every silo in the seed bible and made sure the girls were explicit when it came to what was moving where. I wanted to stay completely on track this year—no fucking up.

The weather made things much easier this time around. By the first week of June it was warm enough to wear shorts and T-shirts, a feat we hadn't accomplished until July the year before. Those high, early temperatures warmed the bay water quickly, actually advancing the oyster's growing cycle by several weeks. It wasn't just on the water. Summer came early everywhere; food crops like tomatoes and squash came out of the ground weeks early while schools of striped bass and herring got a head start on their migration. Farmers everywhere were calling it a record year—and not always for the best. If last year was the Summer That Wasn't, this year would be the Summer That Went by Too Fast.

For our oyster seed, the explosive growth came so rapidly that we were grading by the middle of June. Skip called me on Father's Day just as Dave and I were finishing brunch with my parents, who were in town visiting.

"Are you ready to start grading tomorrow?" he said, with a bit of laughter behind his voice.

"Grading?" I asked incredulously. "I mean, yeah! But wow, that came up quick!"

"I know, I'm down here now looking at the seed and they are absolutely blowing up. I think we need to get on it as soon as possible, like tomorrow," he said.

Eva and I arrived early the next morning to set up our grading stations. We were going over the steps with Michelle when, for a split second, I couldn't remember the terminology for our graded seed.

"What do we call the ones that fall through?" I asked Eva. She smiled like she knew, then stopped herself.

"I honestly don't remember," she said. We were both dumbstruck. Michelle waited patiently for a reply.

"Runts? Midgies?" Eva said, laughing.

"No! But that would be a great name for them," I admitted. "Wasn't it less than or little ones or . . ."

"SUBS!" she cried valiantly. "They're called subs."

"Right!" I replied. "We call them subs!" Michelle looked warily at us both, like we'd completely lost our minds. I credited my temporary memory lapse to old age (couldn't say the same for Eva, who was just twenty-one years old) and to the fact that I likely wiped my memory of last year's grading cycle. Between the misery of last year's weather and so many months out of practice, it took me a while to get my head back into seed mode.

We now had three varieties of seed to look after: ARC, Muscongus Bay, and this year's new batch from a hatchery called Mook Sea Farms (we called them Mookies); within each variety were several groups, differentiated by when they arrived (I labeled them ARC 1, ARC 2, and so on). Keeping everything organized was my only priority, but of course, there were blunders. It was during one of our first big redistributions when we had to move one group of seed to another upweller. I second-guessed which silo was which and in the process thought I mislabeled an entire group of seed. The groups looked very similar this year, so I couldn't use the markings to determine which was which. The result would have been devastating (in my head, anyway). I reluctantly gave Skip the news but when he came down to see if he could determine what was what, he assured me that I hadn't actually screwed anything up.

"The markings on that batch are really deceiving," he admitted. The batch from Muscongus Bay looked almost identical to a batch of ARC seed, which is why I was confused.

"Don Merry had the same problem. But they're definitely from Muscongus Bay," he assured me. "And if they're not," he added, smiling, "we'll just pretend that they are and figure it out later."

His attitude calmed me, as always. After all, we weren't saving the world or doing rocket science. We were growing oysters, plain and simple. Crops could get confused. Seed groups would get mingled. As long as we kept all of the mistakes isolated, he assured me, we would still produce a fine batch of oysters.

The only thing that could possibly throw Skip into a state of panic was physically losing seed, either from bad weather or human error. The reason we were so careful and diligent with washing or transitioning the seed in and out of the upwellers was because we didn't want to lose a single seed. Seed equaled money. Skip's biggest investment. Losing any seed—especially an entire silo of it—would be devastating. And one day, Maggie lost the seed.

The crew was gathered on the dock during a mid-morning lull. We were ready to start grading but Maggie and Pops had one last silo to pull while the rest of us set up our grading stations under the steaming sun. Suddenly, I heard a *sploosh* and looked up to see Maggie's ghost-white face staring at me and the group. I looked down at her hands and realized the silo was gone. Maggie had dropped the rope handles and the box had sunk straight to the bottom of the bay.

It was, as we had often joked, our absolute worst nightmare. Pops sprang into action, ripping his T-shirt off as though he were about to jump in to retrieve it, but Berg, who was standing nearby, pulled Pops away from the upweller and told him to find something with a long handle instead. The entire crew stood there, speechless. Maggie, now terrified, snapped at us.

"Please go do something else," she prodded. The docks were crawling with other growers and farm crews who were all stationed around the docks, grading seed. The last thing she wanted was for a crowd of onlookers to draw attention to her mistake. I calmly went back to the grading station and pretended to stay busy, motioning for Eva and Michelle to do the same. Berg sent the rest of the crew off on errands. Skip would be down to the dock any minute to check on us and Berg wanted to rescue the missing silo before he got there. Pops returned with a long-handled rake that Berg used to pull up the box. Thankfully, the tide was just low enough that the box had dropped like dead weight without tipping over. Berg snagged one of the rope handles and pulled the box up gingerly, raising it up to the surface, where Maggie and Pops pulled it the rest of the way onto the dock. I ran over to see if we'd lost any seed. Nothing in the box, not even the oyster poop that draped the top, had budged. Maggie was in the clear.

"All I could think to myself was where would I come up with the money to replace Skip's seed," Maggie said, still trembling from the episode. Later that day, Maggie, Berg, and I worked up the nerve to confess everything to Skip— and when we did, to our surprise, he actually laughed.

"That happened a few years ago to another girl on the seed crew," he offered. "Actually, she dropped two in one day. I couldn't believe it."

The whole day left me edgy and full of nerves. As the boss and manager of the seed program, I was accountable for everything, including my crew, their work, and even their mishaps. I felt like I'd overfilled my plate. At the office, I was racing to meet deadlines and constantly playing catch-up. On the farm, I was misplacing groups of seed and watching Skip potentially lose thousands of dollars.

My days started to mingle into a million tiny stresses, all of which felt like they might send me over the edge. My life had also become one long stretch of farm—office—farm; I'd taken Maggie up on her offer and was staying in Duxbury almost once a week, living out of the trunk of my car.

But through it all, Dave remained remarkably calm. Something had shifted between us and it felt like we were now in this crazy world together. He helped out around the house where he could, giving me space when I needed nothing but dinner and sleep, and listened patiently as I whined about my moments of mental exhaustion. Best of all, he came down to the farm one morning to hand-pick oysters out on the tide with the crew.

We had a five A.M. call time, so he and I left our dog, Rex, with a friend and drove down to Duxbury to stay the night with Maggie. For dinner, I took him out to the beach shack Blakeman's, where we ate fried clams and big platters of fish-and-chips before taking a walk along Duxbury Beach. The next morning, we were out on the tide as the sun was rising, and I watched Dave stare out at the horizon in awe. Just as the sun peeked out from behind the lip of land that made up Duxbury Beach, the sound of the world waking up rose noisily around us. The bells of Duxbury's church steeple started ringing out across the water, the cackle of gulls drowning in and out while the wind gushed around our ears.

He worked alongside the crew, picking oysters that he thought looked good. I checked on him at times to make sure he was comfortable with what he was picking and just to see how he was holding up. At one point, we stopped to talk about what he was seeing and he leaned in to ask me where all the oysters were.

"We're running short on supply," I explained.

"Yeah, it's pretty empty out here," he said, looking out over the field. We were picking the very last of the field that would soon be planted, but I pointed to our other field, the one covered in last year's seed.

"In about two months, all of that will be ready to harvest," I explained, realizing for the first time that summer that our seed crop from last year was almost fully up to size.

"Funny, isn't it? You've been out here as long as they have," Dave said with a nudge. My babies and I had come such a long way.

After the tide, Dave made his way back to Boston in time to put in a full day at the office. When I got home that night I found him sprawled out on the couch.

"I can't believe you put in another eight hours after being out on the tide like that. I'm beat," he admitted. Finally, he understood why my energy was always zapped. I joined him on the couch, where we lounged for the rest of the night, watching TV.

A few days later, as the girls and I graded under a hot sun, Eva confided that she not only really liked Dave but had developed a new respect for marriage thanks to us.

"You guys go out and do things like go on hikes, go to shows, bartend, work on oyster farms," she observed. "It gives me hope that I might still be cool after marriage."

I blurted out a laugh, surprised that she actually thought I was cool but also pretty pleased for getting her approval.

It was like getting a slap on the back from my twenty-one-year-old self, complete with a good old "You didn't let me down." I must have done something right.

And yet, it reminded me that I wasn't that kid anymore. I was now a thirty-three-year-old adult living with some very adult pangs. Despite all of the responsibility I had taken on at the farm, I genuinely missed elements of my old life: writing, first and foremost. That winter, I'd finally put pen to paper again, mostly to capture some of my moments on the farm. But my former career, the one I'd spent a decade cultivating, was now completely stalled. A part of me wondered what it would take to get back on track. I'd taken this time, a year and a half now, to get my hands dirty and see what it meant to grow food, but in the process, I'd come back to the idea that what I really wanted was to be writing. The urge was so sudden and strong, it overwhelmed me.

There was also another urge, a slower progression of desire and longing that had been welling up over the past year: I wanted to have a baby. Two nieces had arrived that spring (Dave's sister had had a baby, too), giving Dave and me a fresh perspective on what it might mean to have a child. It was inspiring to see my sister, especially, so happy after so many years of struggle. It gave me hope and, quite honestly, made me realize that it's what I wanted all along.

I realized that my time on the farm was coming to an end. I decided that after the seed season ended and Oyster Fest was behind me, I would set an end date.

In the meantime, I wanted to pour myself into farmwork. All too quickly, our seed work was taking over my life—we were now grading daily, pushing tote after tote out to the nursery and once again, the cages were filling up. Before I could move back to the nonoyster world, I needed to finish what I had started here. Like those oysters on the lease, I needed just a bit more time to grow.

A few days into August, we were faced with a devastating development. We'd already deployed a few million seeds out to the nurseries—both in the Back River and out to the cages in the bay—and were to the point where we needed to start cleaning the bags again. Berg had us load up our scrub brushes and head out to the Back River for a few hours of scrubbing seed and flipping bags. But when we got out there, we found that almost all of the bags were carpeted with barnacles.

The scratchy white crustaceans had attached themselves to the underside of almost every bag, blocking water flow and food to the oysters inside. Until now, I'd only known barnacles to attach themselves to dock pilings or the undersides of old boats. Seeing them blanket our bags gave me the willies, as if they'd just sprung up and appeared like gremlins overnight. Their presence was debilitating for our seed crop.

Berg examined all of the bags carefully before calling Skip for advice. Skip was shocked. He'd never in almost twenty years of growing oysters seen a barnacle set that far up the river—he attributed it to the warm weather that had, once again, brought a surprising development to our farming cycle. But we needed to fix the problem quickly—we would switch all of the barnacle-covered bags with new ones immediately, he declared. Starting today.

Berg looked at his crew apologetically and announced the plan. Switching over the bags would take the entire crew almost two weeks to accomplish. Harvesting was put on hold, giving our overharvested lease a much-needed break. Instead, we devoted all of our time to changing over all 1,600 bags that were floating in the Back River. We did the work during low tides so that a few people could stand in the water pulling barnacle-covered bags off the line while another contingent worked in the boats to transfer the seed from old bags to new ones. Along the way, we discovered that, thankfully, most of the oyster seed had survived the barnacles.

The work was endless and absolutely filthy. I stationed myself on the boat, where I could transfer the seed from one bag to another, but that meant I was a prime mud-flinging target. Every time a bag came onto the boat, I was coated in a fresh swath of mud and oyster poop, leaving me covered in layers of grime that took several showers to wash off. A few days of the mind-numbing work and I was ready to throw away my entire summer wardrobe.

It took us two full weeks to finish the project, and the entire crew looked haggard and ready to revolt. But Skip had some good news for us: It was time for our annual float dinner with Jeremy Sewall and his restaurant staff. About thirty people came down from both of Jeremy's restaurants, Lineage and Eastern Standard, on a strikingly balmy summer night. Skip set up an unforgettable spread, this time pulling up a couple pounds of razor clams, which he grilled briefly before cutting each into bite-sized pieces and tossing them with grilled asparagus and roughly chopped tomatoes. He doused the whole thing with garlic dipping oil and a couple squeezes of lemon for a simple, unforgettable razor clam salad. Once again, the crowd dug into steamed lobsters, tossing shells off the side of the Plex as we watched the moon rise up over Duxbury Beach, marveling at our luck for what was turning out to be (barnacles aside) a near-perfect summer season.

After shuttling our guests back to land, shortly after nightfall, we were back on the float swigging beers and scheming up reasons to go joyriding on Don Merry's big, white-cabined boat. Groups of us went out at a time while Skip swung the boat through the harbor at a breakneck speed. At one point, someone loudly suggested that the tide was finally high enough for us to go bridge jumping—that childish Duxbury tradition that I never thought I'd take part in.

Before I knew it we were cruising out to the bridge, leaving our flip-flops on the boat and jumping out onto the beach. I chased Berg up to the road, where we crept noisily along its edge and ran toward the bridge's midpoint. Berg helped me over the bridge's wooden railing, where I watched as he, arms flailing, dropped quietly into the darkness below. For a split second, my conscience yelled at me. Was I really about to *jump off a bridge* just because all my friends were doing it? But it was too late. I launched myself up into the air and fell weightlessly until I crashed into the water below. I kicked up madly, certain that I'd almost hit the bottom, and came up gasping with a scream. The guys hoisted me back onto the boat, where I stood shivering, watching another round of jumpers take to the beach and back up to the railing. I felt my lips turning blue against the now-chilly night air as I watched them plummet one by one into the bay. They looked like a gang from *Lord of the Flies,* young, fearless, and smitten with their own courage. That rush of existing-only-in-this-very-moment lasted until we got back to the dock in search of warmth and another round of beers.

The late summer "we're nearing the finish line" party mentality lasted through early August as we planned a more family-focused event, the first ever Island Creek Oyster Olympics. The Olympics had been discussed for years around the farm with crewmates joking that we should put on a competition that would pit the crews against each other in a series of oyster-related tasks. This year, Skip's daughters, Samantha and Maya, decided it was time to turn the conversation into reality and recruited me to help organize a day of competitive events that adults and kids could participate in.

The girls, with the help of their dad, came up with a strict set of rules and guidelines, mapped out racecourses, and even handcrafted medals made from oyster shells painted gold, silver, and bronze. The games took place on a Saturday in August when the tides were perfectly timed for a mid-afternoon competition. Our battles included diving for oyster bags, a team mud-fling, a long-distance mud run, an oyster sack relay race, and finally an all-encompassing whiffle ball tournament.

We gathered on the oyster floats and divided ourselves into two teams, giving each team an equal distribution of kids and adults. While we hadn't convinced many of the oyster crews to come out on a Saturday, we had a fair number of oyster growers like Don Merry, Mark Bouthillier, and Scott Doyle show up with their families. My own crewmates, including Michelle, Berg, and Quinn, came too, creating a spirited mix of overly competitive adults and willing-to-participate kids.

I managed to compete in every single event, helping Team Bouthillier achieve a pretty astounding victory over Team Bennett and getting absolutely covered in mud in the process. We all did, thanks to the mud fling, which had us literally flinging globs of foul-smelling sea mud at one another to see who could get the dirtiest. It was disgusting and stinky and utterly childish, but it was the most fun I'd had in years.

Later that night, the adult players hopped on the oyster boats and made our way over to the Deck, Plymouth's somewhat rowdy waterside bar. Between that and bridge jumping, I realized I'd accomplished all of the "good stuff" Skip had promised for me way back in the fall. After a few cocktails in the bar that night, I wandered back down to the boat ahead of everyone else and looked out over the inky water. The lights from the bar glistened over the bay almost as brightly as the stars up above. My eye fell on a boat sitting directly in front of me, parked at one of the harbor's slips. The simple words "What Next," stenciled in huge bold letters on the boat's rear end, called out to me. What next, indeed?

Skip's Razor Clam Salad

S kip is the kind of cook I've always admired: inventive and quick on his feet. He came up with the idea for this dish on his way down to the harbor before a float dinner. "I want to grill some razor clams and serve them in a salad," he told me. Razor clams had always intimidated me with their long, razor-sharp shells and meaty, phallic-looking bodies. Having only seen them plated in restaurants or in their shells out on the tide, I had no idea how to prepare them. But, Skip assured me, they were incredibly simple to cook. We made a quick stop at a Duxbury farm stand to gather tomatoes, asparagus, and a fancy bottle of garlic dipping oil. Out on the float, Skip popped the clams (still in their shells) on the grill, instructing me not to overcook them (just a few minutes over the heat). He then grilled up the asparagus, chopped up some tomatoes, and then tossed it all together. "See? Quick. Easy," he declared. And absolutely delicious.

2 pounds razor clams (about 20 to 24
clams), in the shell
1 pound asparagus, trimmed

1 tablespoon extra-virgin olive oil
2 fresh tomatoes, roughly chopped
Juice of 1 lemon
2 tablespoons garlic dipping oil
Salt and pepper, to taste

Light and heat grill to medium. Place the razor clams and the asparagus on the grill, then drizzle the asparagus with oil and close the grill. Let the clams cook for 4 to 5 minutes or until open. Remove clams from the grill and let cool slightly. Continue grilling the asparagus, turning until just charred and tender, about 5 more minutes.

Meanwhile, remove the clams from their shells and chop into bite-size pieces; place them in a large bowl. Once the asparagus is done, remove from the grill, let cool slightly, and then cut into bite-size pieces. Combine the asparagus with the clams, then gently fold in the tomatoes, lemon juice, and garlic dipping oil. Season with salt and pepper and serve.

SERVES 4

CHAPTER THIRTEEN

PAIN TRAIN

The 2010 Island Creek Oyster Festival crept up hard and fast and once again, we faced an impending hurricane. The crews braced for the big winds and high waves of Hurricane Earl, which was positioned to hit us over Labor Day weekend, one week before the fest. I braced for another catastrophe: rain closure, lack of oysters, and gale-force winds on festival day.

I stayed home watching the Weather Channel all weekend, trying desperately to bulk up on rest before the madness of the week set in. I'd gotten one small break a week earlier when Dave and I flew down to Hilton Head, South Carolina, for a quick vacation with my family. For a few days, I basked under the broiling sun, played with my adorable eight-month-old niece Gracyn, and tried unsuccessfully to keep from worrying about whether festival plans were proceeding without me. Returning to an oncoming storm wiped away every ounce of my accumulated relaxation.

But then, miraculously, the big bad hurricane stalled. It was downgraded to a tropical storm before it even hit Cape Cod to the south of us. We were left, instead, with a few inches of pounding rain followed by a sparkling weather forecast.

Now, instead of worrying about the weather, I fretted about tiny details like how quickly our tent would go up and whether or not the portable toilets would arrive on time. We'd expanded the festival site, adding bigger tents to allow for our slightly larger number of attendees, and we'd added three times as many volunteers to this year's staff. It would be a zoo, yes, but at least we'd have a spacious cage.

The weekend kicked off with a volunteer orientation on Thursday night. Our volunteer coordinator and newest committee member Michelle gathered all hundred or so of them under the tents for a pre-event cheerleading session (she did such a stellar job managing the volunteers, she would eventually go on to become the Island Creek Oyster Foundation's executive director). Looking out over the group, I thought back to the previous year and how our volunteer pool consisted of farm friends and a few of the oyster crews. This year felt more official, professional even. The festival was growing up.

After the orientation, Shore and I returned to the office to regroup for the marathon two-day session we were about to put ourselves through. As I gathered clipboards, walkie-talkies, and Sharpie pens to arm myself for the weekend, he pulled a chair up, put his feet up on my desk, and leaned back with a sigh. It was his resting position, one he fell into regularly during office hours. It usually meant he wanted to talk.

"Who are we right now?" he asked, staring up at the ceiling. I'd been wondering that myself for days.

This relatively humble little oyster farm, set in a small, idyllic town on the coast of New England, had turned into a massive operation seemingly overnight. Here we were running a several-thousand-person event, raising hundreds of thousands of dollars for a charity that the farm had created in order to send a team of missionaries halfway around the world to help feed people in an African nation. A few miles up the road, a sprawling and stunning new restaurant was set to open in just weeks, employing hundreds of people, feeding thousands more, and if all went as planned, creating big waves in Boston's food community.

And here we sat, in an office where the rug was stained and dishes overflowed from the sink, wondering how we—and the farm—had gotten here. I gazed around the office and slowly shook my head.

"I don't know. But I'm really grateful to be a part of it," I sighed. Our moment of reflection ended with a hug and a high five and turned out to be my only moment of serenity until the festival madness wrapped up several days later.

There was something special about this year's festival day. The wind blew stiffly. The waves sparkled in the sun and our white tent glistened. Everything fell into place at just the right time and, unlike last year, where chaos ruled, the day was orderly and went almost entirely as planned. Shore and I were actually having fun by the time the doors opened at three P.M. We were, more than we'd ever been before, ready for a party.

We'd added more chefs this time, like Ming Tsai, who brought down an entire camera crew to shoot scenes of the festival for his television show. He rallied and excited the VIP tent before jumping behind his station to fire off grilled oysters with a garlicky black pepper sauce. He was flanked by Rialto's Jody Adams, who had returned with a two-part dish of razor clam chowder and miniature, rabbit-stuffed hoagies, and Jeremy Sewall, who brought his staff from the Island Creek Oyster Bar (they were being trained for the impending opening) and grilled up lobster tails and chorizo. My parents, once again in attendance (and much more pleased with this year's weather) were two of the dozens who crushed around Jeremy's station minutes after he lit his grill, causing him to run out of food within an hour.

There were minor hiccups throughout the day but they mostly involved crowd control, which our hired security team handled smoothly. Despite our massive tent space, there seemed to be only a few channels by which the crowd could travel, causing traffic jams along those routes. It was actually a crowd of people at the front of the main tent that kept me from hearing Shore's announcement to the crowd halfway through the night. Not only did he thank me publicly for my hard work that summer, but he announced that I was being given this year's crown as the Island Creek Oyster "Pearl," a sweet and sentimental award they gave out to their favorite female of the season (it had gone to Lisa the year before). When I finally reached him, he told me the news as tears welled up in his eyes.

"I wish you'd seen it in person," he said, pulling me in for a hug. "Or maybe not since I probably would have cried up there if you were with me," he added, laughing at his own sappiness. The two of us had carried a heavy load together and I couldn't help tearing up at the thought of leaving it all behind.

A little while later, I found Dave up near the stage watching my parents dance to an oldies tune. Mom and Dad came over to congratulate me on a successful event and together, the four of us joined a group of growers and other festival committee members for what had become a festival tradition: singing along to the band at the end of the night. Once again, we belted out the lyrics to a Journey song, danced wildly to the side of the stage, and congratulated each other on another successful fund-raiser.

I carried the highs from that day with me through the ensuing cleanup weeks that followed. Our final number that year was just over $160,000, giving the foundation yet another boost of financing, which would allow Shore to hire Michelle as the executive director and put the foundation on solid footing for years going forward.

Coming down from the adrenaline high proved difficult. I tried to shake off the depression of both concluding such a massive undertaking and facing my last few weeks on the farm. I'd given myself an end date of October 15, the day that Dave and I would leave for a weeklong vacation to the Pacific Northwest.

It wasn't easy to make the decision but once I picked

the date and set a final marker for myself, I realized it was exactly what needed to happen. With both the seed program and oyster festival finished, I'd accomplished all that I'd set out to do that year. On the oyster farm, Skip's summer crew had disbanded, leaving Berg, Gardner, Will, and Quinn to handle the winter farmwork. In the office, Chris had picked up all of the farm's marketing efforts and Shore had hired a woman named Dana, daughter of Skip's friends the Hales, to be the farm's new salesperson. The office would be flush just as soon as she started. There were opportunities for me, too, he said, suggesting I get involved in some permanent way with the restaurant, as a farm-to-restaurant liaison. But I couldn't say yes. As much as I loved being in and around restaurants, I didn't see myself *working* for one.

I was ready to get back to writing. And now, finally, I felt like I had a story to tell.

My final weeks on the farm mostly involved helping Shore and Skip with the final touches of opening the restaurant. Their farm-to-table concept was quickly coming to life as Jeremy finalized the menu and Tom hired and trained the waitstaff. Skip was especially interested in creating a compelling oyster list, which meant we were tasked with the oh-so-torturous task of tasting oysters from around the country. There would be Island Creeks, of course, but he and Jeremy wanted to find representations of all five oyster species: Easterns, Pacifics, Kumamotos, Olympias, and Belons. There would be around twelve to eighteen oysters on the list, giving oyster lovers a sampling of rare and hard-to-find varieties. It would be a place where consumers could learn about Skip's favorite word, "merroir."

To help the restaurant choose its opening list, Skip came up with the idea of setting up a tasting panel, to which we invited a handful of food and wine experts to taste eighteen different oyster varieties. The plan was twofold: to introduce ourselves and Jeremy to the oysters that might make the restaurant's final list as well as to give ourselves and the restaurant staff a list of vocabulary words to use when describing oysters. We had our panelists write down what they tasted, just as they would if taking notes on wine, so that we could compile the language into a larger oyster-tasting tome.

The tasting took place inside the sprawling dining room at Eastern Standard, where our fifteen guests gathered around a large table. The oysters were sent out in flights of three and our list was long and distinguished. It included Island Creeks, Totten Virginicas (an example of an East Coast species grown on the West Coast), Hog Island Oysters from San Francisco, and Kusshi oysters from outside Vancouver, British Columbia. Each flight showed off a range of flavor profiles and sparked discussions about the variations between specific species.

My favorite dialogue took place among the wine experts who we'd brought in from restaurants like the Blue Room, Oleana, Eastern Standard, and a new spot called Bergamot. Because their palates were trained to pick up nuances of flavor, they were using language I'd never applied to oysters. A variety called Raspberry Point from Prince Edward Island invoked descriptors like mushroom stem, "hints of meaty flavor," moss, pepper, and even custard, while the Hog Islands were associated with fennel, white flower, uni, oxidized apple, and green tea.

My vocabulary opened up as I heard their descriptions, and suddenly I was tasting eel grass and marsh from our Island Creeks. No longer restrained to the words "brine" and "sweetness," I walked away realizing I could speak "oyster" fluently. Skip was equally blown away both by this new use of language as well as the oysters themselves. He looked up at me at one point during the tasting, shaking his head in disbelief, and asked why we'd never thought to do this before. Later, as we moved from several rounds of East Coast oysters to a flight of West Coast oysters, and slurped back our first Pacific oyster, the Kusshi, Skip squeezed my arm.

"Oh man," he declared. "I think I just fell in love with oysters again." I laughed at the look of pure joy on his face. Even an oyster farmer needs inspiration.

The exercise not only clinched a few ideas for Jeremy's final Island Creek Oyster Bar list, but it also inspired Skip, Shore, and Chris to create similar tastings for the public. They hoped to use the restaurant as a space where they could introduce guests to several species of oysters at once as a teaching tool. The restaurant's mission would be to educate and incite discussion. Island Creek would be the moderator.

The tasting gave me fodder for my own project: creating an official training manual, called *The Oyster Primer,* for the restaurant's new staff. The primer was to be filled with easy-to-digest but comprehensive data on everything one needed to know about oysters as a beginner. From historical tidbits and oyster lore to anatomical descriptions, breeding habits, farming methods, and species descriptions, it would be a thorough and lengthy work compiling information from dozens of sources in one accessible document. Basically, it would be my thesis.

I recruited help from both Shore and Chris, who contributed to the final piece, but the bulk of the material and information came down to me. Having just spent a year and a half in oyster college, it was extraordinary to see just how much information I'd retained. It covered oyster history, which I'd studied on my own in literature and online but also gathered from the growers and from Skip along the way; oyster anatomy, which I'd received a crash course in while working with the seed; farming techniques and information about aquaculture; oyster species and their origins; oyster lore and myth; and of course, merroir. I found myself fretting over the deadline, rechecking my sources, and studying late into the night to make sure I had covered all of my bases. When I finally handed the thirty-five-page bible over to Tom, I felt like I deserved a diploma.

We passed the primer out to the staff during their first day of training. I think I was more nervous than our new hires were as we gathered inside a tight space at the Hotel Commonwealth. Shore, Skip, Chris, and I stood at the front of the room along with Garrett, Tom, Jeremy, and the rest of the key management team and timidly introduced ourselves to the people who would be representing Island Creek on the floor of the Oyster Bar from here on out. For the four of us from the farm, getting to know the staff would be vital. The restaurant needed to embody and showcase Island Creek's personality and aesthetic. Skip wasn't just putting his name up on the sign. He was creating an extension of the farm.

To bring the staff up to speed, Tom scheduled dozens of classes, seminars, and courses including a panel discussion on sustainable seafood that I moderated between Skip and Jeremy. It was a weeks-long effort to give everyone the tools to understand the menu, Tom's style of service, wine knowledge, and of course, everything oysters.

Besides the primer, I helped out by organizing a massive, all-staff visit to the farm during which our new servers, cooks, and hostesses were given the chance to get out on the water with the growers for a personalized, hands-on tour. We shut down farm operations for a day in the middle of the week in order to get all ninety new hires out on the water.

We picked a day in late September, which of course meant we were faced with high winds and a shaky forecast. But when the restaurant staff arrived that morning, they were greeted with sunshine. I'd stationed the growers and oyster crews all over the harbor: Berg and Gardner each manned a culling station on the floats; Christian, Billy, Scott Doyle, and John Brawley gave guided tours of the bay; and Chris, Shore, and I were stationed on land to offer classes on the seed process and history of Duxbury Bay. It was a full-scale operation, one that ran somewhat successfully until we were socked with pounding winds and a torrential rain. Inevitably, we had to bring all ninety folks indoors and finish up the day huddled together in the Maritime School.

To make up for the weather, we invited all of the growers to the Maritime School and asked them to speak briefly about how they started growing oysters. This was the first time I'd seen so many of the guys in one place, even after a year and a half on the farm. As they started talking to the staff, the stories poured forth. Christian told the group about those first few hairy winters when it was just him and Skip out on the frozen bay, their boat so loaded down with oysters, he was sure they would capsize. Scott Doyle's greatest memory of farming was of the day he brought his first bag of oysters up to the wholesale shop. After years of hard work and effort, he talked of the emotional reward of finally seeing a profit.

The group was mesmerized by Pogie's tale about his scariest moment on the water. A commercial lobsterman and die-hard clammer, Pogie had gone out to dig razor clams on the low tide right before a heavy fog rolled through. In his haste to get picking, he didn't tie up his boat very well and as the tide came in, the boat drifted off, leaving the clam digger stranded on an incoming tide. Billy Bennett was on his way back from pulling lobster traps and saw Pogie's boat drifting without a captain. He alerted the harbormaster and minutes later, there were sirens on the water and a rescue party banded together to search for the missing clam digger. They searched and searched all of Pogie's regular spots, thinking the most courageous of their brethren had most certainly drowned as the waters rose. Hours later, as they reconvened at the harbormaster's hut to figure out a new strategy, Pogie came wandering down the street.

"As soon as I saw the boat was gone, I started to swim," Pogie told the group with a laugh.

"We thought for certain you were a goner," Billy chimed in.

Hearing the guys relive their greatest and scariest moments made me realize I wasn't alone in my passion for the bay. Their stories inspired me but made me nostalgic, too. Despite having once quit my job in the real world to work on an oyster farm, it turned out that quitting the oyster farm would be the hardest decision I'd ever made.

Days later, I stopped by the restaurant to check in with our new staff and see how training was going. I talked to the group about their visit to the farm, asking what they'd taken away. Passion, they called out. Family, hard work, small-town camaraderie. They'd gathered from the growers that there was a deep commitment not only to that place but to the oysters they grew there. I left the discussion satisfied. By conveying how tight-knit the Island Creek community was, we'd given the staff an honest look at what farm life entailed.

A few more weeks of training and preparation and the staff was finally ready for service. Unfortunately, the restaurant was not. We'd watched anxiously as the structural pieces came together under the discerning eye of our architect and designer, Peter Bentel. He'd managed to transform the formerly yawning space into a stunning expression of the farm. There were inspirations from Duxbury intertwined among the décor, such as the bar front that was built to resemble the pilings of the Powder Point Bridge and a massive lighting element at the center of the restaurant that vaguely recalled the bottom of an upweller silo. I stopped by the restaurant regularly to watch as the floors, bar, and walls were put into place followed by the tables, chairs, and final touches of décor. Everywhere I looked I saw traces of the farm. Traces of the world I was about to leave behind.

There were delays securing the liquor license, a common last-minute sidestep for Boston restaurants, so although the opening date had been set for October 4 it was moved to October 5, then October 10, and finally it was settled for Friday, October 15 . . . the day Dave and I would fly out to Portland, Oregon.

I couldn't hide my disappointment. After all of those months working and waiting, I wouldn't be there to watch the space come to life—I would be on a plane. Dave and I did manage to get to one of the preview nights when the restaurant opened to friends and family for a trial run. It was a lovely but clumsy meal where, for the first time, I realized that hidden in a photograph of Skip's oyster lease that took up one entire wall of the restaurant, there was an image of my crewmates and me picking on the tide. It gave me a chill knowing that in some small way, I would always be a part of this place.

During my last week on the farm, I spent one final day working on the water with the crew. It was sparkling and cool, a perfect fall day. I culled with Will and Dana, the farm's future salesperson (she was doing her requisite farm stint before starting in the office), and reminisced about some of the wildest moments of my tenure. I made Will dissect the cull for me since it had changed, once again, to account for a new crop of oysters. These were the oysters that Catie and I had diligently washed, graded, and cared for the summer before and I couldn't help puffing up with pride at how thick and nicely rounded they were. I tried to recall all of the physical pain I'd endured to get these babies out onto the fields but somehow, my mind had blocked it out.

Berg came in from dragging a few hours later and we opened some oysters together. I could taste the sweetness just starting to round out in the flavor. The oysters were already building up glucose in response to the colder water temperature. It would be a few more months until they hit their peak, but today they were full of sea-salty brine and yes, even a vague hint of eel grass.

For a second I wondered if every time I ate an oyster, I would consider the months of care and attention that had gone into growing just one of these precious bivalves. Would I think about lifting silos or standing for hours shaking a wooden-handled grader? Or recall what it felt like to clean cages, oyster bags, or seed, or to work through the aches and pains collecting in my lower back? Would I get a microscopic shiver thinking about the thrill of stacking one last bag in the cooler and calling it a week? I hoped so. I wanted to be able to relive this—every good and bad moment—again and again and again.

Skip came out to the float later that afternoon to help us finish the cull. The afternoon sun had warmed up to the seventies and the whole crew now stood around the tables in T-shirts and baseball hats, finishing up the last of the day's work. Skip and I stood side by side talking about how the oysters were looking and how the crew would prepare for winter. Berg talked about the foundation and his plans to go back to Africa that winter. The farm was moving forward, just as it always had, and somehow, that made me feel okay about moving on, too.

Skip held an oyster up in front of me and, playing his old game, asked, "What would you do with this one?"

"Three," I said with certainty, causing him to look up at me with a grin. I could see sadness behind his eyes. He'd become a mentor, an inspiration, and more than anything else, a very good friend. Being around him on a day-to-day basis was the thing that I would miss the very most.

That night, after a teary drive home, I fell into Dave's arms and sobbed. I didn't think it would be this hard, I tried to tell him. I knew I was making the right decision but I didn't want to say good-bye.

"You don't have to," he said, trying to calm me down. "You can always go back . . ." he offered. In many ways, he wasn't convinced that I was really leaving. But somehow, I knew deep inside that as much as I loved the farm, the people, and the work that I'd done, this had to be the end.

"And even if you don't," he said, holding me tight, "you know you'll always be my farm girl."

Mrs. Bennett's Seafood Casserole

Chef Jeremy Sewall serves this tribute to Nancy Bennett at the Island Creek Oyster Bar nightly.

This dish was inspired by Skip's mom, Nancy Bennett. Being the wife of a lobsterman (now oysterman), she once told me you learned to make dinner with what came out of the lobster traps that day. That means lobster, of course, but also the occasional small cod or floun-

der, clams, and crabs. A lobsterman's wife is versatile in her ability to make chowders, soups, and casseroles—anything that might contain the day's catch. This is a modern version—and my interpretation—of what that might be.

Note: Make sure you have a casserole dish big enough to hold all the ingredients.

1 1½-pound lobster, boiled for 4 minutes, meat removed and cut into small chunks; shells reserved

¼ cup canola oil, divided in half

2 large shallots, sliced thin

3 tablespoons tomato paste

1 cup white wine

1 quart heavy cream

2 sprigs of fresh thyme

Salt and pepper to taste

1 tablespoon lemon juice

3 tablespoons butter

2 cloves garlic, minced

1½ cups bread crumbs

1 tablespoon chopped flat-leaf parsley

4 sea scallops (about 8 ounces)

8-ounce cod filet, cut into 4 pieces

1 Spanish onion, diced into 1-inch pieces

2 celery stalks, sliced ¼-inch thick

1 large carrot, diced into 1-inch pieces

4 small red potatoes, washed and diced
    into 1-inch pieces and boiled in salted
    water for 4 minutes
8 ounces cleaned sweet shrimp

To make the sauce:

Break the lobster shells into smaller pieces (a rolling pin and a towel work great). Heat half the canola oil in a saucepan over medium heat and add the lobster shells; cook for 1 minute, stirring frequently so they don't burn. Add the shallots and cook for another minute. Stir in the tomato paste and let the mixture cook until the tomato paste starts to color the bottom of the pan, then, immediately add the white wine. Bring to a boil, then lower the heat and let simmer for 5 minutes. Add the cream and thyme and continue to simmer gently for 20 minutes. Remove from the heat and let cool for 20 minutes. Strain the stock through a fine mesh sieve. Season with salt, pepper, and lemon juice.

Bread crumb topping:

Melt the butter in a sauté pan over medium-low heat and add the garlic. Cook until the garlic colors very lightly, remove from heat, and stir in the bread crumbs and parsley. Hold at room temperature until ready to use.

To assemble the casserole:

Preheat the oven to 350°. In a large sauté pan heat the remaining canola oil. Sear the scallops and cod together on one side until gently browned, then place them in the casserole dish, seared side up. In the sauté pan, heat the onion, celery, and carrot until they just begin to soften, about 5 minutes. Add the vegetables to the casserole dish along with the boiled potatoes, lobster meat, and shrimp; season with salt and pepper. Bring the lobster sauce to a boil, then pour into the casserole dish over the seafood and vegetables. Sprinkle bread crumbs over top and bake for 25 minutes. Let cool slightly before serving.

SERVES 4

POSEIDON

The end of my time on the farm, like so many endings in life, turned out to be a series of new beginnings. The first was the start of this book. My time at Island Creek inspired me to put my experience on paper, turning both my story and the farm's story into something substantial. With help and encouragement from a core group of people, I turned the idea into a book proposal and later, into the story you just read (and hopefully liked!).

I'm incredibly grateful for my time on the farm but even more so that I decided to leave and get back to writing. Like Skip and his magnetic pull to the water, I've always been pulled to the page by something I can't explain.

Of course, coming off the farm allowed for other beginnings, too. About six weeks after leaving the farm, just a few days before Thanksgiving 2010, Dave and I found that

I was pregnant. It was one of those impeccably timed blessings that made me wonder if it had simply been in the cards all along. Serendipitously, Baby Murray (whom the farm guys have already nicknamed Poseidon) is scheduled to arrive just a few short months before this book will be published, giving me two huge major life events in one year.

I continue to consider the restaurant my home away from home—it has quickly become a Boston institution and is filled nightly with oyster lovers and fans of Island Creek. Dave and I have enjoyed dozens of meals there since the opening and will always consider it our favorite oyster haunt . . . just as soon as I can get back to eating raw oysters again.

As for the farm, I've been back to visit often and still consider them my extended family. I plan on volunteering at the oyster festival this year and for all the years that they'll have me. As I told Shore before I left, "If you really want to get rid of me, you're going to have to drag me away."

My career, from what I can tell at this moment, will be writing from here on out. And while I fully plan on taking breaks to get my hands dirty in the mud or nurture a child or two (somehow more daunting than caring for a million baby oysters), I'll be perfectly content putting words to paper for the rest of my life.

The real difference between where I was when I started and where I am now is actually something I learned from Skip. He taught me that no matter what it is you want to do, do it to the fullest and always find a way to have fun. If you enjoy growing oysters, grow oysters. But make sure you're enjoying every minute of it. If you want to write, then write. And write about what you love. Go after what you want and work hard for it. But never stop dreaming big.